Translation Policies in Legal and Institutional Settings

Translation, Interpreting and Transfer

6

"Translation, Interpreting and Transfer" takes as its basis an inclusive view of translation and translation studies. It covers research and scholarly reflection, theoretical and methodological, on all aspects of the core activities of translation and interpreting, but also similar rewriting and recontextualization practices such as adaptation, localization, transcreation and transediting, keeping Roman Jakobson's inclusive view on interlingual, intralingual and intersemiotic translation in mind. The title of the series, which includes the more encompassing concept of transfer, reflects this broad conceptualization of translation matters.

Series editors
Luc van Doorslaer (KU Leuven / University of Tartu)
Haidee Kotze (Utrecht University)

Editorial board
Lieven D'hulst (KU Leuven)
Daniel Gile (University Paris 3, Sorbonne Nouvelle)
Sara Ramos Pinto (University of Leeds)

Advisory board
Pieter Boulogne (KU Leuven)
Elke Brems (KU Leuven)
Leo Tak-hung Chan (Lingnan University, Hong Kong)
Dirk Delabastita (University of Namur)
Dilek Dizdar (University of Mainz)
Yves Gambier (University of Turku)
Arnt Lykke Jakobsen (Copenhagen Business School)
Reine Meylaerts (KU Leuven)
Franz Pöchhacker (University of Vienna)
Heidi Salaets (KU Leuven)
Christina Schäffner (Aston University, Birmingham)

Translation Policies in Legal and Institutional Settings

Edited by
Marie Bourguignon, Bieke Nouws & Heleen van Gerwen

LEUVEN UNIVERSITY PRESS

This book was published with the support of
KU Leuven Fund for Fair Open Access
and

Published in 2021 by Leuven University Press / Presses Universitaires de Louvain / Universitaire Pers Leuven. Minderbroedersstraat 4, B-3000 Leuven (Belgium).

Selection and editorial matter © Marie Bourguignon, Bieke Nouws, and Heleen van Gerwen, 2021
Individual chapters © The respective authors, 2021

This book is published under a Creative Commons Attribution Non-Commercial Non-Derivative 4.0 Licence.

Further details about Creative Commons licences are available at http://creativecommons.org/licenses/
Attribution should include the following information:
Marie Bourguignon, Bieke Nouws, and Heleen van Gerwen (eds), Translation Policies in Legal and Institutional Settings. Leuven 2021, Leuven University Press. (CC BY-NC-ND 4.0)

ISBN 978 94 6270 294 3 (Paperback)
ISBN 978 94 6166 411 2 (ePDF)
ISBN 978 94 6166 410-5 (ePUB)
https://doi.org/10.11116/9789461664112
D/2021/1869/43
NUR: 610

Cover: Daniel Benneworth-Gray
Typesetting: Crius Group

Table of Contents

Introduction — 7
Marie Bourguignon, Bieke Nouws & Heleen van Gerwen

Government ideologies in translation: An enquiry into past Canadian budget speeches — 23
Chantal Gagnon

The complexity of a translation policy: Interpreting for ethnic linguistic minorities in a local courtroom in China — 47
Shuang Li

Translation guidelines versus practice: A corpus-based study of the impact of the Polish style guide on translations of EU legislation and reports drafted by the European Commission — 67
Katarzyna Wasilewska

Institutional translation practices in South Tyrol: An exploratory study on civil servants working as 'occasional translators' — 87
Flavia De Camillis

Judicial review of translation policy: The case of bilingual Catalonia in monolingual Spain — 109
Albert Branchadell

Investigating the status of Italian as an 'official minority language' within the Swiss multilingual institutional system — 133
Paolo Canavese

Translation, interpreting and institutional routines: The case of Slovakia — 157
Marketa Štefková & Helena Tužinská

Flawless in translation? Legal translations in the Flemish legal professional press (1889–1935) — 181
Sebastiaan Vandenbogaerde

Translating the Belgian Civil Code: Developments after 1961   205
Willem Possemiers

Translation in administrative interactions: Policies and practices at
the local level in the Dutch language area of Belgium   223
Jonathan Bernaerts

About the editors   247

About the authors   249

Index   253

Introduction

Marie Bourguignon, Bieke Nouws & Heleen van Gerwen

1   Context and aim

Today, in 2021, we cannot say that institutional translation and the translation of so-called 'grey literature' is wholly unconsidered by translation studies scholars – or other researchers, for that matter. However, systematic studies on the everyday interaction between governments and their multilingual populations remain relatively rare in comparison to, for instance, research on literary translation. Considering the fact that legal and institutional translation have been practiced since antiquity, the gaps in legal and institutional translation history continue to be considerably larger than what is actually mapped out (see, e.g., Wolf 2015; D'hulst et al. 2016).

This edited volume presents the revised and extended papers of the LITP (Legal and Institutional Translation Policies) 2018 conference, an international and interdisciplinary conference held at KU Leuven (Belgium) in September 2018. The goal of this conference was to bring together translation studies scholars, sociolinguists, political philosophers and legal scholars, in order to reflect on the challenges of translation policies in various multilingual institutional and legal settings. This endeavor was, perhaps surprisingly, one of the first of its kind. We were more than happy to see our call answered by so many researchers, young and accomplished, from different backgrounds and disciplines, conducting studies on so many different regions in the world and aspects of legal and institutional translation. After the stimulating discussions we had during this conference, it was our express goal to publish these papers, presenting the highly original case studies and the data the participants collected. As translation in these two settings is fundamental to understanding translation policies and the interaction between government and citizens, we believe this volume does not come a moment too soon.

The study of legal and institutional translation policies is situated at the crossroads of some recent and continuing trends in translation studies. Ever since its inception, translation studies has been opening up to all kinds of social, political, cultural as well as legal and institutional issues. Each of these research interests has in recent years benefited from the increase of inter- and multidisciplinary academic enterprises. The LITP 2018 conference has sought to honor and enhance this evolution, and we believe the fruitfulness of this scholarly exchange is reflected in the complementarity of the various contributions.

The aim of this book is twofold. Firstly, it wishes to document the state of the art of translation policies in legal and institutional settings. Explicitly opening the book up to studies on the past as well as the present and from several parts of the world allows for a comparison of translation policies in varying contexts. Secondly, we want to highlight the virtues of integrating different types of expertise (theoretical and applied; historical and modern; legal, institutional and political) to further our understanding of past and present translation policies, not to mention their relationship with issues such as linguistic justice, minority rights, multilingualism and citizenship. As of yet, there are few studies that effectively combine insights, concepts and methods from different disciplines and areas of work. Many studies remain firmly rooted within the framework of one or the other discipline, which limits the opportunity to provide productive solutions to present-day challenges, such as the increasing multilingualism of certain areas of the world as a result of considerable mass migration flows. By combining perspectives, methods and results, translation studies scholars, sociolinguists, political philosophers and legal scholars together may arrive at a complete and comprehensive picture of the challenges of and possible roads to a multilingual and inclusive society.

At the onset of this project, we planned to divide this book into three parts, dedicated respectively to studies on the topic of translation policies, legal translation and institutional translation. However, it soon became clear that these domains are not simply complementary fields of research but are fundamentally interconnected. While translations are usually designated 'legal' because of their content (i.e., legal matters), 'institutional' translations are defined by their context (i.e., a certain institution where the translations are carried out). These labels mean their domains may very well, and indeed often do, overlap. For example, while legal translation is often carried out in an institutional setting, some institutional translators certainly carry out legal translations. Even so, each term is associated with its own literature, and they are seldom used in the same article. It is not a coincidence, however, that both subjects were addressed at one and the same conference. We believe this concurrence has everything to do with the fairly recent rise of the concept of translation policy (either explicitly or implicitly understood as 'public' translation policy).

2 Translation policies

As the focus of translation studies has traditionally been on literary and Bible translation, translations for administrative or other 'prosaic' purposes have long remained in the shadows of translation research. Although translation is ubiquitous in many social, political, administrative and judicial institutions, the management and practice of legal and institutional translation seldom attracted extensive attention until the twenty-first century (van Doorslaer 2013, 61–66). Fortunately, however, a growing body of research in this area is evident (see, e.g., Borja Albi and Prieto Ramos 2013; Šarčević 2015; McAuliffe 2016; Biel 2017a, Svoboda et al. 2017; Prieto Ramos 2017 and 2021).[1] As attention to intracultural translations and translations within countries grows, scholars are also increasingly turning to the study of language and translation management in multilingual countries. While elaborate translation policies are rare, even in officially multilingual countries, there is an increased awareness that the absence of translation can be just as meaningful as the translation choices explicitly enshrined in rules and regulations. In the end, as Meylaerts writes, "confronted with multilingual populations, states cannot remain neutral over translation: a translational laissez-faire is no option either" and they therefore automatically make translation choices, even if they are negative (Meylaerts 2018, 222). While the study of translation policies remains a rather small field, the accumulated body of research today extends to numerous countries all over the world.[2]

The concept of translation policy can be considered in different ways. A common view is to see it as the legal rules that officially regulate the use of translations in public institutions. However, Meylaerts and González Núñez (2017) suggest a broader view on translation policies, those not merely restricted to the official management but also including the ideologies and practices that influence them.[3] In this volume, both conceptualizations are applied.

The 'broad' model is explicitly adopted by Shuang Li, while other authors implicitly refer to a definition of translation policy which encompasses two of the three elements. Sebastiaan Vandenbogaerde discusses the 'views' of the translation actors or lawyers, which comprise the way in which they position themselves and the actions they undertake to tackle translation problems,

---

1   See Rogers (2018) for a bibliometric overview of the growing research on specialized translation.
2   See for example O'Rourke and Castillo (2009, 33–51); Suh (2011); D'hulst and Schreiber (2014, 3–31); Ingelbeen and Schreiber (2017, 34–44); Nouws (2019, 44–45).
3   This approach is based on Spolsky's (2004) conceptualization of 'language policy'.

their 'visions', 'strategies' or 'approaches'. In this case, Vandenbogaerde's contribution mentions the legal framework but focuses on ideology and practices. Willem Possemiers refers to the 'development' of translation and analyzes translation practices, explaining the sources used and choices made by translators. Without explicitly mentioning translation policies, Katarzyna Wasilewska focuses on the relation between management and practices; in doing so, she presents an empirical study of the actual influence of the guidelines on the quality of translation practice and products of the Polish language unit at the Directorate-General for Translation (DGT) of the European Union (EU). Flavia De Camillis also confronts language and translation practices and (some aspects of) management in her chapter on multilingual regions of Italy. She opens with an overview of the laws and decrees regulating the language use in official institutions in South Tyrol and, more specifically, Bolzano (Italy). By portraying the legal framework, De Camillis illustrates the multi-layered nature of language management affecting translation practices in this region, as in many other multilingual regions or countries. This first section of her chapter is followed by a scrutiny of actual translation practices in the province's Central Administration. In her contribution on Canadian budget speeches, Chantal Gagnon uses 'policy' to refer to official government policy on budget and languages, yet prefers the word 'politics' when referring to the non-neutral attitude of states regarding translation. While legislation is in the background, Gagnon's chapter essentially focuses on the ideology that translation practices (also called discursive practices) can convey, the nature of the source text being of great importance.

Several authors in this book adopt a narrow definition of the term, in line with Meylaerts's previous definition of public translation policy: "a set of legal rules that regulate translation in the public domain: in education, in legal affairs, in political institutions, in administration, in the media" (Meylaerts 2011a). Jonathan Bernaerts distinguishes translation policies from translation practices, but his definition of translation policies encompasses a set of legal rules in a broad sense, one that comprises local norms, guidelines and recommendations. Bernaerts's contribution, among other contributions in this volume, clearly shows that translation policies form a complex set of laws, rules and guidelines from several authorities that cannot be examined in isolation. In their contribution on translation policy relating to the target groups of Slovakian institutional translation – that is, labor migrants, asylum applicants and refugees, and language minorities – Marketa Štefková and Helena Tužinská also define translation policies as a set of rules. However, their contribution discusses both management (or the objectives, principles and procedures established by the governmental bodies to regulate the translation practices of the language communities) and actual translation practice. The same distinction between translation policy as a set of rules and translation practices is made by Paolo Canavese in his study of the place of Swiss Italian in institutional settings in Switzerland. His chapter focuses on the three elements of translation policy in a broad sense, as he not only assesses the feasibility of full *de jure* and *de facto* equality between the Swiss national languages, but also its desirability, which addresses the ideological component of translation policies. Finally, Albert Branchadell reconciles the strict and broad definitions of translation policy. Translation policies in the strict sense, understood as a set of rules, are a part of the management component of translation policies seen in their broad sense.

Meylaerts's typology of translation policy regimes is frequently referenced, critically discussed and complemented by the authors in this volume. This typology identifies four possible regimes (see Meylaerts 2011b). The first regime is that of total institutional monolingualism, which results in an official, national language and the absence of translation (i.e., a ban on translation) by the state. The second is that of institutional monolingualism accompanied by temporary or occasional translations. There is limited multilingualism among institutions and thus the recognition of a right to translation in specific situations. This regime is discussed in the chapters by Li and by Štefková and Tužinská. The third regime is complete institutional multilingualism with compulsory translations from and to the different languages involved. This regime is illustrated by the EU's translation policy, where the large amount of translations is supposed to increase legitimacy in the EU, as Wasilewska discusses in her contribution. The fourth regime is local monolingualism combined with multilingualism and compulsory multidirectional translations. This model allows citizens of different languages within the same country to remain monolingual. Regarding the last regime, Koskinen (2014) has shown that central monolingualism (the first regime) can be combined with local multilingualism, which resulted in Meylaerts adding 'vice-versa' at the end of the description of the last model. Branchadell's contribution on bilingual Catalonia (Spain) refers to this second conception of the last regime. Canavese fits Switzerland into the fourth category: the local level is monolingual and the central level is multilingual with obligatory multidirectional translations. However, he nuances that those multidirectional translations do not necessary imply language equality, as a clear asymmetry between the subdirections may occur both on a quantitative and qualitative level. Finally, the contributions by De Camillis and by Štefková and Tužinská illustrate how a state can correspond to several types of translation policy, depending on the languages taken into account. Regarding Slovakia, for example, official translations exist in Czech whereas occasional translations are done in English. De Camillis explains that among 'recognized' minority languages, several degrees of protection are granted.

In 2010, Oscar Diaz Fouces suggested another typology, which places translation policies between two extremes. At one end of this spectrum, we find institutional monolingualism with administrations and citizens communicating only in the official language. At the other end, there is institutional multilingualism where citizens can communicate in their own language(s) or the language(s) of their choice with the administration. Among the scenarios located on these extremes, one is multilingualism with official – not multidirectional – translation, which relates to Canavese's nuance of the fourth model of Meylaerts. Branchadell's contribution further compares and combines the two typologies.

The place of a particular state or region's translation policy on the continuum also depends on a particular period of time. For instance, Vandenbogaerde's insights on nineteenth-century Belgium show that it fits somewhere between the first and the second models, while the period analyzed by Possemiers corresponds to a multilingual state. Most states are multi-layered, and one regime can apply at the state level, whereas others can be found at the local level, as demonstrated in Bernaerts's contribution. Even though present-day Belgium is a federal multilingual state with territorial monolingual regions, further research on the local level (in this case an officially monolingual territory) prompted Bernaerts to design three models that may complement Meylaerts's regimes. The first one is called a 'strict Dutch-only policy' with the exceptional use of interpreters, the second an 'in-between policy' with regular use of interpreters, and the third a 'flexible language (and translation) policy' with few rules on the use of translation. As several contributions in this volume show, Meylaerts's model of translation policy offers four comprehensive regimes, but they cannot be applied to all situations or used as an absolute guideline for classifying the many different and complex translation policies that exist. The debate remains as to which concepts and models can be fruitful for the analysis and comparison of translation policies in different countries.

Keeping these distinctions in mind, we now turn to two areas that are often studied from the perspective of translation policy: legal and institutional translation. We will briefly outline what can be understood by legal and institutional translation and explore how these concepts are discussed in the contributions to this volume.

3   Legal translation

This first pillar of the research field we address in this book is hardly a wasteland in translation and interpreting studies. To delineate this area of research, however, remains difficult, not in the least because the concept of law itself is open to multiple interpretations.

Legal translation studies emerged as a sub-discipline in the 1970s (Prieto Ramos 2014), while in the 1980s, comparative legal approaches developed with Gemar's jurilinguistics in Canada (De Groot 1987, 2012). The current focus mostly lies on the design of specific translation methods for legal texts, on the translation of texts produced in the context of multilingual governance and on interdisciplinarity in legal translation (Prieto Ramos 2014; Biel 2017b). Research into historical aspects of legal translation, as the studies conducted by Possemiers and Vandenbogaerde in this volume, still remain the exception (Glanert 2014, 257).[4] A historical approach is not without its merits, however, as Dullion has pointed out, since it "can also help to understand current institutional policies and practices and put them in perspective, serving as a reminder that multilingual law is not a new phenomenon" (2018, 397). Equally rare were studies on the people conducting legal translations, their education and social profiles (see D'hulst 2015), though they have been studied more extensively over the last decade (see, e.g., Borja Albi and Prieto Ramos 2013; Cadwell et al. 2016; Rossi and Chevrot 2019; Scott 2019; Nartowska 2019; Simonnæs and Kristiansen 2019 and a special issue of *Interpreter and Translator Trainer* (2015) on legal translator training). In this volume, the studies of Vandenbogaerde and of Štefková and Tužinská richly contribute to the exploration of this too-long uncharted territory.

As several of the contributions in this volume demonstrate, there is often no simple correlation between the 'practical' status of texts, that is, as source vs. target texts, and the legal status of texts. Moreover, we are reminded that legal translations can take on various degrees and forms of 'equality'. Possemiers, for instance, describes the different stages that the Dutch translation of the Belgian Civil Code went through before reaching status equal to the French original. A similar story is told by Canavese with regard to the Swiss Italian versions of Swiss legal texts, before the creation of a dedicated parliamentary commission.

While full equality of all language versions is often considered as the *nec plus ultra* to strive for, several authors once again point out that uniformity

---

4   See for example Dullion (2017) and van Gerwen (2019) for studies of historical legal translation practices.

between different versions and within the translated text itself is a constant struggle. Firstly, translators sometimes lack the instruments, such as the EU's Vademecum (see Wasilewska's contribution), to guide them in their translations. Such was the case, as De Camillis explains, for the institutional translators for German in South Tyrol, before the foundation of a Terminology Commission in 1994. Secondly, the standardization of (legal) terminology can be the object of ideological debate. Possemiers illustrates how this was the case for the Dutch translation of the Belgian Civil Code, which, according to some, had to be less 'Dutch' (variant spoken in the Netherlands) and more 'Flemish' (variant spoken in northern Belgium). Štefková and Tužinská argue, in addition, that terminology should be plain and clear, and that sentences should be short with single clauses in the active voice.

As Canavese points out, full equality between various linguistic versions is a fiction, and there is often a gap between *de jure* and *de facto* equality of citizens belonging to different language communities. The same conclusion can be drawn from different contributions with regard to interpreting. Li observes that the equal treatment of citizens speaking a minority language can be compromised by a lack of detailed guidelines on when and how to apply translations in court. She is able to draw this conclusion based on interviews with key players of a trial conducted in a local courtroom in a multilingual region in China, where legal stipulations proved to be far too imprecise to steer the actual language decisions that had to be made in the courtroom.

Branchadell scrutinizes both the translation of normative texts and the translation policies pertaining to the judiciary in Spain's multilingual regions, especially Catalonia. He not only demonstrates again that official language regulations do not give a clear-cut image of actual practices, but also exemplifies that there is more to translation policies than laws, decrees and statutes by governing authorities. He argues that case law should be taken into account for a fuller picture of the regulations coordinating translation practices. Moreover, Branchadell makes an interesting comparison between translation policies in Catalonia and other multilingual regions in- and outside of Spain. He particularly uses the case of South Tyrol as a reference, making his study perfectly complementary with De Camillis's contribution on translation practices in the South Tyrolian Provincial Administration.

Legal translation is often linked to institutional translation policies – or the lack thereof. The institutionalization of legal translation tends to avoid several translations of the same legal text, whereas a lack of agencies and of clear guidelines may generate legal translations of poor quality, as Possemiers demonstrates in his contribution. In South Tyrol, the institution responsible for the translation of acts published in the Official Bulletin is settled by decree. However, as pointed out by Wasilewska, a large number of guidelines may affect their implementation and hinder legal certainty. The discrepancies between management and practice may also be due to a lack of legitimacy of the institution, as in Possemiers's discussion of the Van Dievoet Commission.

4   Institutional translation

In 1988, Brian Mossop (1988, 65) pointed to an important void in translation studies: "There is an important participant missing in existing models of translation: the translating institutions (corporations, churches, governments, newspapers) which directly or indirectly use the services of translators." However, his call to fill this gap largely remained a dead letter until the scope of translation studies started to widen from intercultural literary translation to other kinds of translation, and as the study of interpreting practices was integrated in mainstream translation studies. Indeed, in recent years institutional translation studies has been cultivated to a considerable extent by leading, younger scholars, offering good prospects for the field to be explored further in the coming years. Regulatory functions assigned to institutional translation have received some attention, as have translation practices in institutional settings (Kang 2014; Koskinen 2008, 2014; Schäffner et al. 2014; Svoboda et al. 2017; Prieto Ramos 2017, 2021). However, a lot of research still needs to be done, such as on the way practices and guidelines influence institutional translators, as stated by Wasilewska in citing Kang (2014).

Koskinen observes that governmental institutions in multilingual environments can and often do employ translation in performing their regulatory and organizational functions, and that they therefore "govern by translation" (Koskinen 2014, 479–481). The idea of 'government by translation' has since then been adopted by several scholars and is further institutionalized in the present volume by Gagnon and Canavese, who consider their respective cases (Canada and Switzerland) to be examples of the phenomenon. The concept is also mentioned by Štefková and Tužinská as the inspiration for the design of their study on Slovakia. According to these authors, 'institutional translations' are the translations used in this very act of governing by translation. De Camillis gives an explicit definition of the term in this volume, describing it as "translation practices in government entities". Most other authors implicitly adopt a similar conception of 'institutional translation', by referring to a particular type of public institution. It is worth noting that this take on the term is narrower than when Koskinen describes it as follows:

> [W]e are dealing with institutional translation in those cases when an official body (government agency, multinational organization or a private company, etc.; also an individual person acting in an official status) uses translation as a means of 'speaking' to a particular audience. Thus, in institutional translation, the voice that is to be heard is that of the translating institution. As a result, in a constructivist sense, the institution itself gets translated (2008, 22).

In a broader and interdisciplinary sense, 'institutional translation' can be seen as "[a]ny translation that occurs in an institutional setting, (…) consequently the institution that manages translation is a translating institution" (Schäffner et al. 2014, 493). This definition overlaps with the one given by De Camillis, who considers institutional translation as translation practices in public entities. As illustrated in this book, those public entities can take many forms, such as supranational administrations, national parliaments, parliamentary commissions, commissions on behalf of governments, administrations, courts and tribunals. Since legal translations have particular features because of the specificity of legal language and affairs, it can be noted that institutional translations are a specific kind of translation as well, as they derive from specialized institutional language. Štefková and Tužinská moreover indicate that citizens in contact with institutions may enter an established communication hegemony (Briggs 1984). The "language for institutions is constitutive, that is, the means by which the institution forms a coherent social reality" (Vráblová 2018). In this book, the term 'institutional translation' or 'institutional translators' themselves are only mentioned by four authors and only regularly by De Camillis and by Štefková and Tužinská. However, almost all contributions address institutional translation in the broad sense by referring to a particular type of institution.

The EU is arguably the institution producing the highest amount of translations. Wasilewska describes the confrontation between the guidelines emanating from the Commission's DGT and the translations into Polish. She explains that the language unit revises translations but that the revision procedure does not seem to guarantee a high quality. Wasilewska's study reminds us that institutional translations in practice are not necessarily "collective, anonymous and standardized", the three qualities Koskinen (2008) identified as typical of institutional translations.

The role of parliaments and central governments is also discussed extensively in several contributions in this book. As major players in a democratic society, the study of these institutions is particularly interesting, yet still under-researched. Gagnon, for instance, highlights the great but seldom recognized value of parliamentary debates, as they are "the site of major power struggles" and have a high symbolic value. The study of these debates therefore provides new perspectives on institutional translation. Starting from translation practices, Gagnon demonstrates that official multilingual institutions convey certain ideologies through translation, possibly impacting citizens' identities.

A special role in (multilingual) administrations is played by civil servants who interact directly with citizens. Several case studies presented in this book show that this communication happens in a great variety of ways. Bernaerts, for example, illustrates that, despite a uniform legal framework, various approaches to language use and translation manifest themselves in bilingual municipalities in Belgium. He therefore advises to draft and implement guidelines on the use of translation and interpreting. In her study on the provincial administration in South Tyrol, De Camillis describes the phenomenon of 'occasional translation' within an institutional setting. The frequency of translation depends mostly on the availability of translators. This "spontaneous self-organization" system assures communication between institution and citizens, yet results in a lack of standardization and requires general regulation. De Camillis further calls for the acknowledgment of translation "as one of many necessary steps of the administrative process" and denounces a lack of evaluation of the translations by the institution: an issue similar to complaints discussed by Wasilewska, with regard to translations in the Polish language unit in the EU, and by Štefková and Tužinská, in their contribution on institutional translation in Slovakia. Canavese mentions the lack of availability of Italian translations of Swiss administrative websites and full reports of the activities of the federal departments and offices for Italophone Swiss citizens, despite the official status of Swiss Italian. Finally, Canavese briefly touches upon another type of public institution: the educational system, where the lack of legal courses in Swiss Italian reflects the inequality of languages and the choices made by this institution.

Another institutional context where translation plays an important role, and which has been studied by scholars of interpreting studies in particular, is that of the courts. Court translation is at the heart of three contributions in this volume. In her research on interpreting in Chinese local courts, Li observes how interactions between multilingual participants in a trial are difficult to predict and influence the reactions of other participants, but that the court's translation still shows some kind of pattern. Štefková and Tužinská focus on yet another application of public service interpreting, studying asylum procedures in particular. In their research, based on asylum hearings and interviews conducted with several actors of the hearing, court interpreting is considered part of a larger process. This broad scope allows them to conclude that there is a lack of awareness of the context of communication. They observe that institutional translation and interpretation partly overlaps with parallel concepts such as community, social liaison, as well as public service translation and interpretation. Branchadell's contribution is concerned with court translation and aims at illustrating that case law is an important part of translation policy, in addition to the laws and decrees proclaimed by legislative bodies in the strict sense.

Vandenbogaerde tackles another aspect of judicial translation when analyzing the legal journals in which laws and case law are published, translated and discussed. His discussion of the translation practices of legal editorial boards, struggling to find fixed methods for standardized translations, bears interesting resemblances to translation practices in other political and public institutions examined in this book.

Finally, the importance of providing institutional translation for vulnerable groups in society, such as migrants and minorities, is addressed in this volume, particularly in the contributions of De Camillis and of Štefková and Tužinská. Both contributions point out the importance of spoken forms of translation and the use of children as intermediaries or community interpreters. In this context, the degree of institutionalization of language services for non-native speakers is linked with the position of vulnerable groups in society.

By sharing this collection of original contributions on translation policies in legal and institutional settings, often based on highly valuable empirical data, we hope to ignite many new discussions and studies on similar topics and to enhance the development of just and effective translation policies, with respect to the specific linguistic and political context. Due to their obvious link with languages policies, we strongly believe translation policies can lead to more linguistic as well as political equality. Furthermore, we wish to demonstrate that normative sources such as laws should be considered together with observations in real-life situations as much as possible. Empirical studies and field work have proved incredibly valuable for gaining insight into actual translation practices.

As translation practices are typically variable in time and space, we need flexible tools to examine, describe and compare public translation practices in different times and places, without losing sight of the complexity and uniqueness of each case. Based on the concepts and methods developed so far, it is hoped that researchers will undertake further innovation (by looking, for example, at new types of sources as suggested by Gagnon), so as to take those particularities into account and connect them with existing results. We believe the contributions in this book offer very interesting case studies and provide an important stepping stone for future research on translation policies in institutional and legal settings. We hope that many researchers, be they translation scholars, legal historians or political scholars, will be inspired by them to continue on this promising path.

References

Biel, Łucja. 2017a. "Quality in Institutional EU Translation: Parameters, Policies and Practices." In *Quality Aspects in Institutional Translation*, edited by Tomáš Svoboda, Łucja Biel and Krzysztof Łoboda, 31–57. Berlin: Language Science Press.

———. 2017b. "Researching Legal Translation: A Multi-perspective and Mixed-method Framework for Legal Translation." *Revista de Llengua i Dret, Journal of Language and Law* 68: 76–88. https://doi.org/10.2436/rld.i68.2017.2967.

Biel, Łucja, Jan Engberg, Rosario M. Martín Ruano, and Vilelmini Sosoni, eds. 2019. *Research Methods in Legal Translation and Interpreting*. London: Routledge.

Borja Albi, Anabel, and Fernando Prieto Ramos, eds. 2013. *Legal Translation in Context: Professional Issues and Prospects*. Oxford: Peter Lang.

Briggs, Charles. 1984. *Learning how to Ask: A Sociolinguistic Appraisal of the Role of the Interview in Social Science Research*. Cambridge: Cambridge University Press.

Cadwell, Patrick, Sheila Castilho, Sharon O'Brien, and Linda Mitchell. 2016. "Human Factors in Machine Translation and Post-Editing among Institutional Translators." *Translation Spaces* 5 (2): 222–243. https://doi.org/10.1075/ts.5.2.04cad.

D'hulst, Lieven, and Michael Schreiber. 2014. "Vers une historiographie des politiques des traductions en Belgique durant la période française." *Target* 26 (1): 3–31. https://doi.org/10.1075/target.26.1.01hul.

D'hulst, Lieven. 2015. "Quels défis pour l'histoire de la traduction et de la traductologie?" *Meta* 60 (2): 281–298. https://doi.org/10.7202/1032858ar.

D'hulst, Lieven, Carol O'Sullivan, and Michael Schreiber, eds. 2016. *Politics, Policy and Power in Translation History*. Berlin: Frank & Timme.

Derlén, Mattias. 2015. "A Single Text or a Single Meaning: Multilingual Interpretation of EU Legislation and CJEU Case Law in National Courts." In *Language and Culture in EU Law: Multidisciplinary Perspectives*, edited by Susan Šarčević, 53–72. Farnham: Ashgate.

Diaz Fouces, Oscar. 2010. "(Eco)linguistic Planning and Language-Exchange Management." *MonTI: Monografías de Traducción e Interpretación* 2: 283–313.

Dullion, Valérie. 2017. "La traduction des décisions de justice dans les revues juridiques suisses: développement d'un régime de traduction privée (1856–1912)." *Parallèles* 29 (1): 75–89.

Dullion, Valérie. 2018. "Legal History." In *A History of Modern Translation Knowledge*, edited by Lieven D'hulst and Yves Gambier, 397–400. Amsterdam: John Benjamins.

Glanert, Simone. 2014. "Law-In-Translation: An Assemblage in Motion." *The Translator* 20 (3): 255–272.

González Núñez, Gabriel and Reine Meylaerts. 2017. *Translation and Public Policy: Interdisciplinary Perspectives and Case Studies*. London: Routledge.

Ingelbeen, Caroline, and Michael Schreiber. 2017. "Translation Policies in Belgium during the French Period (1792–1814)." *Parallèles* 29 (1): 34–44.

Kang, Ji-Hae. 2014. "Institutions Translated: Discourse, Identity and Power in Institutional Mediation." *Perspectives* 22 (4): 469–478. https://doi.org/10.1080/0907676X.2014.948892.

Koskinen, Kaisa. 2008. *Translating Institutions: An Ethnographic Study of EU Translation*. Manchester: St. Jerome.

———. 2014. "Institutional Translation: The Art of Government by Translation." *Perspectives* 22 (4): 479–492. https://doi.org/10.1080/0907676X.2014.948887.

McAuliffe, Karen. 2016. "Hidden Translators: The Invisibility of Translators and the Influence of Lawyer-Linguists on the Case Law of the Court of Justice of the European Union." *Language and Law / Linguagem e Direito* 3 (1): 5–29.

Meylaerts, Reine. 2010. "Multilingualism and Translation." In *Handbook of Translation Studies*, vol. 1, edited by Yves Gambier and Luc van Doorslaer, 227–230. Amsterdam: John Benjamins.

———. 2011a. "Translation Policy." In *Handbook of Translation Studies Online*, vol. 2, edited by Yves Gambier and Luc van Doorslaer. Amsterdam: John Benjamins. https://doi.org/10.1075/hts.2.tra10.

———. 2011b. "Translational Justice in a Multilingual World: An Overview of Translational Regimes." *Meta* 56 (4): 743–757. https://doi.org/10.7202/1011250ar.

———. 2018. "The Politics of Translation in Multilingual States." In *The Routledge Handbook of Translation and Politics*, edited by Jonathan Evans and Fruela Fernandez, 221–237. London: Routledge.

Mossop, Brian. 1988. "Translating Institutions: A Missing Factor in Translation Theory." *TTR: traduction, terminologie, rédaction* 1 (2): 65–71.

Nouws, Bieke. 2019. "'Van de woede der Noormannen en vertalers verlos ons heer!' Opvattingen over vertaling en juridisch vertaalbeleid in België, 1830–1914." unpublished PhD diss., KU Leuven.

O'Rourke, Bernadette, and Pedro Castillo. 2009. "Top-Down or Bottom-up Language Policy: Public Service Interpreting in the Republic of Ireland, Scotland and Spain." In *Interpreting and Translating in Public Service Settings: Policy, Practice, Pedagogy*, edited by Raquel de Pedro Ricoy, Isabelle Perez and Christine Wilson, 33–51. Manchester: St. Jerome.

Prieto Ramos, Fernando. 2014. "Legal Translation Studies as Interdiscipline: Scope and Evolution." *Meta* 59 (2): 260–277. https://doi.org/10.7202/1027475ar.

———, ed. 2017. *Institutional Translation for International Governance: Enhancing Quality in Multilingual Legal Communication*. London: Bloomsbury.

———, ed. 2021. *Institutional Translation and Interpreting*. New York: Routledge.

Rogers, Margaret. 2018. "Specialised Translation Today: A View from the JoSTrans Bridge." *The Journal of Specialised Translation* 30: 3–22.

Rossi, Caroline, and Jean-Pierre Chevrot. 2019. "Uses and Perceptions of Machine Translation at the European Commission." *The Journal of Specialised Translation* 31: 177–200.

Šarčević, Susan, ed. 2015. *Language and Culture in EU Law*. London: Routledge.

Schäffner, Christina, Luciana Sabina Tcaciuc, and Wine Tesseur. 2014. "Translation Practices in Political Institutions: A Comparison of National, Supranational, and Non-Governmental Organisations." *Perspectives* 22 (4): 493–510.

Scott, Juliette R. 2019. *Legal Translation Outsourced*. Oxford: Oxford University Press.

Simonnæs, Ingrid, and Marita Kristiansen. 2019. *Legal Translation. Current Issues and Challenges in Research, Methods and Applications*. Berlin: Frank & Timme.

Spolsky, Bernard. 2004. *Language Policy*. Cambridge: Cambridge University Press.

Suh, Joseph Che. 2011. "The Role of Translation in the Implementation of Language Policy in Cameroon." *Translation Journal* 15 (3). https://translation-journal.net/journal/57cameroon.htm.

Svoboda, Tomáš, Łucja Biel, and Krzysztof Łoboda, eds. 2017. *Quality Aspects in Institutional Translation*. Berlin: Language Science Press.

van Doorslaer, Luc. 2013. "Belgian Translation Policy. The Case of the German-Language Community." In *Multilingualism for Empowerment: Studies in Language Policy in South Africa*, edited by Pol Cuvelier, Theodorus Du Plessis, Michael Meeuwis, Reinhild Vandekerckhove and Vic Webb, 60–71, Pretoria: Van Schaik.

van Gerwen, Heleen. 2019. "Studying the Forms and Functions of Legal Translations in History: The Case of 19th-Century Belgium." *Translation and Interpreting: The International Journal of Translation and Interpreting Research* 11 (2): 106–118. https://doi.org/10.12807/ti.111202.2019.a09.

Vrábľová, Júlia. 2018. *Specifics of Institutional Management of the National Language in Slovakia*. In *National Language Institutions and National Languages: Contributions to the EFNIL Conference 2017 in Mannheim*, edited by Gerhard Stickel, 85–99. Budapest: Research Institute for Linguistics, Hungarian Academy of Sciences.

Wolf, Michaela. 2015. *The Habsburg Monarchy's Many-Languaged Soul: Translating and Interpreting, 1848–1918*. Translated by Kate Sturge. Amsterdam: John Benjamins.

Government ideologies in translation

An enquiry into past Canadian budget speeches

Chantal Gagnon

Abstract

This chapter deals with parliamentary language in translation, an under-researched area in translation studies. In particular, the study investigates translated budget speeches in the federal government of Canada, in the last quarter of the 20th century. Using critical discourse analysis and Koskinen's work on governing by translation, the investigation argues that the nature of government by translation creates a particular translation practice and that the federal government of Canada can be seen as a typical example of governance through translation. The main corpus investigated is comprised of every budget speech delivered between 1970 and 1995. The translation of the ideologically laden word 'federal' is examined in this budget corpus, and it shows translation shifts attributed to power struggles between Canadian nationalist and Québécois nationalist discourses. In fact, through their translation choices, the work of translators has helped to assert the federal government's presence in the minds of the province of Quebec audience.

1 Introduction

In any society, the state plays many roles at the economic, political, social or cultural level. Over the last centuries, these roles have evolved and have had inevitable repercussions on governments' budgets and fiscal policies. Studies on government budgets and fiscal issues help to understand the progression of societies, since the growth and diversification of the public sector are linked, in part, to the evolution of a society's ideas, to innovation in the communication media and to the development of trade (Bernard 1992, 3). As we are reminded by political scientist Bernard (1992, 1ff), these studies can be developed from several academic perspectives, including economics, law, and political science. We argue that the translation studies perspective is also highly relevant, especially when studying fiscal and budgetary communication in a multilingual government. A country like Canada, with its officially bilingual federal government and its history of clashes between its two official linguistic communities, is an ideal example to illustrate the pertinence of the translation studies perspective when investigating multilingual budgetary communication, such as budget speeches in the Canadian Federal Parliament.

Parliamentary language has been an object of study in linguistics for some time, but Calzada Pérez (2018a) argues that it is still an under-researched area within linguistics and related fields. In translation studies, specifically, parliamentary discourse is particularly under-researched (with some exceptions, such as Calzada Pérez (2001, 2018b)). Moreover, to our knowledge, budget speeches in the Canadian Federal Parliament have almost never been studied. Yet budget speeches are the site of major power struggles, and they should be investigated for what they symbolize and for the ideologies they convey, in translation, to the general public.

Political science research has shown that budgetary forecasts are impacted by party ideology and hence are sometimes subject to political manipulation. In certain instances, for example, right-leaning governments in Canada tend to underestimate their revenues (Couture and Imbeau 2009). Since budgets symbolize, in many ways, the priorities of a government at a certain period in time, it is quite possible that aside from being part of the left/right political spectrum, budget speeches represent other types of ideas and values, such as a nation's identity. In translation studies, we have shown elsewhere that economic speeches delivered by Canadian politicians at the Economic Club of New York sometimes present translation shifts which could be explained by identity-related factors (Gagnon and Kalantari 2017). One of the hypotheses of the present chapter is that a similar phenomenon is (to be) found in Canadian budget speeches. Exploring translation shifts in budget speeches could provide new perspectives on institutional translation, since such speeches are at the center of parliamentary life and are seldom studied in translation studies. Specifically, budget speeches were chosen because they are regarded as some of the most important speeches of the Canadian Parliament. These key speeches receive wide attention from the media and the public in general, and both their original text and translation are carefully crafted. We wish to investigate how the federal government of Canada has spread the idea of the Canadian nation through these speeches delivered between 1970 and 1995, a period marked by power struggles between Canadian nationalist and Québécois nationalist discourses. Quebec is the only Canadian province with a Francophone majority.

2 Framework of analysis and corpus design

When investigating the politics of translation in multilingual states, we are reminded by Meylaerts (2018, 222) that "confronted with multilingual populations, states cannot remain neutral over translation." Since its founding in 1867, Canada has chosen to embrace translation, mainly into French and into English, the dominant languages of its linguistic communities. Translation plays a major role in Canadian society by putting forward the federal[1] government's values (Mossop 1990; Gagnon 2014a, b). It should be noted that only recently has the Canadian Government started to provide some translation into Indigenous languages (Lemieux 2019), and mostly through interpreting. Much remains to be done regarding Indigenous linguistic rights and research on Indigenous translation in Canada, but for reasons of space and lack of translation data, this research will focus on Canada's official languages, English and French.

Political scientists such as Hanson, Kopstein and Lichbach (2000/2014) have established that institutions reinforce certain identity groups by promoting their ideas. In translation studies, research has shown that translations feature widely in debates about identity (e.g., Cronin 2006; Hostová 2017) and that translation is at the heart of multilingual institutions (e.g., Meylaerts 2011, 2013). Moreover, Koskinen argues that the central function of any institution is to govern (2014, 481) and that multilingual institutions generally use translation when governing. Hence, for this scholar, official multilingual institutions govern by translation. The present chapter investigates how Koskinen's idea of governing by translation can be applied, from a critical discourse analysis perspective (Fairclough 1989/2015; van Dijk 2001; Schäffner 2003; Fairclough and Fairclough 2012), in a translation corpus made up of budget speeches delivered in Canada during the twentieth century. We will argue that the nature of government by translation creates a particular translation practice where the act of translating takes place in a structured and structuring institutional environment. The political function of translation in a bilingual institution such as the federal government of Canada can be seen as a typical example of governance through translation. It is from this perspective that we will analyze the federal government's budget speeches from the last quarter of the twentieth century. This historical time frame was chosen because Quebec's nationalist discourse was particularly strong during this period, as evidenced by the first election in Quebec of a pro-independence government (1976) and the holding of two referendums on Quebec sovereignty (in 1980 and 1995).

---

1   Canada is a federal state with ten provinces and three territories.

During this period, direct confrontations between the federal government of Canada and the government of the province of Quebec increased. It is therefore an ideal context to study how the federal government has presented its institutional discourse in translation.

According to critical discourse analysis, language is a form of social practice (Fairclough 1989/2015, 1992). Our project investigates the translation of parliamentary budget speeches in Canada, a social practice that is available in two languages and two cultures. In particular, we consider possible translation shifts between the French and English speeches in the corpus. Because the concept of 'ideology' refers to the collective values of a social group (Hatim and Mason 1997), it is an excellent tool for studying the question of identity. We are reminded by van Dijk (1998, 118) that "whenever a group has developed an ideology, such an ideology at the same time also defines the basis for the group's identity." In the present study, we wish to investigate ideological markers informed by the notion of institutional identity. Such a notion is characterized by the degree to which actors position themselves towards an institution's ideology. For Benwell and Stokoe (2006), in critical discourse analysis, the way people interact in social or institutional situations reflects existing power struggles. Therefore, institutional identity is a function of power relations within the institution (Benwell and Stokoe 2006, 87). In our analysis we will try to see from a discursive and translation studies point of view whether there is a connection between certain translation choices and the values of a translator's institution, which is in our case the federal government of Canada. For instance, Drew and Sorjonen (1997/2011) identify certain characteristic features of institutional discourse, such as lexical choices (including specialized vocabulary). Investigating the translation of specific lexical choices could provide insight into the discursive practices of Canada's best-known translating institution.

We have already shown, in another project dealing with identity crises and translating institutions in Canada, that in order to promote Canadian nationalism, the federal government proposed democratic values, in French, using terms such as *citoyens* (citizens), while for the same English excerpts, it put forward patriotic values, employing 'fellow Canadians' (e.g., Gagnon 2006). From these past results, it emerged that the question of language was closely associated with membership in an identity group, and that it necessarily highlighted ideology issues in the linguistic communities. These were first attempts at understanding political discourse in Canada. We are, here, proposing a new study consisting of a body of budget speeches delivered in the Canadian House of Commons by former finance ministers. In particular, we wish to verify whether the subject of the speech (a country's finances) and the form of the speech (parliamentary speech) have repercussions for the reproduction of ideologies in translation, hence the importance of comparing the results of the present project with those obtained in our past research.

The corpus investigated in the present study is comprised of every budget speech delivered between 1970 and 1995. We start in 1970 because some of Canada's most significant identity crises and language issues took place in the 1970s (for historical and sociopolitical background, see Larrivée 2003; Howard 2007; Dickinson and Young 2014), and these crises may have had an impact on the wording of the budget speeches. With the referendum on Quebec's sovereignty and the narrow victory of the NO camp,[2] the year 1995 marked a turn in Quebec's nationalist discourse, which explains the end date of the corpus period. There are twenty-six budget speeches within the period, all of them available electronically (Parliament of Canada n.d.) in Canada's official languages, that is, French and English. The corpus of budget speeches presented here consists of 227,993 English words and 241,964 French words, or 469,957 words in total.

The results obtained in the budget corpus will be compared to other corpora from our previous research (e.g., Gagnon 2019). These corpora for comparison can be divided into two categories: seven televised addresses to the nation discussing identity crises, delivered between 1970 and 1995 (10,036 words in English, 10,644 words in French, for a total of 20,680 words) and five parliamentary speeches about these same crises (27,256 words in English, 29,006 in French, for a total of 56,262 words). Some crises involved more than one televised speech, which explains the difference between the number of televised addresses and the number of parliamentary speeches.

Between 1970 and 1995, the Liberal Party of Canada led the federal government of Canada slightly more often than its political rival, the Progressive Conservative Party of Canada. The Liberals led the government for fifteen of the twenty-five years. During this time, Canada had six prime ministers, three from either party, and ten finance ministers, that is, seven Liberals and three Conservatives. This distribution means there could be a greater variety of writing styles in Liberal speeches than in Conservative speeches, and a difference between the parties.

---

[2] In Quebec, during the 1995 referendum campaign, 'YES' and 'NO' supporters were organized in committees. The 'YES' camp was led by the then Premier of Quebec, Jacques Parizeau, while the 'NO' camp was led by the Leader of the Opposition of the Quebec government, Daniel Johnson. The 'NO' side narrowly won the campaign with 50.58%.

3 Contextualization

3.1 Historical and political contextualization

In Canada, and particularly in Quebec, questions of finance, taxation or even currency have often gone hand in hand with the question of language. For instance, with the 1935 creation of the Bank of Canada arose a debate about the language(s) to appear on Canadian bank notes. Some members of Parliament, such as Conservative politician Thomas Langton Church, were strongly opposed to a bilingual note, preferring the status quo, that is, notes in French for Quebec and in English for the rest of Canada. He said, in June 1936, in the House of Commons: "I shall, however, refer to the statement of the minister that in future there will be bilingual notes instead of some being in English and some in French. (…) [It] is inconvenient, and what is more it is not desired by the banking people or by the taxpayers (…)." (Canada. Parliament 1936a, 3340)

That Langton Church refers to "banking people" shows that at that time, English was the dominant language of business not only throughout English Canada but also in Francophone Quebec (Burnaby 1996, 162). Indeed, as the Royal Commission on Bilingualism would show in 1969, Quebec Francophones' minority status also subsumed subordinate economic status (d'Anglejan 1984, 28–30). Furthermore, the fact that French was a minority language also meant that a majority of English-speaking taxpayers were probably inclined to oppose bilingual notes. Days after his House of Commons statement, Langton Church would go on to add:

> Canada is not and never was a bilingual country. It is a country where the two languages are official languages, but the law courts have set out the length and depth and breadth of the two languages (…) This particular legislation will be here forever. Those who vote for this bill are voting that this country is to be a bilingual country by order of a militant minority. (Canada. Parliament 1936b, 3757–3758)

Canada had already introduced bilingual postage stamps in 1927 (Fraser 2007), but for this member of Parliament, bank notes were the true symbol of Canada's imposed bilingualism. For Francophones in Canada, bilingual notes were a step towards the recognition of their linguistic rights, but in no way did this act represent the end of their fight (Fraser 2007). The divergence of perspectives is not only striking but is also evidence of the linguistic divide in Canada during that period.

Another strong symbol combining language and finance is Quebec Premier Maurice Duplessis's Income Tax Act in 1954, which gave back to the province of Quebec control over its own taxes. To this day, Quebec is the only province where separate tax returns are filed with both the federal and provincial governments. In other provinces, the federal government collects all the income taxes and gives back a part thereof to the provincial governments. In Quebec, both governments collect their own tax. As argues Tillotson (2017, 266), Duplessis closely linked the power of taxation with the power to govern, which was particularly important in a government whose mission was to preserve the French Canadian people. More than sixty years later, this political legacy is still valuable to Quebecers. According to Canadian journalist Daniel Leblanc (2018), "Quebec is jealous of its responsibility for its provincial income-tax system, which was created (...) as part of a quest for greater autonomy [from the federal government]." Struggles between the Canadian and Quebec governments and, in particular, around their conception of fiscality are at the heart of the present research.

3.2 Budget speeches in Canada

The question of power regarding taxation regularly comes up, directly or indirectly, in budget speeches by the federal government. Budget speeches are part of a long-standing tradition in the Canadian House of Commons. On a day designated by the government (most often in February or March), usually after the financial markets have closed, the finance minister delivers the Budget Speech (Bosc and Gagnon 2017). As a parliamentary convention, the content of the Budget Speech is kept secret until the minister presents it in the House. Since the speech is used as a tool for communicating with the general public, technical information such as the fiscal framework is presented in the budget plan rather than included in the House of Commons speech (Tellier 2019). The budget plan is published at the same time as the speech.

According to Tellier (2019, 116), a minister's budget speech generally involves four themes: a country's (or province's) economic situation, the government's spending initiatives, the government's tax initiatives, and the government's financial position (i.e., deficit and debt). These subject matters are of utmost importance for both the Parliament and the government: Smith and Pu (2015/2019, 1) argue that one of Parliament's fundamental roles is to comment on and approve the government's taxation and spending propositions. The approval of Parliament is required for any measure associated with taxes or public funds spending. Hence, the Budget Speech ranks next to the Speech from the Throne – Canada is a constitutional monarchy – in terms of the most important events in the House of Commons (Smith and Pu 2015/2019, 6).

3.3 Translation production contextualization

Since 1935, translators at the Translation Bureau (the federal government's translation service) have been translating the House of Commons Debates by night, in order to reduce the delay between the production of the English and the French versions of these proceedings (Delisle 1984). However, important government speeches are usually written and translated in advance to facilitate their distribution to the Canadian media in both official languages. Prepared translations also give finance ministers a chance to practice their budget speech, including the parts delivered in their second language. Indeed, when searching the Canadian National Archives (Library and Archives Canada. Michael Wilson Fonds 1990), we noticed that finance ministers and their staff carefully choose the parts of the budget speeches to be delivered in English, and the parts to be delivered in French. In each case, the language choice was made on the basis of the intended addressee, for instance, French Quebec or English Canada. Unfortunately, the various archives consulted contained little or no information on the translators of the budget speech. On interviewing the current chief of the Language Services for the Department of Finance Canada (Bétoté Akwa 2019), we learned that the speech has been translated in the private sector for at least the past ten years.

When we asked a former political adviser of the Pierre Elliott Trudeau era how translation worked in the 1970s and 1980s, he said public policy speeches were written and translated by civil servants and revised (sometimes heavily) by political advisers (see also Gagnon 2010). The political adviser we spoke to was kind enough to search in his personal archives, where he found a memorandum that sparked the present research. In the memo, the adviser discusses the ideas submitted to him by a fellow political aide:

CABINET DU PREMIER MINISTRE
MEMORANDUM
Le 11 juillet 1978
J'ai lu avec grand intérêt votre note (…). Il y est question du poids émotif des mots dans la lutte qui nous oppose aux Péquistes et des avantages qu'il y aurait à substituer systématiquement au terme « fédéral » le terme « canadien » afin de mieux rejoindre le cœur et l'esprit des Québécois.

J'admets volontiers avec M. Préfontaine que le mot « fédéral » n'a pas très bon cours au Québec où les gens l'associent au statu quo, aux tendances centralisatrices, aux disputes stériles entre Ottawa et les provinces et au rejet systématique de toute forme de nationalisme québécois.

(I read with great interest your memo (…). It discusses the emotional weight of words in the fight with Quebec's separatists, as well as the benefits of systematically replacing the word *fédéral* [federal] with the word *Canadien* [Canadian], to better connect with the heart and minds of Quebecers. I readily agree with Mr. Préfontaine that the word *fédéral* does not go down very well in Quebec, since people associate it with the status quo, centralizing tendencies, counterproductive disputes between Ottawa and the provinces and the systematic rejection of any form of Quebec nationalism.)

At first glance, the word *Canadien* seemed popular among Pierre Trudeau's staff, especially when compared with the word *fédéral*. However, in the rest of the memo, the political adviser did not agree with his colleague: he was not sure that the word *Canadien* was such an agreeable word and, in any case, there should be no abuse of it. We learned that Trudeau agreed that the word *Canadien* should not systematically replace the word *fédéral*. These discussions about the terminology to be used to refer to the federal government show the extent of the power struggle between the Quebec government and the federal government of Canada in the 1970s and 1980s. However, we should note that research on public policy has shown that "Canada is along with Switzerland one of the more decentralized industrial countries in the world, with Quebec being one of the strongest subnational units in a federal system (…)" (Vaillancourt 2010). It is clear that the decentralization noted by experts did not prevent the struggle between Quebec and Canada. The fight for power between the Canadian federal government and the Quebec government was very real and is still relevant to this day.

All of this led us to investigate how the word 'federal' has been translated in our budget corpus and how it has been used in the French translation of the budget, throughout the period 1970–1995.

4   Results

We have seen that at least during the Pierre Elliott Trudeau era, that is, in the 1970s and the early 1980s, some Francophone political advisers thought that the word 'Canada' referred to a strong and positive force. In previous studies, we have investigated translation shifts around the lemma CANADA in several translation corpora, such as televised and parliamentary speeches during political crises, or budget speeches (e.g., Gagnon 2006, 2019). These studies were helpful in understanding ideologies in translated political speeches as a whole, but also in verifying whether translation shifts and the ideological variation they sometimes conveyed differed from one political genre to the next. For example, in Figure 1 below, when looking at the lemma[3] CANADA as used in the different corpora of our past studies, we notice, in every corpus, a small difference between the French and English speeches.

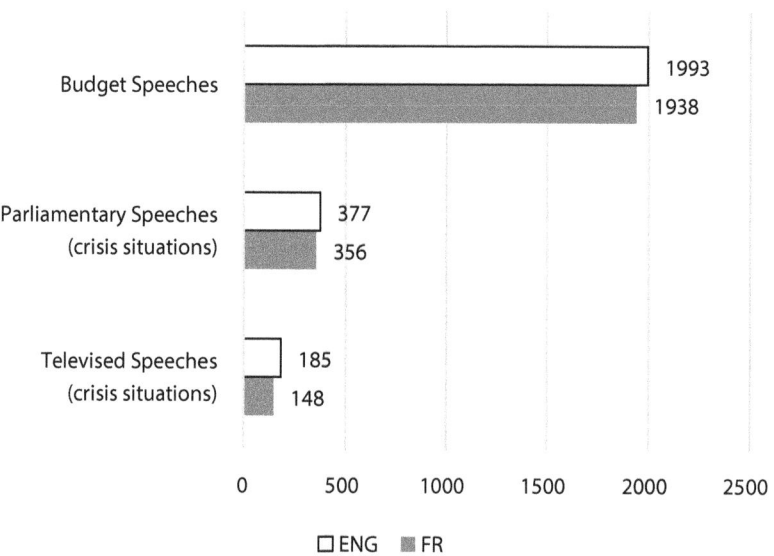

Figure 1. Number of raw occurences of the lemma CANADA (1970-1995)

In Figure 1, we observe that in all three corpora, the lemma CANADA is used more often in English than it is in French. With significant differences between the number of occurrences of CANADA in French and English, translation

---

3   For this research, we do not use a classical definition of the term 'lemma.' Usually, a lemma is the canonical form of a word: it represents a group of words that can be treated as variants of the same word (Knowles and Don 2004, 71). Take, for example, the French adjective *canadien*. Its feminine form *canadienne* and the plural forms *canadiens/canadiennes* would typically all fall under the headword CANADIEN. With such a definition, all variants relate to only one word class and one definition, and in that case, CANADA and CANADIEN would represent two distinct French lemmas. However, in translation, names are often translated using another word class (e.g., Vinay and Darbelnet 1977; Chesterman 1997/2016). For the purpose of our study, lemmas will not be restricted to one word class.

shifts were to be expected. In fact, our research has shown that some of the translation shifts were potentially based on an ideological struggle between different national discourses in Canada. Some of these results could also be explained by the fact that Romance languages, such as French or Italian, try to avoid repetitions in texts (Scarpa 2010). Moreover, in a widely used Canadian translation manual (Delisle and Fiola 2013), translation students are told to find synonyms for the word 'Canada' in their French translations, in order to avoid repetitions and hence improve on the style of their texts.

The memo in the previous section showed that for some political aides the words 'Canada' and *fédéral* were often synonyms in French political speeches, but that they carried different connotations: the former was seen as having a positive (or neutral) connotation, whereas the latter was seen as having a negative connotation. Here is an example taken from a 1977 issue of the Quebec news magazine *L'actualité*, which illustrates the negative connotation of *federal* (our emphasis): "On est tanné d'aller frapper [au gouvernement] pour quémander de l'argent (…). Un dollar dépensé [dans la province canadienne de l'] Ontario, c'est dans l'industrie secondaire. **Une piastre dépensée au Québec par le fédéral, c'est pour de l'assistance.**" ("We are tired of going cap in hand [to the government] (…). A dollar spent [in the Canadian province of] Ontario goes to the industrial sector. **A buck spent in Quebec by the federal goes to social assistance.**") (Godin 1977, 10)

This excerpt was taken from an interview with a member of Parliament (henceforth referred to as MP) from the Parliament in the province of Quebec, that is, the *Assemblée Nationale*. This MP was a representative of the *Parti Québécois*, a political party whose main objective is the independence of Quebec from Canada. The MP presented here an argument often upheld in Quebec, particularly by sovereignists (Intellectuels pour la souveraineté 1995), which states that for decades in the twentieth century, the federal government's economic policy has given priority to the city of Toronto (in the province of Ontario), thereby helping it to become the vital centre of the Canadian economy. During the same period, the argument goes, Quebec did not benefit as much from these federal investments, but it received significant funding for its social programs. As a result, Ontario has acquired the image of a wealthy province, while Quebec has been perceived as a province in need. Some consider this situation unfair, since the province of Quebec is ideally situated for trade and possesses diversified resources (Intellectuels pour la souveraineté 1995). (At the turn of the twentieth century, Montréal – Quebec's most important city – was considered Canada's economic center, but its economic vitality has since faded, to Toronto's advantage.) According to sovereignists, the federal government's policy has resulted in an imbalance in Canada's economic development.

The member of Parliament who made these comments was Gérald Godin. Prior to his involvement in politics, Godin was known, among other things, for his poetic works (e.g., Godin 1967). His poetic writing was characterized by its use of Quebec's popular language to defend the financially deprived (Royer 1994). His mastery of different language registers is recognizable in his interview with *L'actualité* magazine. For instance, when talking about Quebec's economic situation, Godin uses the familiar register (the expression *le federal* supposes an ellipsis of the word *gouvernement*) and vernacular language (the Quebec word *piastre*), but when talking about Ontario he uses the formal register, devoid of the vernacular or ellipsis, but including technical vocabulary (*secteur industriel*). In Quebec, writers have often used the vernacular language as a means of socioeconomic contestation (e.g., Saint-Jacques 1974; Gauvin 1976), particularly in the 1960s and 1970s, and Godin's use of words was meaningful in the quote above. It is clear from Godin's statement that *fédéral* has a negative connotation.

A year after Godin's interview, a poll published in the daily newspaper *La Presse* revealed that Quebecers disapproved of the federal government's attitude towards their home province. To summarize the content of a part of the survey, the journalist wrote: "Mauvaise attitude du fédéral envers le Québec" (Bad Attitude of the Federal towards Quebec) (Gravel 1978, A7).

We note that the French word *fédéral* has engendered among Quebecers' unfavorable opinions about their federal government, at least at some point in Quebec's history. In fact, according to *La Presse* journalist André Pratte, this negative connotation remains in the Quebec discourse (2006, A38): "Au Québec, le mot « fédéralisme » a une connotation négative. (...) Le fédéralisme est associé par plusieurs à un gouvernement fédéral centralisateur, à la déception engendrée par de pénibles épisodes de notre histoire politique, au scandale des commandites, etc." ("In Quebec, the word 'federalism' has a negative connotation. (...) Federalism is often associated with a centralizing federal government, with the disappointment caused by painful episodes in our political history, with the sponsorship scandal, etc.")

We thus decided to investigate the lemmas FÉDÉRAL and FEDERAL in our three corpora; that is, we looked at the number of occurrences of FÉDÉRAL and FEDERAL in each corpus. The results are shown in Figure 2.

In the televised and parliamentary speeches delivered in times of crises, the lemma FEDERAL is used almost as often in English as the lemma FÉDÉRAL is used in French. However, when we look at budget speeches, there are more occurrences of FÉDÉRAL in French. Considering the results described in

Figure 1, the results of Figure 2 were not expected. As we explained earlier, the French language tends to avoid repetitions, and the word 'fédéral' in French can have a strong negative connotation. We expected results similar to those in Figure 1, that is more occurrences of the lemma FEDERAL in English. The variation between the French and the English in the budget corpus occurs in both Liberal and Conservative speeches, as can be seen in Figure 3. Hence, this is not a trend associated with a single political party, but rather a global trend within the budget corpus.

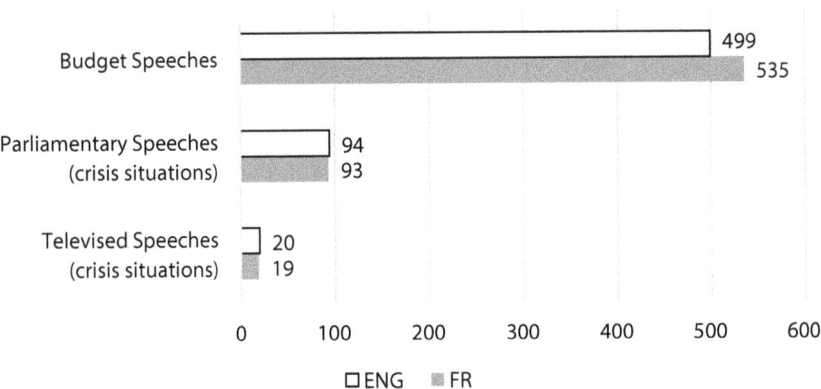

Figure 2. Number of occurrences of the lemmas FÉDÉRAL/FEDERAL

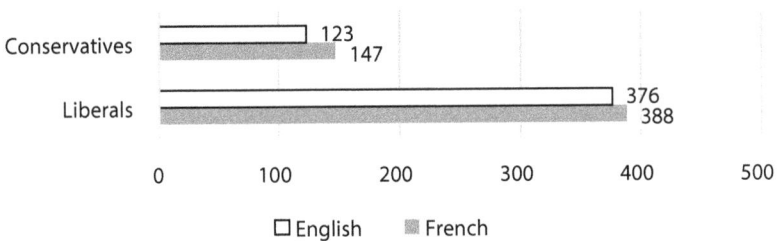

Figure 3. Number of occurrences of the lemmas FÉDÉRAL/FEDERAL distributed by political parties (1970-1995)

To better understand this phenomenon, we looked at all 527 occurrences of FEDERAL and FÉDÉRAL.[4] In a comparison of the French and the English speeches, we labelled all the translation shifts according to a typology heavily based on Chesterman's work in *Memes of Translation* (1997/2016). The

---

4   Sometimes, in the corpus, the lemma FEDERAL is not translated by FÉDÉRAL, and vice versa. The number 527 accounts for all the references where either FEDERAL or FÉDÉRAL appears.

categories of the typology can be found in Appendix 1. As we have explained elsewhere (Gagnon 2006), Chesterman's 'translation strategies' are text-based, and such use of the concept 'strategy' can be ambiguous. Indeed, whereas translation shifts are almost always text-based, it is not so with translation strategies, since they can be seen from an array of perspectives. For Molina and Hurtado Albir (2002), strategies are procedures used by translators to solve problems. For all these reasons, we adapted Chesterman's typology, using the concept of 'translation shifts' rather than 'translation strategies', and we slightly adapted the typology to reflect this change.

In labelling the occurrences of FEDERAL and FÉDÉRAL in the budget corpus, we found that a majority of 'federal' occurrences (354, around 67%) were translated literally, that is, 'federal' was translated as *fédéral*. This was expected: after all, from a Canadian terminological perspective, the adjectives 'federal' and *fédéral* generally refer to the very same political reality. According to *Termium* (Translation Bureau 1999), the Canadian federal government's terminological database, 'federal' should be translated as *fédéral* or one of its quasi-synonyms (e.g., *fédéraliste* or *fédéré*).

When looking at the non-literal translation – that is, the shifts – we found that one type stood out: explicitness change. Indeed, as shown in Figure 4, almost half of the shifts belong to this category (eighty-five explicitness changes out of 173 translation shifts). For a detailed presentation of all the types of shifts in the budget corpus, see Appendix 2.

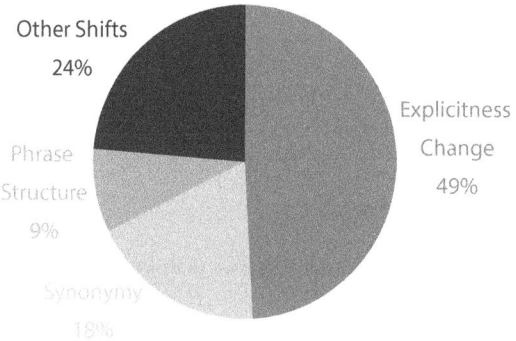

Figure 4. Distribution of translation shifts out of 173 shifts

As we are reminded by Chesterman (1997/2016, 108), explicitness changes are very common, and they refer to the way translators add explicitly, in the target text, components which are only implicit in the source text (explicitation), or the opposite (implicitation). Because of their importance, the discussion will focus solely on explicitness changes. Here are examples of such changes as found in the budget corpus:

(1)
EN: The paper will outline proposals for consultation between the **government** and the provinces, and business, labor and other interest groups.
FR: Le document fera des propositions pour la consultation entre le **gouvernement fédéral** et les provinces, les entreprises, le mouvement ouvrier et les autres groupes intéressés.
(Donald MacDonald, Minister of Finance, 1977)

(2)
EN: A three-per-cent surtax will be imposed on **federal** personal income taxes commencing July 1, 1986.
FR: Une surtaxe de trois pour cent sera imposée sur le revenu des particuliers à compter du 1er juillet 1986.
(Michael Wilson, Minister of Finance, 1986)

(3)
EN: In creating this budget, no activity of **government** has gone unexamined.
FR: Dans la préparation de ce budget, aucune activité du **gouvernement fédéral** n'a été laissée de côté.
(Paul Martin, Minister of Finance, 1995)

The examples (1) to (3) are representative, in that most occurrences of explicitation involved the use of *fédéral* in French, but there are exceptions, as we can see in example (2). If we detail the explicitness changes into implicit and explicit changes, we get fifty-four explicitations and thirty-one implicitations. Furthermore, not all instances of explicitation dealt with the addition of the word *fédéral* in French. Sometimes, the focus was on the word 'government':

(4)
EN: We will eliminate new **federal** borrowing in financial markets after 1993–1994.
FR: Nous éliminerons les nouveaux emprunts du **gouvernement fédéral** sur les marchés financiers après 1993–1994.
(Michael Wilson, Minister of Finance, 1991)

The majority of our examples are similar to excerpts (1) and (3): of the fifty-four explicit changes, thirty-five 'add' the word *fédéral* in French. As explained above, this explicitation comes as a surprise in many ways, since we have seen that the French word *fédéral* sometimes has a negative connotation. Furthermore, the French language tends to avoid repetitions for stylistic reasons. In the corpus, we expected more implicitations and fewer explicitations.

What is striking from our results is that a significant portion of the shifts 'add' the word *fédéral* in the French text and that translators do not seem to do it for reasons of style. In both of my interviews, one with the chief of Language Services and the other with a political adviser (see Section 3.3), it was clear that translators were not given direct guidelines about the translation of 'federal', and that throughout the period under study (1970–1995), they nonetheless chose similar strategies, that is explicitating the word *fédéral* in French. We have two related hypotheses to explain this finding. First, Quebec's desire for fiscal autonomy is the locus of a power struggle with the federal government of Canada. As shown in a report on Quebec fiscal policy (Godbout et al. 2005), a majority of Quebecers believe that there is a fiscal imbalance in the Canadian federation and that it must be corrected by transferring federal taxes to provincial governments. One of the co-authors of the report, political scientist Jean-Herman Guay, stated in a newspaper interview that his results had convinced him that there is a strong fiscal nationalism in Quebec (Paquet 2005). Two years later, *Journal de Montréal* columnist Antoine Robitaille (2017, 58) argued that 'fiscal autonomy', which refers to the Quebec government's ability to define its own tax policies, is important for the Quebec nation: "**Le gouvernement Couillard profite d'un rapport de force avec Ottawa qu'il a bien failli abandonner il y a deux ans.** De quoi je parle ? De « l'autonomie fiscale ». Autrement dit, de la capacité du gouvernement du Québec de définir ses propres politiques fiscales." ("The Couillard government is taking advantage of a position of strength vis-à-vis Ottawa that it came close to relinquishing two years ago. What am I talking about? 'Tax autonomy.' In other words, the Quebec government's ability to define its own tax policies.")

Here, the journalist hinted that 'fiscal autonomy' was a vital tool for addressing inequality issues between the federal and the provincial governments. The title of his article was *Essentiel nationalisme fiscal* (Essential Fiscal Nationalism). Fiscal autonomy is therefore clearly presented as closely linked to fiscal nationalism. The nationalist discourse in other nations without a state, such as Catalonia, also refers to the fiscal issue. For instance, Serrano (2013, 534) has argued that contemporary Catalan nationalism is based on identity issues, but it could also be associated with an "alleged fiscal unfair treatment by the state".

In the translation corpus, the strong use in French of the word *fédéral* could therefore be part of an adversarial discourse over fiscal policies in Quebec and in Canada. As explained by Vaillancourt (2010, 372), an economist and public policy expert, growth of support for sovereignty in the 1965–1995 period occurred against the backdrop of Quebec's increasing fiscal autonomy and lack of agreement on constitutional reform. Growth in tax autonomy resulted from changes in the sharing of the personal (PIT) and corporate tax fields (CIT). The federal government gave more and more tax autonomy to provinces, particularly Quebec.

All of which leads us to our second hypothesis. Since budget speeches are widely discussed on radio and television and in the press, and since journalists often quote isolated excerpts of these speeches, it is possible that, consciously or unconsciously, professional translators chose to clarify the source of the speech, that is, the federal government in Ottawa. Without proper context, a reader, for example, could perhaps mistake a statement from the federal level for a statement from the Quebec government. In the examples we looked at earlier, many statements could have been uttered by a Quebec finance minister, hence the explicitation added by the professional translators.

5 Conclusion

So, how does our study illustrate governance through translation? We have shown that over the decades and through the budget speeches of various Liberal and Conservative governments, translators have been instinctively making linguistic choices that hint at ideological differences. Through their translation choices, the work of translators has helped to assert the federal government's presence in the minds of the Quebec audience, and has, perhaps, even helped Francophone Quebecers to overcome potential ambiguities. We can say that such discursive and translation practice is in line with the governance of a Canadian institution that is confronted with identity and fiscal policy issues. It can be argued that the translators of the federal government, between 1970 and 1995, internalized the federal government's strong institutional discourse, and it made governance through translation possible. Such institutional discourse was not equally noticeable throughout the various corpora: certain text genres, such as budget speeches, revealed more power struggles between federal and provincial governments than did other genres. This could mean that text genres and their content have a strong impact on the use of translation shifts. Of course, more work is needed to understand the question of discourse internalization, a matter definitely worth investigating.

Acknowledgement

This chapter draws on research supported by the Social Sciences and Humanities Research Council of Canada.

References

Benwell, Bethan, and Elizabeth Stokoe. 2006. "Institutional Identities." In *Discourse and Identity*, edited by Anna De Fina, 87–128. Edinburgh: Edinburgh University Press.

Bernard, André. 1992. *Politique et gestion des finances publiques, Québec et Canada*. Sillery, Québec: Presses de l'Université du Québec.

Bétoté, Akwa, Doumbé. 2019. Interview by Chantal Gagnon. Personal Interview over the phone. Montréal and Ottawa, 15 April 2019.

Bosc, Marc, and André Gagnon. 2017. *House of Commons Procedure and Practice*. Ottawa: House of Commons.

Burnaby, Barbara. 1996. "Language Policies in Canada." In *Language Policies in English-dominant Countries: Six Case Studies*, edited by Michael L. Herriman and Barbara Burnaby, 159–219. Clevedon: Multilingual Matters.

Calzada Pérez, María. 2001. "A Three-Level Methodology For Descriptive-Explanatory Translation Studies." *Target. International Journal of Translation Studies* 13 (2): 203–239.

———. 2018a. "Researching the European Parliament with Corpus-Assisted Discourse Studies." *Revista Española De Lingüística Aplicada* 30 (2): 465–490.

———. 2018b. "What Is Kept and What Is Lost without Translation? A Corpus-Assisted Discourse Study of the European Parliament's Original and Translated English." *Perspectives* 26 (2): 277–291.

Canada. Parliament. *House of Commons Debates*, 1936a, 2 June (Mr. Thomas Langton Church). 1st session, 18th Parliament, Volume IV: 3340. https://parl.canadiana.ca/view/oop.debates_HOC1801_04.

———. *House of Commons Debates*, 1936b, 16 June (Mr. Thomas Langton Church). 1st session, 18th Parliament, Volume IV: 3757–3758. https://parl.canadiana.ca/view/oop.debates_HOC1801_04.

Chesterman, Andrew. 1997/2016. *Memes of Translation: The Spread of Ideas in Translation Theory*. Amsterdam: John Benjamins.

Couture, Jerôme, and Louis M. Imbeau. 2009. "Do Governments Manipulate their Revenue Forecasts? Budget Speech and Budget Outcomes in the Canadian Provinces." *Studies in Public Choice* 15 (3): 155–166.

Cronin, Michael. 2006. *Translation and Identity*. New York: Routledge.

d'Anglejan, Alison. 1984. "Language Planning in Quebec: An Historical Overview and Future Trends." In *Conflict and Language Planning in Quebec*, edited by Richard Y. Bourhis, 29–52. Clevedon: Multilingual Matters.

Delisle, Jean. 1984. *Bridging the Language Solitudes: Growth and Development of the Translation Bureau of the Government of Canada, 1934–84*. Translated by the Translation Bureau. Ottawa: Secretary of State.

———, and Marco A. Fiola. 2013. *La traduction raisonnée: manuel d'initiation à la traduction professionnelle de l'anglais vers le français*. 3rd ed. *Pédagogie de la traduction*. Ottawa: Presses de l'Université d'Ottawa.

Dickinson, John, and Brian Young. 2014. *A Short History of Quebec*. 4th ed. Montréal: McGill-Queen's University Press.

Drew, Paul, and Marja-Leena Sorjonen. 1997/2011. "Dialogue in Institutional Interactions." In *Discourse Studies: A Multidisciplinary Introduction*, edited by Teun van Dijk, 191–216. London: Sage.

Fairclough, Isabela, and Norman Fairclough. 2012. *Political Discourse Analysis: A Method for Advanced Students*. New York: Routledge.

Fairclough, Norman. 1989/2015. *Language and Power*. 3rd ed. New York: Routledge.

———. 1992. *Discourse and Social Change*. Cambridge, UK: Polity Press.

Fraser, Graham. 2007. *Sorry, I Don't Speak French: Confronting the Canadian Crisis That Won't Go Away*. Toronto: McClelland & Stewart.

Gagnon, Chantal. 2006. "Ideologies in the History of Translation: A Case Study on Canadian Political Speeches." In *Charting the Future of Translation History*, edited by Paul Bandia and Georges Bastin, 201–223. Ottawa: University of Ottawa Press.

———. 2010. "When Text and Translation Production Meet: Translation in the Prime Minister's Office." In *Political Discourse, Media and Translation*, edited by Christina Schäffner and Susan Bassnett, 164–177. Newcastle upon Tyne: Cambridge Scholars.

———. 2014a. "January/February 1977: Independence, Secession, Political Duels… Or Lévesque and Trudeau in the United-States." In *Translation Effects, The Shaping of Modern Canadian Culture*, edited by Kathy Mezei, Sherry Simon and Luise von Flotow. Montréal: McGill-Queens University Press.

———. 2014b. "Québec et Canada: entre l'unilinguisme et le bilinguisme politique." *Meta* 59 (3): 598–619.

———. 2019. "Gouverner par la traduction au Canada: le cas des discours sur le budget." *Onomázein. Journal of Linguistics, Philology and Translation* (V): 4–23.

———, and Esmaeil Kalantari. 2017. "Canadian Translated Politics at the Economic Club of New York." *The Translator* 23 (1): 17–30.

Gauvin, Lise. 1976. "Problématique de la langue d'écriture au Québec, de 1960 à 1975." *Langue française* (31): 74–90.

Godbout, Luc, Jean-Herman Guay, and Matthieu Arseneau. 2005. *Que reste-t-il du Rapport Séguin ?* Sherbrooke, Chaire de recherche en fiscalité et en finances publiques. Cahier de recherche no 2005-04.

Godin, Gérald. 1967. *Les cantouques: poèmes en langue verte, populaire et quelquefois française, Collection paroles*. Montréal: Editions Parti pris.

———. 1977. Interviews. Gérald Godin: Un an de pouvoir. Jean Paré. *L'actualité* (11): 6–10 ; 56–58.

Gravel, Pierre. 1978. "La majorité désapprouve l'attitude générale d'Ottawa face au Québec." *La Presse*, A7.

Hanson, Stephen E., Jeffrey Kopstein, and Mark Irving Lichbach. 2000/2014. "The Framework of Analysis." In *Comparative Politics: Interests, Identities, and Institutions in a Changing Global Order*, edited by Jeffrey Kopstein, Mark Irving Lichbach and Stephen E. Hanson, 15–36. Cambridge: Cambridge University Press.

Hatim, Basil, and Ian Mason. 1997. *The Translator as Communicator*. New York: Routledge.

Hostová, Ivana. 2017. "Introduction. Translation and Identity." In *Identity and Translation Trouble*, edited by Ivana Hostová, 1–18. Newcastle upon Tyne: Cambridge Scholars.

Howard, Martin, ed. 2007. *Language Issues in Canada: Multidisciplinary Perspectives*. Newcastle upon Tyne: Cambridge scholars.

Intellectuels pour la souveraineté (IPSO). 1995. La nécessaire souveraineté : Dix arguments pour le Québec. In *Comité national du OUI*. Montreal: Presses du comité national du OUI.

Knowles, Gerry, and Zuraidah Mohd Don. 2004. "The Notion of a 'Lemma'. Headwords, Roots and Lexical Sets." *International Journal of Corpus Linguistics* 9 (1): 69–81.

Koskinen, Kaisa. 2014. "Institutional Translation: The Art of Government by Translation." *Perspectives* 22 (4): 479–492. https://doi.org/10.1080/0907676X.2014.948887.

Larrivée, Pierre, ed. 2003. *Linguistic Conflicts and Language Laws: Understanding the Quebec Question*. Houndmills: Palgrave Macmillan.

Leblanc, Daniel. 2018. "Ottawa Rejects Quebec Proposal to Collect, and Transfer, Federal Income Tax." *The Globe and Mail*, 18 May. https://www.theglobeandmail.com/politics/article-ottawa-rejects-quebec-proposal-to-collect-and-transfer-federal/.

Lemieux, René. 2019. "Reconnaissance des langues autochtones au Canada. Un commentaire sur le projet de loi C-91." *Trahir – le blog*, 31 March 2019. https://trahir.wordpress.com/2019/03/31/lemieux-c-91/.

Library and Archives Canada. Michael Wilson Fonds. 1990. Orator Draft of Budget Speech. In *MHW Speeches—February 1990*. Ottawa.

Meylaerts, Reine. 2011. "Translational Justice in a Multilingual World: An Overview of Translational Regimes." *Meta* 56 (4): 743–757.

———. 2013. "Multilingualism as a Challenge for Translation Studies." In *The Routledge Handbook of Translation Studies*, edited by Carmen Millán and Francesca Bartrina, 519–533. New York: Routledge.

———. 2018. "The Politics of Translation in Multilingual States." In *The Routledge Handbook of Translation and Politics*, edited by Jonathan Evans and Fruela Fernandez, 221–237. New York: Routledge.

Molina, Lucía, and Amparo Hurtado Albir. 2002. "Translation Techniques Revisited: A Dynamic and Functionalist Approach." *Meta* 47 (4): 498–512.

Mossop, Brian. 1990. "Translating Institution and 'Idiomatic' Translations." *Meta* 35 (2): 342–354.

Paquet, Stéphane. 2005. "Moins pour Ottawa, plus pour Québec." *La Presse*, 23 February, A6.

Parliament of Canada. n.d. "Parlinfo—Budgets." Government of Canada, accessed December 17. https://bdp.parl.ca/sites/ParlInfo/default/en_CA/Parliament/budgets.

Pratte, André. 2006. "L'idée fédérale." *La Presse*, 6 juin, A38.

Robitaille, Antoine. 2017. "Essentiel nationalisme fiscal." *Journal de Montréal*, 11 November, 58.

Royer, Jean. 1994. "Gérald Godin: Une vie réussie (1938–1994)." *Lettres québécoises. La revue de l'actualité littéraire* 76:7.

Saint-Jacques, M. 1974. "Le Québec à la recherche de son identité." *Études de Linguistique Appliquée* 15: 103–106.

Scarpa, Federica. 2010. *La traduction spécialisée: une approche professionnelle à l'enseignement de la traduction*. Translated by Marco Fiola. Ottawa: Presses de l'Université d'Ottawa.

Schäffner, Christina. 2003. "Third Ways and New Centres: Ideological Unity or Difference?" In *Apropos of Ideology: Translation Studies on Ideology—Ideologies in Translation Studies*, edited by María Calzada Pérez, 23–41. Manchester: St. Jerome.

Serrano, Ivan. 2013. "Just a Matter of Identity? Support for Independence in Catalonia." *Regional & Federal Studies* 23 (5): 523–545.

Smith, Alex, and Shaowei Pu. 2015/2019. *The Parliamentary Financial Cycle, Library of Parliament Background Papers*. Ottawa: Library of Parliament.

Tellier, Geneviève. 2019. *Canadian Public Finance: Explaining Budgetary Institutions and the Budget*. Translated by Käthe Roth. Toronto: University of Toronto Press.

Tillotson, Shirley. 2017. *Give and Take: The Citizen-Taxpayer and the Rise of Canadian Democracy*. Vancouver: University of British-Columbia Press.

Translation Bureau. 1999. Federal. In *Termium*. Ottawa: Public Services and Procurement Canada.

Vaillancourt, François. 2010. "The Costs and Benefits of Constitutional Options for Quebec and Canada." In *Political Economy of Inter-Regional Fiscal Flows: Measurement, Determinants and Effects on Country Stability*, edited by Nura Bosch, Marta Espasa Queralt and Albert Sole Olle, 371–388. Cheltenham: Edward Elgar Publishing.

van Dijk, Teun A. 1998. *Ideology: A Multidisciplinary Approach*. London: Sage.

———. 2001. "Critical Discourse Analysis." In *Handbook of Discourse Analysis*, edited by Deborah Tannen, Deborah Schiffrin and Heidi Ehernberger Hamilton, 352–371. Oxford: Blackwell.

Vinay, Jean-Paul, and Jean Darbelnet. 1977. *Comparative Stylistics of French and English: A Methodology for Translation*. Translated by Juan C. Sager. Amsterdam: John Benjamins.

Appendix 1: Chesterman's modified taxonomy[5]

Syntactic shifts	Semantic shifts	Pragmatic shifts
G1 — Loan, calque (borrowing items from another language)	S1 — Synonymy (not the 'obvious' equivalent)	P1 — Adaptation (reality from SL replaced with a reality specific to the TL)
G2 — Transposition (word-class change)	S2 — Antonymy (using a negation element)	P2 — Explicitness change (explicitation/implicitation)
G3 — Unit shift (units are: morpheme, word, phrase, clause, sentence, paragraph)	S3 — Hyponymy (superordinate — hyponym)	P3 — Information change (addition, omission: cannot be inferred)
G4 — Phrase structure change (number, definiteness, person, tense, mood)	S4 — Converses (same state of affair from opposing viewpoints, as in 'buy-sell')	P4 — Coherence change (logical arrangement of information, often paragraph change)
G5 — Clause structure change (order, active/passive, finiteness, transitivity)	S5 — Abstraction change (from abstract to concrete level, or from concrete to abstract level)	P5 — Partial translation (summary, transcription, symbolist translation)
G6 — Sentence structure change (main/subordinate clause changes)	S6 — Distribution change (expansion or compression of semantic components)	P6 — Visibility change (footnotes, comments, glosses)
G7 — Cohesion change (intra-textual references, ellipsis, pronominalization, repetition)	S7 — Emphasis change (adds to, reduce, or alters the emphasis or thematic focus)	P7 — Transediting (tidying badly written parts or whole texts)
G8 — Level shift (levels are phonology, morphology, syntax and lexis)	S8 — Paraphrase (disregard of semantic components in favor of pragmatic sense)	P8 — Layout change
G9 — Scheme change (changes in rhetorical schemes)	S9 — Trope change (change in figurative expressions)	P9 — Choice of dialects

---

5   This modified taxonomy has slightly changed since its first publication (see Gagnon 2006). For instance, literal translation is no longer considered a shift but, rather, a basic translation strategy.

Appendix 2: Type of shift and frequency

Type of shift	Frequency
Transposition	1
Phrase structure change	8
Clause structure change	15
Sentence structure change	1
Cohesion change	8
Level shift	10
Adaptation	7
Explicitness change	85
Synonymy	32
Abstraction change	2
Distribution change	2
Emphasis change	1
Paraphrase	1

The complexity of a translation policy

Interpreting for ethnic linguistic minorities in a local courtroom in China

Shuang Li

Abstract

The topic of translation policy is of unprecedented relevance, as it is intrinsically concerned with decisions on how to enable communication between linguistically diverse populations. Translation-related decisions take the forms of not only policy texts (i.e., translation management), as well as everyday social practices (i.e., translation practices) and ideological factors (i.e., translation beliefs). While it has been observed that translation management, translation practices and translation beliefs are sometimes contradictory and relate to each other in complex ways, the mechanisms that underpin their interactions remain to be studied. Little is known about why and how translation policies have become as they are in specific contexts. This chapter aims to develop qualitative explanations for a particular translation policy followed by a local court in China, with specific attention to a trial that involves ethnic linguistic minorities. To this end, this study adopts some conceptual tools of complexity theory: the concepts of 'constraints', 'attractors' and 'trajectories'. By taking into account both realized and unrealized possibilities, this study sheds light on the nonlinear causality in the emerging process of a translation policy. It shows that the translation policy investigated in this study gravitated between the attractor featured by a correct information exchange and the attractor featured by information gaps. Such a translation policy emerged from nonlinear interactions between a series of constraints and attractors. While the qualitative explanations developed in this chapter are local in time and place, this study sheds light on the mechanisms underlying a translation policy process and illustrates why translation management, translation practices and translation beliefs can be contradictory.

1 Introduction

The world we live in faces the challenge of enabling communication between linguistically diverse populations. To rise to this challenge, we need to decide whether to provide translation services, who to entrust with the task of translating, what to translate, and how to translate. These questions are central to translation policy design. In other words, a translation policy is intrinsically about "deciding how people communicate" (González Núñez 2017, 152) and is therefore highly relevant to the challenges we are facing. In their exploration of the role of translation policies, Meylaerts and González Núñez (2017, 2) identify – following Spolsky (2012) – the study of a translation policy as the study of translation management, translation practices and translation beliefs. According to them, translation management refers to decisions concerning translation activities made by people with authority. Translation practices then refer to the actual translation activities in a language community. Translation beliefs are the values assigned by members of a language community to translation management and translation practices for particular linguistic groups. The model developed by Meylaerts and González Núñez (2017, 2) draws our attention not only to the roles of legislation or policy texts, but also to the roles everyday social practices and ideological factors play in shaping both *de jure* and *de facto* translation policy. This insight paves the way for a further description and conceptualization of the dynamics of a translation policy.

2 A complexity theory approach to translation policy

It has previously been observed that translation management, translation practices and translation beliefs are sometimes contradictory and relate to one another in complex ways, bringing about unexpected effects (González Núñez 2016; González Núñez and Meylaerts 2017; Meylaerts 2017; Qian and Li 2018). However, the mechanisms that underpin the interactions between translation management, translation practices and translation beliefs remain to be studied. Little is known about why and how translation policies become as they are in specific processes.

This chapter aims to develop qualitative explanations for a particular translation policy followed by a local court[1] (hereinafter referred to as the

---

1   In the interests of interviewee privacy, all names and references to people, institutions and places have been rendered anonymous in this study.

Court) in China, with specific attention to a trial (hereinafter referred to as the Trial) that involves ethnic linguistic minorities.[2] This study is underpinned by complexity theory, which provides conceptual tools that not only fit but also explain the complex reality of translation policies, as demonstrated by a growing body of literature, either from policy studies or from translation studies (e.g., Morçöl 2012; Cairney 2012; Marais 2014; Meylaerts 2017; Marais and Meylaerts 2019). For example, in policy studies, Morçöl (2012, xii, 269) argues that the core problem of applying complexity theory to public policy is the agency-structure problem or micro-macro problem: how do properties and actions of actors relate with structural properties and change? He considers the concept of 'emergence' as an answer to the agency-structure problem (Morçöl 2012, 269). The concept of 'emergence' refers to the process in which higher-order properties arise from the interactions of constituent parts lacking these properties (Deacon 2013, 169). That is, structural properties or patterns of a policy emerge from the interactions among actors and are irreducible to the intentions or actions of individual actors (Morçöl 2012, 269). This development has important implications for understanding the nonlinear relationship between "policy goals of governmental actors or those of others" (i.e., micro properties) and the outcomes of policy texts (i.e., macro properties) (Morçöl 2012, 269).

This process reflects the idea of 'nonlinearity', which means "disproportionate relationships between cause and effect" (Marais 2014, 34) and "sensitive dependence on initial conditions" (Marion 1999, 17). That is, a small change might have drastic effects, and a small change in the initial conditions may produce widely divergent outcomes. The concept of 'nonlinearity' has important implications for how we understand the discrepancies between translation management, translation practices and translation beliefs. Morçöl (2012, 270) is also aware of the downward causation from structural properties to individual behaviors and illustrates this downward causation by integrating Giddens's structuration theory. Likewise, the concepts of 'emergence' and

---

2   China is home to fifty-six ethnic groups, including the Han majority and fifty-five ethnic minority groups, which only account for 8.49% of the total population (Ministry of Education of the People's Republic of China 2013). As for the languages, Han, together with Hui and Manchu, use *Hanyu* (Chinese), which is extensively used by the majority in major public sectors. In this study, *Hanyu* (Chinese) refers to both written Chinese and spoken Chinese. Spoken Chinese includes Mandarin Chinese, which is the standard spoken Chinese language, and other Chinese dialects with local accents. It is worth noting that some people of ethnic minority origin speak other indigenous languages as their mother tongues and have limited proficiency in *Hanyu* (Chinese). These people are considered to be the ethnic linguistic minorities in China. The indigenous languages used by the ethnic linguistic minorities are minority languages in China.

'nonlinearity' have also prompted translation studies scholars (e.g., Marais 2014; Marais and Meylaerts 2019) to reconsider the structure-agency relation in translation studies. As the leading author that links translation studies and complexity theory, Marais (2019, 53–72) develops an understanding of emergence by adopting Deacon's (2013, 192–193) notion of 'constraints' and the concepts of 'attractors' and 'trajectories'. These conceptual tools are usefully applied by Marais (2019) to illustrate both upward and downward causation. Meylaerts's (2017, 46–47) study of Belgian translation policies in the nineteenth century demonstrates a need to supplement an approach that looks for "generalization, reproducibility, predictability and systematization" with a complexity theory approach, which is useful in conceptualizing the contradictions, exceptions, complexity and change of translation policies. One important epistemological implication of complexity theory for studies about translation policies is, as suggested by Meylaerts (2017, 57), that we need to study processes of interaction in which different actors interact at different levels with different purposes. In other words, translation policies should be studied dynamically as processes that emerge and evolve over time. Methodologically, however, it is not clear yet which methodological options provided by complexity theory could be usefully applied to studies about translation policies (Meylaerts 2017, 57).

Drawing upon Marais's (2019) study, this chapter adopts the concepts of 'constraints', 'attractors' and 'trajectories' as analytical instruments, because they are effective tools for developing causal accounts. Constraints can be used both in an extrinsic sense and in an intrinsic sense (Deacon 2013, 192–193). When used in an extrinsic sense, a constraint refers to 'an external limitation, reflecting some extrinsically imposed factor that reduces possibilities or options' (Deacon 2013, 192). One example is that "citizens are constrained in their behavior by laws" (Deacon 2013, 193). When used in an intrinsic sense, constraints refer to the states or tendencies that are not exhibited but that could have been (Deacon 2013, 192), or in Marais's words, "unrealized possibilities" (Marais 2019, 56). The unrealized possibilities become causally relevant because, by not having been realized, they limit some possibilities or tendencies and give rise to other possibilities or tendencies. Some examples given in Section 4 will attempt to illustrate this relevance. It is worth noting that a constraint limits but does not exclude a certain possibility or tendency: it affects the probability that a tendency might emerge. Several examples provided in Section 4 will illustrate how constraints can simultaneously reduce and open up possibilities (see also Juarrero 1999, 133; Cilliers 2001, 139).

In social sciences terms, "an attractor is a 'region' within the range of possible states that a dynamical system is most likely to be found within"

(Deacon 2013, 547). In this study, the states towards which the translation policy to be investigated is most likely to gravitate are identified as attractors. As behavioral patterns of a participant also constitute the states towards which the translation policy tends to gravitate, a participant's tendencies to behave in certain ways and to have certain beliefs are also identified as attractors. It is worth noting that a participant does not stay in the same state all the time, as will be shown in Section 4. In other words, a translation policy might gravitate towards one attractor and then switch to another attractor. The term 'trajectory' was used to describe the way a translation policy gravitates towards and cycles through different attractors. Social phenomena, including translation policies, show 'strange attractors' (Marion 1999, 22). Strange attractors have complex trajectories, which "show a pattern or form or habit but not an exactly duplicated pathway as with a pendulum (which is a periodic attractor)" (Marais 2019, 58). In other words, a translation policy in a certain context could be predicted to emerge in the vicinity of certain attractors, but the exact way in which it gravitates towards and cycles through the attractors can never be foreseen (Marais 2019, 59).

The concepts of 'constraints', 'attractors' and 'trajectories' alert us to the variety of possibilities (i.e., both realized and unrealized possibilities). The concept of 'constraints', in particular, reflects the causal influence of absence on the emergence of a translation policy trajectory. Through taking account of both realized and unrealized possibilities, we are more likely to see the nonlinear dynamics of courtroom interactions and thus avoid the pitfalls of linear and deterministic thinking when we explain a translation policy.

This study uses an ethnographic approach to trace and explain the emerging process of a translation policy. Specifically, the empirical data for this study is collected through observing the Trial, both in person and via online videos, and conducting semi-structured interviews with people involved. These ethnographic approaches aim to establish a contextualized and holistic understanding of the people, events and ideas being investigated, along with the connections within and between them. This context-oriented and relational way of thinking coincides with the insights of complexity theory. Based on the ethnographic investigations, this study will explain why and how the translation policy of the Trial emerged between the moment when the judge decided how to enable the courtroom interactions at the Trial and the moment when the defendants decided whether or not to appeal against the court judgment for reasons of language issues.

3 Initial conditions

As indicated in the idea of 'nonlinearity', a small change in the initial conditions of a process might result in a vastly different trajectory. Therefore, the first step of tracing the translation policy trajectory of the Trial is to describe its initial conditions.

The participants of the Trial (e.g., the judge, the court interpreter, the defendants and the prosecutor) served as one initial condition. With different participants, the courtroom interactions of the Trial could have involved different views on translation management, different translation beliefs and translation practices, as they are subject to the participants' social engagement and previous experiences. Table 1 provides an overview of the roles that the participants played at the Trial, their professional and educational backgrounds, their ethnic origins and their language skills. This sketch may to some extent enable us to compare how participants with different demographic details think of court interpreting activities and act accordingly.

Table 1. The participants of the trial

pseudonym	role in a trial	occupation	educational background	ethnic origin	language skill(s)
Judy	judge	judge (criminal cases)	law	Han	monolingual (Chinese)
Lawrence	court interpreter	judge (civil cases)	law	Lahu	bilingual (Chinese and Lahu)
Jenny	prosecutor	prosecutor	law	Hani	monolingual (Chinese)
Alan	defendant	farmer	primary school (fourth grade)	Lahu	Lahu (mother tongue) Chinese (limited proficiency)
Zoey	defendant	farmer	uneducated	Lahu	monolingual (Lahu)

The status and use of the languages involved in the Trial, as a cultural given, served as another initial condition. At the Trial, the judge and the prosecutor are monolingual in *Hanyu* (Chinese), while the defendants speak the *Lahu* language as their mother tongue and have great difficulty in communicating in *Hanyu* (Chinese). China's current constitution emphasizes all ethnic groups' rights to use and develop their own spoken and written languages.[3] In other words, *Hanyu* (Chinese) and the *Lahu* language, in the legal sense, are on an equal footing. However, when it comes to language practices, the *Lahu* language is not as extensively used as *Hanyu* (Chinese) in public sectors in the county (hereinafter referred to as the County) where the Court is located. Instead, the *Lahu* language is mainly spoken in private lives, with the use of its written script limited in scope (Ministry of Education of the PRC 2004). This situation indicates that *Hanyu* (Chinese) and the *Lahu* language possess different functions and values in reality. A language hierarchy manifests itself in the context of courtroom interactions, during which the language of the court is often *Hanyu* (Chinese) because people in positions of authority are monolingual in *Hanyu* (Chinese). As Blommaert, Collins and Slembrouck (2005, 198) note, "communication problems in such situations are the result of how individuals and their communicative 'baggage' are inserted into regimes of language valid in that particular space." Such particular language environment dominated by *Hanyu* (Chinese) incapacitates the ethnic minorities who speak other languages as their mother tongues unless they are bilingual, thus resulting in communication problems. Translation serves as a way to enable courtroom communications, but at the same time it helps preserve the existing language hierarchy.

The laws that were in place at the moment when the judge decided how to enable the courtroom interactions, as a legal given, accounted for another initial condition. China has established legislation to mandate the use of minority languages and the provision of translation and interpreting services in judicial settings, as exemplified by its constitution[4] and other national laws, such as the Criminal Procedure Law,[5] the Administrative Litigation Law,[6] the Civil Procedure Law,[7] the Organic Law of the People's Courts[8] and the Law on Regional National Autonomy. The current legislation involves translation management in judicial settings. For example, any individual with limited proficiency in the spoken or written language(s) commonly used in the locality is entitled to translation and interpreting services in court proceedings (ibid.).

---

3   中华人民共和国宪法 (The Constitution of the People's Republic of China (PRC)) (The National People's Congress (NPC) 1982, article 4).
4   中华人民共和国宪法 (The Constitution of the PRC) (NPC 1982, article 139).
5   中华人民共和国刑事诉讼法 (The Criminal Procedure Law of the PRC) (NPC 1979a, article 9).
6   中华人民共和国行政诉讼法 (The Administrative Litigation Law of the PRC) (NPC 1989, article 9).
7   中华人民共和国民事诉讼法 (The Civil Procedure Law of the PRC) (NPC 1991, article 11).
8   中华人民共和国人民法院组织法 (The Organic Law of the People's Courts of the PRC) (NPC 1979b, article 6).

The laws also explicitly mandate the use of the language(s) commonly used in the locality for trials and written documents (e.g., indictments, judgments and notices) in the areas where a specific ethnic minority group lives in a concentrated community or where a variety of ethnic groups live together (ibid.). As mentioned above, in the County, *Hanyu* (Chinese) is widely used in public sectors, whereas the *Lahu* language is frequently spoken at home. As the Court is staffed by bilingual judicial personnel for the *Lahu* language and other minority languages, there is a certain degree of institutional multilingualism, with *Hanyu* (Chinese) as the dominant language. Current laws provide a valid legal basis for the Trial to be conducted either in the *Lahu* language or in *Hanyu* (Chinese). In other words, the courtroom interactions at the Trial can be enabled either through a bilingual judge's direct use of the *Lahu* language or with the help of a court interpreter. What the Court usually does is to employ court interpreters among local bilinguals or bilingual judicial personnel from the same Court for its criminal trials, and to appoint a bilingual judge to enable courtroom interactions for its civil trials. This practice has become one of its standing operating procedures regarding languages.[9] As the Trial is a criminal trial, another initial condition was that the Trial was held by a judge who is monolingual in *Hanyu* (Chinese) with the involvement of a court interpreter.

The layout of the courtroom also represents one of the initial conditions of the Trial. As shown in Figure 1, the courtroom has a hierarchical but interactive seating arrangement. In the front of the courtroom, the judge and two people's assessors[10] were seated on the highest position. One step lower were the prosecutor, the clerk on behalf of the local people's procuratorate,[11] the clerk for this trial, and the court interpreter. On the lowest position were the two defendants, the plaintiff of the collateral civil action, the two bailiffs and the audience. Despite the three-level seating positions, this seating arrangement allowed face-to-face interactions among the two defendants, the court interpreter, the judge and the prosecutor. The trial was video-recorded and simultaneously displayed on the two screens hung on either side of the front wall, respectively. Screen B was made up of several parts, showing close-ups of different participants.

---

9 Judy (pseudonym), interview by author, 18 April 2018; Lawrence (pseudonym), interview by author, 19 April 2018; online videos of the trials posted by the Court on http://tingshen.court.gov.cn/, an official website for making China's trials public.
10 In China, people's assessors are drawn from members of the public. They assist judges and evaluate evidence. They do not rule on matters of law but can decide on a verdict with judges.
11 In China, the people's procuratorates are state organs for legal supervision (NPC 1983, article 1). The people's procuratorates at all levels have the authority to initiate and support public prosecutions of criminal cases and to supervise the judicial activities of people's courts (NPC 1983, article 5).

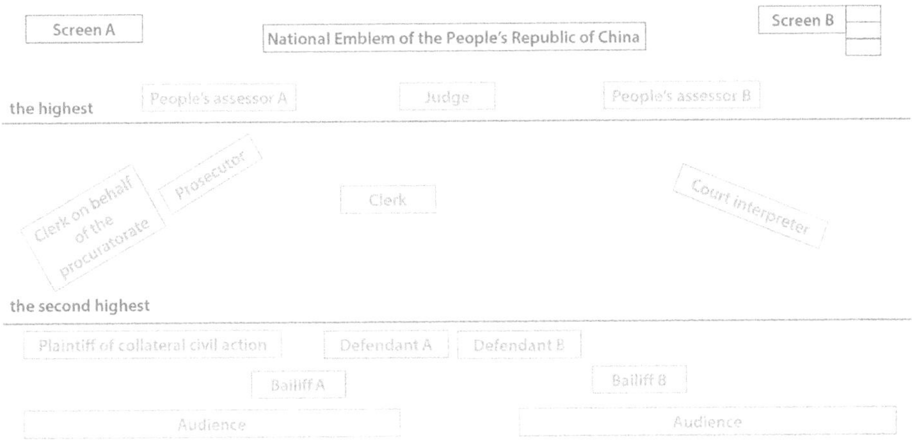

Figure 1. Visual Map of the Courtroom

4 Tracing the translation policy trajectory of the Trial

Admittedly, current translation management emphasizes the importance of court interpreting in guaranteeing citizen's basic rights and achieving language equality, which leads to an attractor that judicial personnel at the Court feel obliged to provide court interpreting services.[12] However, current translation management has not specified who to entrust with the task of translating or interpreting, what to translate or interpret, and how to translate or interpret. Constrained by this lack of clear guidelines, the Court's judicial personnel tend to equate bilinguals with interpreters, thus routinely designating its bilingual legal professionals or bilingual locals to serve as court interpreters for criminal trials. To my knowledge, only the Civil Procedure Law and the Administrative Litigation Law have articles that require interpreters to recuse themselves from a given task whenever a conflict of interest on their part exists.[13] A party in a case is entitled to request the disqualification of a court interpreter, when (s)he deems that the interpreter has an interest in the case, which may affect the impartial trial of the case (ibid.). However, these articles do not mention whether a conflict of interest involves circumstances where a court appoints its own judicial personnel as

---

12 Judy (pseudonym), interview by author, 18 April 2018; Jenny (pseudonym), interview by author, 19 April 2018.
13 中华人民共和国民事诉讼法 (The Civil Procedure Law of the PRC) (NPC 1991, article 44); 中华人民共和国行政诉讼法 (The Administrative Litigation Law of the PRC) (NPC 1989, article 55).

the interpreter. Neither do the articles include the possibility to disqualify a court interpreter based on insufficient language proficiency, insufficient interpreting knowledge, or other professional skills. Despite the lack of official guidelines, judicial personnel are apparently aware of the need to employ the court interpreters who are not affiliated with the same court to ensure neutrality.[14] Unfortunately, in day-to-day reality this need for neutrality is often neglected due to time constraints. In one interview, another judge, who works for the same Court, indicated that the Court usually only designates an external bilingual interpreter if there are no strict time constraints. For instance, if a trial is held in a local village, judicial personnel will consult local village committees and judicial teams to find a bilingual local. However, if time is limited, judges often turn to their bilingual colleagues despite the neutrality concern, since bilingual judicial personnel are more familiar with court procedures and are legal professionals.[15] This practice indicates that legal concerns are given priority over language concerns. In addition, China currently does not have accreditation tests for qualifying the competence in translation and interpreting between *Hanyu* (Chinese) and ethnic minority languages. The absence of sworn translators and interpreters for ethnic minority languages is another constraint that increases the possibility of employing non-professional interpreters. In the present investigation, for example, the Trial called upon a bilingual judge who works on civil cases at the same Court to conduct the court interpreting.

It is noteworthy that the court interpreter of the Trial (i.e., Lawrence) showed quite different tendencies when he was asked to interpret the same information[16] at the beginning of the Trial and at the beginning of another

---

14   Judy (pseudonym), interview by author, 18 April 2018.
15   Judy (pseudonym), interview by author, 18 April 2018.
16   From the receiver's point of view, information can be provided only if there is uncertainty, and information is provided when this uncertainty is then removed or reduced (Deacon 2013, 380). For example, when a judge already knows what answer a defendant is going to give, the defendant's answer provides no information. When a court interpreter alters information in the interpreting, he or she either increases uncertainty and thus conveys less information or reduces more uncertainty and thus conveys more information. When there are information gaps between the message to be interpreted and its interpreting, there can be either more information in the interpreting or less information in the interpreting. From the sender's point of view, 'information' is 'associated with the amount of freedom of choice we have in constructing messages' (Shannon and Weaver 1964, 13). The amount of information that a situation allows a sender to convey is related to the alternatives the sender has. The more alternatives a sender has in constructing messages, the greater uncertainty the sender could reduce, the more information the sender is likely to convey. For example, when a court interpreter interprets a wh- question into a yes/no question for a defendant, he or she limits the defendant's choice to two alternatives and reduces the amount of information that the sender could convey.

trial, which was held three months earlier than the Trial. Specifically, at the beginning of the Trial, the judge of the Trial (i.e., Judy) showed a tendency to divide the questions about the defendants' names, birthdays, ethnic origins and educational backgrounds into four separate questions. Such a tendency saved the need for the court interpreter to memorize a fairly large amount of information at a time. The absence of such a need became a constraint, reducing the likelihood of the court interpreter leaving certain information uninterpreted and increasing the possibility of a correct information exchange. The court interpreter not only interpreted each question raised by the judge (i.e., Judy), but also interpreted each answer given by the defendant into *Hanyu* (Chinese). These tendencies of the court interpreter drove the translation policy of the Trial to gravitate towards an attractor featured by a correct information exchange. However, by contrast, at another trial, another judge (i.e., Lily) summarized the questions about the defendant's names, birthdays, ethnic origins and educational backgrounds in an imperative sentence. Constrained by the absence of any note taken by the court interpreter and lack of memory capacity, the court interpreter forgot to check the defendant's ethnic origin and educational background. In addition, the use of an imperative sentence rather than an interrogative sentence entailed the absence of a question. Constrained by the absence of any question raised by the judge (i.e., Lily), the court interpreter was unlikely to provide Lily with answers as to the defendant's name, birthday, ethnic origin and educational background. In fact, the court interpreter did not interpret his conversation with the defendant into *Hanyu* (Chinese). Constrained by the non-interpreting of the conversation between the court interpreter and the defendant, the judge (i.e., Lily) was unlikely to understand the conversation and thus unlikely to correct the court interpreter. In other words, constrained by what the court interpreter had not interpreted, Lily was likely to react in certain ways and to deliver certain utterances rather than others. This example reflects the idea of nonlinearity: a small initial change such as a different judge could lead to different tendencies of the same court interpreter and a different translation policy trajectory. In other words, the two different judges showed different tendencies, which entailed different unrealized possibilities. Constrained by different constraints, the same court interpreter showed different tendencies, which accounted for the differences between the translation policy trajectories of the two trials. This example also attests to the need to compare the tendencies of the same actor in different translation policy processes.

As pointed out earlier, a constraint limits but does not exclude a certain possibility or tendency – it affects the probability that a tendency might emerge. The tendency of the judge of the Trial to divide a string of words into smaller parts saved the need for the court interpreter to memorize a large amount of information at a time. The absence of such a need constrained the court interpreter from forgetting to interpret certain information, but did not exclude the possibility of the court interpreter altering information. For instance, although the judge of the Trial introduced each right of the defendants one by one, the court interpreter did not interpret the information embedded in the legal term 'right to defense', as he did not reduce the uncertainty about the fact that the defendants could defend themselves. Instead, he added information by reducing the uncertainty for the defendants about what they could do, that is, to tell the court whether they had done anything wrong. Constrained by the information gaps in the court interpreting, the defendants were unlikely to have a heightened awareness of the opportunity to defend themselves in the case. In other words, information that was not interpreted limited the possibility of certain reactions. Even though the messages to be interpreted did not involve a large amount of information, the court interpreter still tended to alter information. For example, he did not explicitly repeat in the *Lahu* language that the victim had drunk alcohol. Instead, he simply asked the defendant (i.e., Zoey) whether she had any comments and even implied that she should say no. By doing so, the court interpreter filtered out information, as he did not reduce the uncertainty about the content of the evidence that the judge had introduced. Meanwhile, the court interpreter also added information, as he reduced the uncertainty about what exact answer the defendant should give. As a matter of fact, most of the time at the Trial the court interpreter tended to alter information in his interpreting. At the Trial, no one else besides the court interpreter was bilingual in *Hanyu* (Chinese) and the *Lahu* language. Constrained by the absence of any correction to the court interpreting, the information gaps in the court interpreting were unlikely to get bridged. In addition, another constraint, that is, the lack of specific regulations on court interpreting, allowed court interpreters to switch between the tendency to alter information and the tendency not to alter information.

Furthermore, the attractor featured by the information gaps gained traction, constrained by the limited role of the court interpreter at the Trial. As indicated by the judge in the interview,[17] the involvement of a court interpreter might limit the possibilities of trial efficiency and direct communication between the judge and the defendants. Constrained by these unrealized possibilities, the judge tended to limit the use of court interpreting at the Trial. More specifically, she either interacted with the defendants directly in *Hanyu*

---

17 Judy (pseudonym), interview by author, 18 April 2018.

(Chinese) when it was possible or asked the court interpreter to summarize rather than interpret sentence-by-sentence. For example, even though one of the defendants (i.e., Zoey) was known to have no knowledge of *Hanyu* (Chinese), the judge directly asked both the defendants in *Hanyu* (Chinese) whether they understood the evidence that the prosecutor had presented. Such a tendency of the judge to interact with the defendants directly in *Hanyu* (Chinese) limited the involvement of the court interpreter and limited the possibility that the defendants received the information in their mother tongue. Constrained by the lack of knowledge of *Hanyu* (Chinese), Zoey was unlikely to understand the information in *Hanyu* (Chinese), as demonstrated by how she reacted in most occasions at the Trial. However, Zoey answered in the *Lahu* language that what the prosecutor had said was right. It is difficult to gauge whether Zoey really understood the piece of evidence presented by the prosecutor. However, no request on the part of Zoey for the interpreting of what the prosecutor had presented, as a constraint, limited the involvement of the court interpreter and reduced the possibility of further courtroom interactions in the *Lahu* language. In addition, since Zoey replied to the judge in the *Lahu* language rather than in *Hanyu* (Chinese), it was impossible for the judge to understand Zoey's answer. Constrained by this unrealized possibility, the judge was unlikely to continue the conversation with Zoey in *Hanyu* (Chinese). The judge could have turned to the court interpreter for help, but again she did not allow the court interpreter to have the floor. Instead, the judge asked the other defendant (Alan) – who understands *Hanyu* (Chinese) to a limited degree – to check with Zoey whether she understood the general message. Such a tendency of the judge contradicted the tendency that she had shown at the beginning of the Trial. Specifically, at the beginning of the Trial when the judge checked the name with Zoey, Alan interrupted and informed the judge that Zoey has no knowledge of *Hanyu* (Chinese). The judge forbade Alan from answering on behalf of Zoey and asked the court interpreter to interpret for Zoey. Such a contrast in the tendencies of the judge reveals the possibility of random fluctuations in a participant's behaviors. This situation indicates that a translation policy is likely to gravitate towards different or even contradictory attractors. It is also noteworthy that Alan answered on behalf of Zoey without actually interpreting the judge's question for Zoey. The non-interpreting of the judge's question constrained Zoey from actually participating in the courtroom interactions. In addition, although the judge was then informed that Zoey had only understood a fraction, she still moved on to the next piece of evidence rather than turning to the court interpreter. As a result, the judge's tendency of not turning to the court interpreter along with no objections from Zoey to the non-interpreting together constrained the possibility of information exchange in the *Lahu* language.

Apart from interacting with the defendants directly in *Hanyu* (Chinese), during the court debate session, the judge explicitly asked the court interpreter to simply summarize that what the two defendants had done constitutes a crime. Constrained by the judge's instruction, the court interpreter did not interpret the entire statement made by the prosecutor, which resulted in the non-interpreting of certain content, including the reasons why both defendants should serve the same sentence and what they are supposed to do in the future. In an interview, the prosecutor stated that legal knowledge could be disseminated to the defendants with the aid of interpreting.[18] However, the judge's tendency to ask the court interpreter to summarize rather than interpret entailed an unrealized possibility of making full use of court interpreting. Constrained by the limited use of court interpreting, the presence of a court interpreter did not necessarily imply that all information was interpreted. This non-interpreting constrained the level of information exchange and knowledge dissemination.

Paradoxically, although the judge is the one who asked the court interpreter to summarize due to time constraints, during the interview, she herself complained about the fact that some court interpreters tend to generalize what has been said.[19] The judge then tended to doubt whether court interpreters interpret all the information. In the interview, the judge claimed that she wished either to be bilingual herself or to have machine interpreting for minority languages.[20] Unfortunately, these wishes are unlikely to come true in the near future. Constrained by these unrealized possibilities, the judge has to continue to rely on court interpreters whose involvement she tends to limit. This, in turn, might result in the non-interpreting of certain information and thus information gaps. In this way, information gaps can be both the effect and the cause of the judge's decision to limit the use of court interpreting.

Constrained by the court interpreter's tendency to alter information in the interpreting and the judge's tendency to limit the involvement of the court interpreter, the translation policy of the Trial tended to gravitate towards an attractor featured by information gaps. Such a trend could have taken a different turn if either of the two defendants had questioned the way the court interpreting was conducted. However, neither of them showed a tendency to require the involvement of the court interpreter or to require further

---

18   Jenny (pseudonym), interview by author, 19 April 2018.
19   Judy (pseudonym), interview by author, 18 April 2018.
20   Judy (pseudonym), interview by author, 18 April 2018.

explanations. A possible explanation given by a people's assessor is that many defendants are unaware of their right to an interpreter, let alone openly questioning the court interpreting quality.[21] Another reason could be the psychological impact of this particular legal circumstance. As the people's assessor indicates, "犯了罪当事人已经很害怕了" ("the defendants already feel very afraid because they have committed crimes"), and thus "只能是让干嘛就干嘛" ("they would do whatever they are told to do"). Interestingly, the people's assessor also associates this with the typical personality traits of *Lahu* people. The people's assessor believes that *Lahu* people tend to be more childlike, innocent and weak. In any case, the absence of objections to the court interpreting practices enabled the existing attractor (i.e., information gaps through interpreting) to gain traction.

5 The translation policy of the Trial and other processes

It is worth noting that the translation policy of the Trial is not an isolated process. It is related to other emerging processes in a way that the initial conditions of the translation policy process at the Trial are the subsequent conditions of another process. In other words, the factors that cause the initial conditions of the translation policy process at the Trial might be the initial conditions, attractors or constraints of another process. For example, if we want to explain why one initial condition of the Trial is to employ a court interpreter, we will have to examine the process of judicial appointment in the Court. The initial conditions of the judicial appointment process include the availability of bilingual judges at the moment, the number of the criminal trials that involve multilingual populations, the number of the civil trials that involve multilingual populations, etc. Constrained by a low level of bilingualism among prosecutors[22] and people's assessors, the criminal trials at the Court tend to involve monolingual prosecutors and monolingual people's assessors, who can only understand *Hanyu* (Chinese). Consequently, bilingual judges alone would hardly suffice for the courtroom interactions between different participants, and thus the criminal trials have to inevitably rely on court interpreters. This reliance could explain why the

---

21 Interview by author, 21 April 2018. The people's assessor is drawn from members of the public and is of *Lahu* origin. He used to work as a teacher in an ethnic school. He taught a course on politics, which consisted of a series of lectures about legal system. After his retirement, he sometimes engages in dubbing or translating movies that are in the *Lahu* language and sometimes serves as a people's assessor at the Court.

22 All but one prosecutor are monolingual speakers of *Hanyu* (Chinese).

Court has appointed all the monolingual judges to criminal courtrooms and all the bilingual judges to civil courtrooms. A subsequent condition of the appointment process is to employ a court interpreter for the Trial.

The translation policy process at the Trial also paves the way for new processes. What has (not) been achieved, as the subsequent conditions of the translation policy process at the Trial, may serve as the initial conditions of new processes, causing certain attractors and constraints rather than others. At the Trial, certain patterns of practices and interactions emerged from the initial conditions and constraints identified in Section 3 and Section 4. For example, the judge tended to reduce her reliance upon the court interpreter, the court interpreter tended to alter information in his interpreting, and the defendants tended to cooperate with the court. These tendencies and patterns of interactions that emerged from the Trial may constrain the participants of the Trial in their future engagement in other translation policy processes. Follow-up studies will be conducted to delve into the tendencies of the same judge and the same court interpreter in different translation policy processes. In addition, studies of different translation policy processes at the Court may allow us to compare the attractors and constraints that contributed to the translation policy trajectory of the Trial with those that contributed to other translation policy trajectories at the Court.

Therefore, a translation policy is a path-dependent process. That is, a translation policy process is constrained by past interactions and at the same time constrains future interactions. In addition, it can be discerned that an initial condition in a process could be a subsequent condition in a previous process. Likewise, a subsequent condition in a process might become an initial condition in a following process. This also reflects the reciprocal relationship between cause and effect, that is, "causes might thus sometimes be effects" (Marais 2019, 62).

6 Conclusion

By adopting some conceptual tools of complexity theory (i.e., the concepts of 'constraints', 'attractors' and 'trajectories'), this chapter develops qualitative explanations for a particular translation policy of a trial at a local court in China. As this chapter shows, the translation policy of the Trial gravitated between the attractor featured by a correct information exchange and the attractor featured by information gaps. The emergence of the translation policy trajectory was a collective result of nonlinear interactions between the constraints and the attractors identified in this study. What the participants of the Trial tended to do (i.e., attractors) and what the participants of the Trial tended not to do (i.e., constraints) interacted in a nonlinear way and contributed to the emergence of the translation policy. The participants of the Trial all played an important role in shaping the translation policy trajectory of the Trial, even though each of them was in a different position in the courtroom interactions. Yet because of nonlinear interactions and a translation policy's sensitivity to initial conditions, it is impossible to deal with matters pertaining to translation policy by linear intervention.

Admittedly, the qualitative explanations developed in this chapter are local in time and place, and the sample is limited to only one trial. However, the focus on local processes of interaction corresponds well with complexity theory, which considers knowledge as 'inherently local rather than universal' (Byrne 2005, 97). From the perspective of complexity theory, explanation is possible only if explanation is local in time and place (ibid.). It should be also noted that the constraints identified in this study are some (but not the only) potential means through which a certain attractor might be reached. To be sure, the objective of this study is not to reduce the causality to a limited number of factors. On the contrary, it intends to explain possible translation policy trajectories by examining the roles of constraints based on the data available. As pointed out in previous sections, further comparisons are needed to enrich the understanding of the attractors and constraints that have contributed to the past translation policy trajectories or might contribute to future translation policy trajectories at the Court.

In addition, by taking account of both realized and unrealized possibilities, this study sheds light on the nonlinear causality in the emerging process of a translation policy. For example, the same court interpreter does not necessarily always show similar tendencies when interpreting similar information, due to what is called sensitivity to initial conditions. Additionally, the same constraint (e.g., the absence of the need for the court interpreter to memorize a large amount of information at a time) may lead to multiple or even contradictory attractors (e.g., the court interpreter's tendencies to alter information and not to alter information). In other words, a constraint affects the probability that a tendency might emerge, but it does not set clear what tendencies will definitely take place or not take place. This role illustrates why translation management, translation practices and translation beliefs can be contradictory. Translation management, translation practices and translation beliefs constrain but *do not determine* each other. The perspective of complexity theory allows for a conception that embraces the coexistence of contradictory translation management, translation practices and translation beliefs, all of which constitute the reality of translation policy.

References

Blommaert, Jan, James Collins, and Stef Slembrouck. 2005. "Spaces of Multilingualism." *Language & Communication* 25 (3): 197–216.

Byrne, David. 2005. "Complexity, Configurations and Cases." *Theory, Culture & Society* 22 (5): 95–111.

Cairney, Paul. 2012. "Complexity Theory in Political Science and Public Policy." *Political Studies Review* 10 (3): 346–358.

Cilliers, Paul. 2001. "Boundaries, Hierarchies and Networks in Complex Systems." *International Journal of Innovation Management* 5 (2): 135–147. https://doi.org/10.1142/S1363919601000312.

Deacon, Terrence W. 2013. *Incomplete Nature: How Mind Emerged from Matter*. New York: W. W. Norton & Company.

González Núñez, Gabriel, and Reine Meylaerts, eds. 2017. *Translation and Public Policy: Interdisciplinary Perspectives and Case Studies*. New York: Routledge.

González Núñez, Gabriel. 2016. "On Translation Policy." *Target* 28 (1): 87–109.

———. 2017. "Law and Translation at the U.S.–Mexico Border: Translation Policy in a Diglossic Setting." In *Translation and Public Policy: Interdisciplinary Perspectives and Case Studies*, edited by Gabriel González Núñez and Reine Meylaerts, 152–170. New York: Routledge.

Juarrero, Alicia. 1999. *Dynamics in Action: Intentional Behavior as a Complex System*. Cambridge: MIT Press.

Marais, Kobus, and Reine Meylaerts, eds. 2019. *Complexity Thinking in Translation Studies: Methodological Considerations*. New York: Routledge.

Marais, Kobus. 2014. *Translation Theory and Development Studies: A Complexity Theory Approach*. New York: Routledge.

———. 2019. "'Effects Causing Effects': Considering Constraints in Translation." In *Complexity Thinking in Translation Studies: Methodological Considerations*, edited by Kobus Marais and Reine Meylaerts, 53–72. New York: Routledge.

Marion, Russ. 1999. *The Edge of Organization: Chaos and Complexity Theories of Formal Social Systems*. London: Sage.

Meylaerts, Reine, and Gabriel González Núñez. 2017. "Interdisciplinary Perspectives on Translation Policy: New Directions and Challenges." In *Translation and Public Policy: Interdisciplinary Perspectives and Case Studies*, edited by Gabriel González Núñez and Reine Meylaerts, 1–14. New York: Routledge.

Meylaerts, Reine. 2017. "Studying Language and Translation Policies in Belgium: What Can We Learn from a Complexity Theory Approach?" *Parallèles* 29 (1): 45–59.

Ministry of Education of the People's Republic of China. 2004. "The Written Scripts of Ethnic Minority Languages in China." Accessed 23 May 2019. http://www.moe.gov.cn/s78/A19/yxs_left/moe_812/s234/201412/t20141225_182378.htm.

Ministry of Education of the People's Republic of China. 2013. "Languages and Their Written Scripts in China." Accessed 23 May 2019. http://www.moe.gov.cn/jyb_sjzl/s5990/201111/t20111114_126551.html.

Morçöl, Göktuğ. 2012. *A Complexity Theory for Public Policy*. New York: Routledge.

Qian, Duoxiu, and Shuang Li. 2018. "Language and Translation Policies Toward Minority Languages in China and the USA." In *Handbook of the Changing World Language Map*, edited by Stanley D. Brunn and Roland Kehrein, 1–16. Cham: Springer.

Shannon, Claude, and Warren Weaver. 1964. *The Mathematical Theory of Communication*. Urbana-Champaign: The University of Illinois.

Spolsky, Bernard. 2012. "What Is Language Policy?" In *The Cambridge Handbook of Language Policy*, edited by Bernard Spolsky, 3–15. Cambridge: Cambridge University Press.

The National People's Congress. 1979a. "The Criminal Procedure Law of the People's Republic of China." Accessed 31 May 2019. http://www.gov.cn/flfg/2012-03/17/content_2094354.htm.

———. 1979b. "Organic Law of the People's Courts of the People's Republic of China." Accessed 31 May 2019. http://www.npc.gov.cn/zgrdw/npc/xinwen/2018-10/26/content_2064483.htm.

———. 1982. "The Constitution of the People's Republic of China." Accessed 31 May 2019. http://www.gov.cn/guoqing/2018-03/22/content_5276318.htm.

———. 1983. "Organic Law of the People's Procuratorates of the People's Republic of China." Accessed 29 January 2020. http://www.gov.cn/ziliao/flfg/2005-09/12/content_31168.htm.

———. 1989. "Administrative Litigation Law of the People's Republic of China." Accessed 31 May 2019. http://www.npc.gov.cn/wxzl/gongbao/2014-12/23/content_1892467.htm.

———. 1991. "Civil Procedure Law of the People's Republic of China." Accessed 31 May 2019. http://www.npc.gov.cn/wxzl/gongbao/2012-11/12/content_1745518.htm.

Translation guidelines versus practice

A corpus-based study of the impact of the Polish style guide on translations of EU legislation and reports drafted by the European Commission

Katarzyna Wasilewska

Abstract

Translation plays a crucial role in the European Union (EU). To ensure high quality of translations, the translators at EU institutions are bound by specific institutional practices and guidelines. The guidelines, especially language-specific ones, evolve over time and their contents adjust to the current needs of the language. The aim of this chapter is to empirically investigate to what extent the new rules integrated into the successive versions of the Polish style guide *Vademecum Tłumacza* are incorporated into the translators' practice. To this end, the distribution of selected expressions in Polish language versions is examined on a yearly basis using the methods of corpus linguistics. The patterns are identified on the basis of applicable versions of the Polish style guide. The analysis is conducted on the corpora of legislation and reports drafted by the European Commission. It is argued that the changes introduced to the *Vademecum* are not always taken into consideration. The study shows that there is generally little variation in the distribution of the items indicated in the guidelines as "undesired". This lack of response to the new rules is attributed to the combination of time pressure, requirement of consistency, the use of translation memories, translators' habits and a high volume of instructions.

1 Introduction

The European Union (EU) currently comprises twenty-seven states and twenty-four official languages, which makes it an organization in which translation plays a crucial role. Translation of all important documents drafted by its institutions[1] enhances transparency, thereby strengthening

---

1   Not all documents drafted at the institutions are translated into all official languages (Wagner et al. 2012, 9–10).

the legitimization and democratic nature of the EU (Nesti 2010, 31–32). The institutions use the term 'language version' instead of 'translation' in order to highlight the equality of all the official languages (Wagner et al. 2012, 8–9; Koskinen 2014, 484). Translation of such a vast quantity of politically sensitive and often legally binding texts is a huge endeavor, which entails a significant level of quality control to ensure that all documents produced at the institutions reliably and consistently fulfill established norms. Thus, translators at EU institutions are bound by specific practices and guidelines, which leave them little freedom of choice as regards vocabulary, syntax or style (Koskinen 2008, 24; Kang 2014, 475; Schäffner et al. 2014, 494).

The topic of style guides used in international organizations has already been studied by various researchers. In 2003, Mason (2012) conducted a small corpus study that cast doubt on whether guidelines used in international organizations actually affect translator behavior by exploring shifts in transitivity[2] in translations done at the European Parliament and UNESCO. More recently, the subject of EU style guides has been included in articles by Svoboda (2017), Strandvik (2017) and Drugan, Strandvik, and Vuorinen (2018). Svoboda (2017) surveyed the content of the resources websites – the online collection of guidelines for translation contractors – of all the language units at the European Commission's Directorate-General for Translation (DGT). Strandvik (2017) described quality assurance practices at the DGT, and Drugan, Strandvik, and Vuorinen (2018) analyzed translation quality management in the EU institutions. However, the actual influence of the guidelines on the quality of translation practice and products was not examined. In her overview of research into translation in various institutions, Kang (2014, 471) states that the manner and extent to which institutional translators are shaped by imposed practices and guidelines have not been sufficiently studied. It seems that this observation still holds true. This chapter elaborates on the discussion by empirically investigating the extent to which the behavior of translators in the Polish unit of the DGT is affected by the instructions provided in their in-house style guide, *Vademecum Tłumacza*.

---

2   Transitivity is a text parameter that pertains to the way processes are viewed and presented; it includes the expression of agency, state and process (Mason 2012, 400).

2 Translation guidelines at EU institutions

The functioning of the EU is heavily dependent on whether its institutions are able to reach out to the Europeans who give them their mandate (Koskinen 2008, 50; Drugan et al. 2018, 41). Translation is a tool for the EU to communicate with most of its citizens.[3] If it is not effective, not only the image but also the future of the EU may be at stake. Therefore, EU institutions have developed a complex system of translation quality management (Strandvik 2017; Drugan et al. 2018), where guidelines and manuals play a crucial role.

The main purpose of the guidelines is to ensure clarity and consistency in drafts and translations, but they are also supposed to bring administrative texts closer to the readers. Documents drafted by various institutions, both domestic and international, are not generally reader-friendly. Some of the most conspicuous traits of administrative style include nominalization, depersonalization and the overuse of analytical structures (including complex prepositions) (see, e.g., Harvey 1995; Wilkoń 2000; Biel 2014; Lewandowski 2015). Each of these features has its pros and cons: nominalization serves condensation and makes the text more concise, but when used in excess it may also make the text unintelligible; depersonalization tends to enhance objectivity, but it induces detachment from the text and the reader; analytical structures are used to ensure precision, but they often result in prolixity. All of these structures are factors of incomprehensibility, though also strong markers of style (Czerwińska 2016). Although the guidelines instruct drafters to avoid them whenever possible, they cannot be eliminated altogether.

EU institutions use a broad range of resources to standardize drafting and translation. The types of resources used at the European Commission have been surveyed by Svoboda (2013, 2017). They cover guidelines, manuals, style guides, glossaries and translation memories, among other resources. They are intended to be used by translators as a toolbox for finding solutions to problems encountered in their work. These aids are used both in-house and by external contractors, who are obliged to follow the same quality requirements as in-house translators.[4] This is particularly important due to the fact that, in general, only 10% of the samples of the outsourced translations are thoroughly

---

3   There are many voices that claim that the multilingual language regime of the EU is costly and insufficiently justified (see Van Parijs 2011 for an overview). However, Council Regulation No. 1 of 1958 provided for equality of all official languages of the Communities in order to satisfy people's identity interests and avoid conflicts, so the EU is formally committed to using translation as a means of communication (see Stefaniak 2013, 58; De Schutter and Robichaud 2015, 90).
4   See tender specifications, for example OMNIBUS-15 https://infoeuropa.eurocid.pt/files/database/000064001-000065000/000064078_2.pdf (accessed 15 May 2019).

evaluated, that is, only one in ten pages of a document translated by an external contractor undergoes in-house revision (Strandvik 2017, 59–60).

The institutions have issued various manuals: from more general ones, aimed at achieving consistent drafting and translation[5] of documents in all official languages, to more specific ones, which answer detailed questions regarding the drafting/translation procedure or language particularities. The guidelines available in all language versions include:

- *Interinstitutional Style Guide* – an online resource published by the Publications Office and updated on a regular basis. It contains uniform stylistic rules and conventions for the drafting of all written documents, developed by an interinstitutional group involving translators, lawyer-linguists, proofreaders and terminologists. Three parts of the *Guide* cover issues applicable to all the official languages, and the last part is language-specific. The *Guide* is the only obligatory resource, the provisions of which need to be observed by drafters and translators. Updates are listed in the News section and marked with a colored font or a strikethrough in the text, so they may be easily traced;
- *Joint Practical Guide of the European Parliament, the Council and the Commission for persons involved in the drafting of European Union legislation*[6] – a guide prepared by the legal services of the three institutions. It provides twenty-two basic legal drafting guidelines with comments and examples. Its main aim is to facilitate the drafting of clear legal acts. The second and most recent edition[7] was published in 2015;
- *Joint Handbook for the Presentation and Drafting of Acts subject to the Ordinary Legislative Procedure* – a handbook drawn up by the legal services of the Parliament, the Council and the Commission. It contains detailed drafting rules regarding the presentation and standard wording of final versions of legal acts adopted under the ordinary legislative procedure. The most recent edition[8] was produced in January 2018;

---

5   Drafting and translation at the EU institutions are intertwined; therefore, the drafting resources are also applied during the translation process.
6   The Council issued a document with similar contents to the *Joint Practical Guide* – the *Manual of Precedents for Acts Established within the Council of the European Union*. Its publicly available version of 2002 was published in ten official languages; the current version is an internal document (Robertson 2013).
7   The first edition was published in 2003; translations for the MS that joined in 2004 were issued in 2008.
8   It is not the first edition, as earlier versions are mentioned in other works (e.g., Drugan et al. 2018), but there is no reference in the document specifying which version this is or what changes have been introduced.

- *How to write clearly* – a booklet that contains ten very general hints[9] facilitating clear and simple text production, recommended for all types of documents; it is a result of the Clear Writing Campaign, a reflection of the plain language movement at the European Commission (Wagner et al. 2012, 74).

Apart from these EU-wide manuals, most of the language units at the DGT have their own in-house style guides (Svoboda 2017, 96). Although the name could suggest that the guides are only used internally, they are publicly available on the website for contractors for most languages.[10]

3   Guidelines and EU genres

EU institutions produce texts that belong to a range of genres (Biel et al. 2019, 68). Various types of documents are subject to different quality requirements. For example, the rules provided in the *Joint Practical Guide* and *Joint Handbook* apply to legal acts only; thus, they would not be of much use in the translation of websites. Information on which manuals to take into account while translating different types of documents may be found in the *DGT Translation Quality Guidelines* (DGT 2015), issued in 2015 as an operationalization of the DGT Quality Management Framework (Drugan et al. 2018, 47). The main aim of the *Guidelines* is to ensure that the translations fulfill their communicative purpose. They distinguish four main text categories: A – Legal documents, B – Policy and administrative documents, C – Information for the public, and D – Input for EU legislation, policy formulation and administration (DGT 2015, 4). Each category covers several types of texts produced in the EU institutions, along with their specification, the intended effects, risks and recommended minimum level of quality control.[11] High-stakes documents, which fall into text category A, have strict quality control requirements, such as obligatory full revision even under extreme work pressure (DGT 2015, 6). Texts in category B do not need full revision; in this case, review of key parts of documents may be sufficient (DGT 2015, 11). The different requirements

---

9   The provisions in the booklet are called "hints" in order to highlight their non-compulsory nature.
10   https://ec.europa.eu/info/resources-partners/translation-and-drafting-resources/guidelines-translation-contractors_en (accessed 15 May 2019).
11   DGT distinguishes between two types of quality control to ensure suitability of texts for a given purpose: revision–bilingual examination of target language text against source language text; and review–monolingual examination of target language text (DGT 2015, 3).

may affect the level of quality of texts that belong to different genres – full revision should provide a flawless text, whereas errors could be missed in the case of sole review. Accordingly, the type and purpose of the text may influence the extent to which translators follow the guidelines. It is expected that translators adhere to the guidelines more closely in the case of category A documents than in the case of category B documents. In order to check this claim, the study at hand focuses on two genres: legislation and reports.

Legislation has the highest status in the hierarchy of legal genres: it prescribes law, creates legal norms and establishes rights and obligations (Biel et al. 2019, 70). It has a huge impact on the everyday life of Europeans. Legal acts have twenty-four language versions, all of which are equally authentic: they convey the same meaning and produce the same legal effect in all the Member States (DGT 2015, 5). The authorship of legal acts is collective and the drafting passes multiple stages – the first draft and translations into all official languages are usually carried out by the European Commission, and further amendments are dealt with by the European Parliament and the Council.[12] The interdependency of the institutions in the multilingual law-making process may induce errors, which could lead to litigation and financial, political and image-related damage (DGT 2015, 6). Therefore, legislation entails the highest quality requirements as regards translation and revision. The *Guidelines* instruct translators to necessarily comply with the drafting rules in the manuals (the *Interinstitutional Style Guide*, *Joint Practical Guide*, the *Manual of Precedents*, the *Joint Handbook*, language-specific style guides), to use Normative Memories, LegisWrite and other sector-specific templates, and to revise the translations even under extreme work pressure (DGT 2015, 5).

Reports drafted at the European Commission are informative texts, aimed at the presentation and evaluation of the activities of the EU. In the functional classification developed by Prieto Ramos, they fall into two categories: monitoring (covering documents which help EU institutions supervise Member States' compliance) and administrative (devoted to the functioning of the institution itself) (Prieto Ramos 2019, 39–40).[13] However, they also serve to create a positive image of the institutions and to legitimize their functioning. They are drafted by the Directorates-General (DGs) of the European

---

12   See the Ordinary Legislative Procedure http://www.europarl.europa.eu/ordinary-legislative-procedure/en/ordinary-legislative-procedure.html (accessed 15 May 2019).
13   In the classification by Prieto Ramos (2019, 39–40), reports also fulfill secondary law- and policy-making functions. Such technical reports, which are a part of the preparatory legislative work, are not included in this study.

Commission mainly for experts or semi-experts, but they may also be read by members of the general public interested in the subject. The risks caused by erroneous translation are not as substantial as in the case of legislation, and are generally image-related. Inconsistencies between language versions may cause damage to the political credibility and incur complications in negotiations between Member States or in public consultation. Reports fall into text category B, which requires the translations to be accurate, factually correct, complete and idiomatic, to focus on meaning rather than words, though with attention to terminology (DGT 2015, 10). The guidelines recommended for the translation of reports are the *Interinstitutional Style Guide*, language-specific style guides and the *How to write clearly* booklet. Revision is not obligatory; it may be limited to a revision or review of the key parts of the texts or skipped altogether if there is insufficient time.

The two genres, legislation and reports, differ significantly with regard to their application, status and the standards of quality control. These factors are likely to influence the translation process in all the language units and thus be reflected in the corpora of the Polish versions of the documents.

4   The quest for quality at the Polish language unit

Poland joined the EU in the "big bang" enlargement in 2004. The accession of a new Member State has always been a challenge with regard to translation, but enlargement by ten additional states was exceptional and brought major changes both to the practice of drafting and translating and to quality assurance at the EU institutions (Wagner et al. 2012, 102–103; Strandvik 2017, 53).

The legislation of every newly joined Member State needs to be harmonized with EU legislation upon accession. This means that the *acquis*, involving primary and secondary legislation,[14] as well as the most important parts of the case law of the Court of Justice, must be translated at the responsibility of national governments, revised by the EU institutions and published in a special edition of the Official Journal (Wagner et al. 2012, 103–104). The candidate countries were instructed to set up a special Translation Coordination Unit, after which they were free to decide how to manage the translations (Rzewuska 2002, 2145; Wagner et al. 2012, 104).

---

14   Primary legislation covers treaties; secondary legislation is derived from primary legislation and includes regulations, directives, decisions, recommendations and opinions (https://europa.eu/european-union/law_en).

The translation of the *acquis* into Polish was assigned to the Office of the Committee for European Integration (UKIE)[15] in Poland, where a Translation Coordination Unit was established in 1997. The Unit dealt with the revision of translations commissioned to translation agencies. However, those engaged personally in the process admit that the procedure chosen for the management of translation did not ensure a high quality; the translations submitted by agencies were revised only in part (10–20%) and returned to the agencies along with a list of the most common mistakes to be corrected in the text; not all of the final versions were checked afterwards (Rzewuska 2002, 2146). These shortcomings did not reflect any intentional disregard of quality requirements but, rather, stemmed from the lack of adequate resources and experience in such a huge translation project. The Unit developed glossaries and a manual for translators of EU legal acts into Polish, which was updated along the way in order to enhance translation quality. Nevertheless, hasty translation and inadequate quality control resulted in numerous errors in the translated documents, which were widely commented on, even in the press (e.g., PAP 2004; Uhlig 2005; see Biel 2014, 74).

Upon accession, the responsibility for translating legislation and other documents into Polish was shifted to EU institutions. The newly recruited translators were selected in rigorous competitions, aimed at employing high-caliber staff. Consequently, the quality of translations improved. This enhancement was based on two pillars: the multi-faceted quality assurance process at the translation departments and the high language awareness of the translators. Translation of EU documents entails, among other things, the creation of new terms (Stefaniak 2017; Temmerman 2018). These neologisms usually attract much attention and criticism, which develops into the general idea of badly-translated EU texts (see Biel 2014, 73). However, EU translators actually put a great deal of effort into ensuring the highest possible language quality. They sought answers to complex linguistic problems using various language guidance services provided by universities and other organizations, such as the Council for the Polish Language at the Presidium of the Polish Academy of Sciences (Kołodziejek 2014, 64). This cooperation soon needed to be systematized, which led to the appointment of an EU coordinator based at the Publications Office at the end of 2005 (Markowski 2007, 22), whose duty was to select and group the questions and transfer them on to the Council for the Polish Language. Moreover, the Council conducted several training sessions for translators on correct language use.

---

15 Polish: *Urząd Komitetu Integracji Europejskiej*.

One of the outcomes of these activities was the development of the Polish style guide at the European Commission, *Vademecum Tłumacza* (*Translator's Vade Mecum*). The first drafts of the guide were written in 2006,[16] but the first publicly available version (already called the second version) was issued in November 2007. The *Vademecum* brings together solutions to problems encountered by the translators drawn from different sources: internal arrangements, materials from training sessions, aids developed by the Publications Office and the Legal Service, and by the UKIE (DGT 2016, 7). The applicability of the rules crosses the borders of EU institutions – it is a highly useful tool for translators of various texts, often recommended by universities to their students or by translation agencies to their employees.

The *Vademecum* has evolved over time, and its contents have been adjusted to the needs of the language. In total, seventeen versions have been published up to 2019, with approximately a year between two subsequent versions.[17] The length of the guide has expanded from the initial seventy-five pages to 151 in the seventeenth version. However, the general scope of information has remained unchanged in most of them. The parts that are present in all versions cover correct language use and general translation problems regarding orthography, punctuation, style and grammar, as well as the specificity of the translation of EU legal acts – document structure, punctuation, lexical and legal issues. The two latest editions saw modifications in the layout as well as the deletion of the chapter on where to look for information, documents and terminology.[18] The most significant differences in the remaining content may be seen in the style and grammar part. New patterns to avoid and problematic words and expressions have been added over time. A survey of these changes is provided in the following section of the present study.

EU translators receive notifications of the amendments in order to incorporate them into their practice. This study empirically investigates to what extent these amendments to successive versions of the *Vademecum* are applied by translators at the DGT.

---

16   Personal communication with Karolina Stefaniak, quality officer at the DGT Polish unit, 3 September 2018.
17   Three versions were published in 2007 and in 2012.
18   The chapter mainly included references to EUR-Lex and IATE, which are also mentioned in other guidelines, such as the *Interinstitutional Style Guide*.

5   Corpus design

This study uses corpus-based methods. The analysis is conducted on the corpora of Polish versions of legislation and reports drafted by the European Commission in 2011–2015, which were compiled for the purposes of the Polish Eurolect project (Biel 2016). It is supplemented by early-accession corpora, containing legislative acts from 2004 and reports from 2004 and 2005,[19] as well as the most recent corpora of legislation and reports from 2018, in order to broaden the picture. The corpora of legislation cover binding acts, that is, regulations, directives and decisions, downloaded from EUR-Lex.[20] The corpora of reports contain reports drafted by the DGs of the European Commission, downloaded from the register of Commission documents.[21] Table 1 shows the key data on the corpora.

Table 1. Key data on the corpora used in the study

	2004	2011	2012	2013	2014	2015	2018
LEGISLATION							
texts	388	462	344	348	427	320	325
tokens	553 434	1 815 850	1 318 678	2 385 869	2 218 478	880 164	642 735
types	24 881	93 090	48 028	61 853	56 384	39 248	26 770
REPORTS							
texts	99	162	155	168	158	152	193
tokens	333 449	711 788	764 866	867 754	814 044	712 823	779 400
types	25 963	35 069	35 812	39 664	37 016	34 771	36 562

The study was conducted with Wordsmith Tools 7.0 (Scott 2016). The results were normalized to one million words in order to eliminate the influence of the sizes of the corpora.[22] The statistical significance of the results was tested

---

19   The extension of the time frame for the reports corpus was necessary due to an insufficient number of documents translated into Polish in 2004, and thus a severe lack of comparability between the corpora of legislation and reports from 2004.
20   https://eur-lex.europa.eu/homepage.html.
21   http://ec.europa.eu/transparency/regdoc/.
22   The detailed statistics of the analyzed items may be found at https://eurolekt.ils.uw.edu.pl/files/2021/01/Translation-guidelines-vs-practice.xlsx (accessed January 2021).

with the Log Likelihood (LL) test, and their effect size was measured with the Effect Size for Log Likelihood (ELL).[23]

6   The impact of the *Vademecum* on translators' practice

As mentioned above, one of the most explicit changes in the content of the subsequent versions of *Vademecum* may be observed in the section on problematic words and expressions. The section presents problems arising from the fact that the most obvious Polish equivalents of some foreign words and phrases do not work well in the contexts in which they appear in translated documents, thus resulting in stylistically unfortunate translations (DGT 2016, 51). The *Vademecum* provides suggestions for better solutions. A summary of the changes in the scope of problematic expressions is illustrated in Figure 1.

Only three expressions in English seemed to be problematic for translators from the very beginning ('strengthen', 'ensure that' and 'relevant'), but the section soon expanded, and the seventeenth version of the style guide includes ten times more items. The problematic words and expressions in English cover various forms, and the style guide provides preferred equivalents for most of them. The Polish part includes only complex prepositions, such as *na rzecz* ('for') or *w zakresie* ('in the scope of'), and the *Vademecum* instructs translators to avoid them where possible, mainly in order to decrease the level of nominalization and wordiness. The list of Polish problematic items is not a closed set, which is indicated in the body of the provision. However, the items in the heading clearly stand out and may influence the translators' awareness of these expressions. Nevertheless, for the sake of clarity, the editors reduced the number of the expressions in the heading in the latest versions of the *Vademecum*.[24]

Problematic expressions in Polish were chosen for the purpose of the present study, as their quantity is expected to decrease if the guidelines are followed. Each of the corpora was surveyed in search of the items identified above. They were divided into two groups: those added earlier, in 2010, *na rzecz* ('for'), *w zakresie* ('in the scope of') and *w celu* ('for the purpose of'),

---

23   The LL provides information on statistical significance, that is, whether the observations are incidental or not, whereas the ELL informs researchers about the practical significance of the study and indicates whether the result is meaningful (see Ridge and Kudenko 2010, 272). Both measures were calculated using the Lancaster calculator available at http://ucrel.lancs.ac.uk/llwizard.html (accessed 15 May 2019).

24   Personal communication with Karolina Stefaniak, quality officer at the DGT Polish unit, 11 January 2021.

	v 2 Nov 2007	v 3 Dec 2007	v 4 Dec 2007	v 5 Feb 2009	v 6 Apr 2010	v 7 Jan 2011	v 8 Jan 2012	v 9 Sep 2012	v 10 Dec 2012	v 11 Jul 2013	v 12 Jan 2014	v 13 Jan 2015	v 14 Jan 2016	v 15 Oct 2016	v 16 Mar 2018	v 17 Jan 2019
Polish				na rzecz, w zakresie, w celu										+ w dziedzinie w przypadku w ramach w kontekście	−	w przypadku
Version																
English				strengthen, ensure that, relevant							+ it is appropriate	+ promote, contribute, objectives, effort		+ export/import, however, if appropriate, legislation, legislative, may not, provide for, see, specific, unless, without prejudice		+ enter into force, apply, take effect, established in vs. nationality, transpose vs. implement

Figure 1. Changes in the scope of problematic expressions in the versions of the *Vademecum*

which should be well incorporated in translators' practice; and those added only in 2016 – *w dziedzinie* ('in the field of'), *w przypadku* ('in the case of'), *w ramach* ('within') and *w kontekście* ('in the context of').

The results for the first group are presented separately for 2011–2015, as the trends may be seen year on year, and then including the corpora of 2004 and 2018. The trends in the figures for 2004–2018 need to be treated with caution, due to the omission of data for 2005–2010 and 2016–2017. Figure 2 shows the distribution of the items in 2011–2015.

The expressions *na rzecz* ('for'), *w zakresie* ('in the scope of') and *w celu* ('for the purpose of') are more frequent in the corpora of reports, and the fluctuations are generally less marked; the changes year on year are statistically insignificant. Although a decrease in the frequencies of all items may be seen in 2015, the trend is growing for all but one expression (*w zakresie*, 'in the scope of'). Nevertheless, the effect size of the differences is minimal (the maximum value of ELL is 0.00002[25] and may be seen with regard to *na rzecz* ('for') in the corpora of legislation). Figure 3 shows a broader perspective of the three expressions, including the data for 2004 (and 2005 for reports) and 2018.

---

25   ELL varies between 0 and 1; the higher the value, the more important the difference (Johnston et al. 2006).

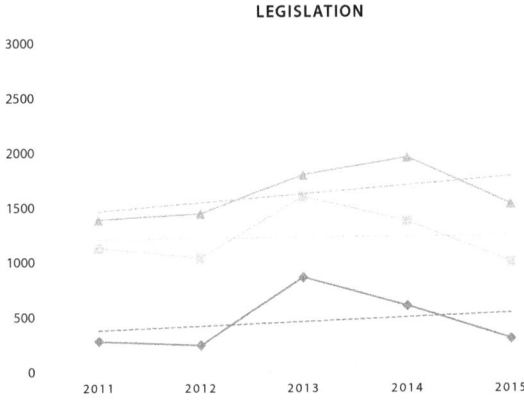

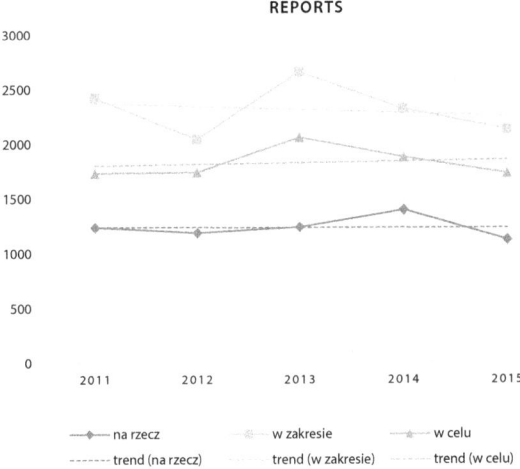

Figure 2. Problematic expressions *na rzecz* ('for'), *w zakresie* ('in the scope of') and *w celu* ('for the purpose of') in 2011–2015

Again, there is more fluctuation in the frequencies of the problematic expressions in the corpora of legislation. The trends of *na rzecz* ('for') and *w zakresie* ('in the scope of') are increasing. The only downward trend may be noted with regard to *w celu* ('for the purpose of'), but it is still more common in 2018 than it was in 2011–2015. The corpora of reports generally show a steady increase in the number of instances, and only the trend of *w celu* ('for the purpose of') is flat. The values for 2018 are higher than for 2015 in all cases. However, the effect size again indicates that the differences are not of considerable magnitude, with ELL between 0.00000 and 0.00002.

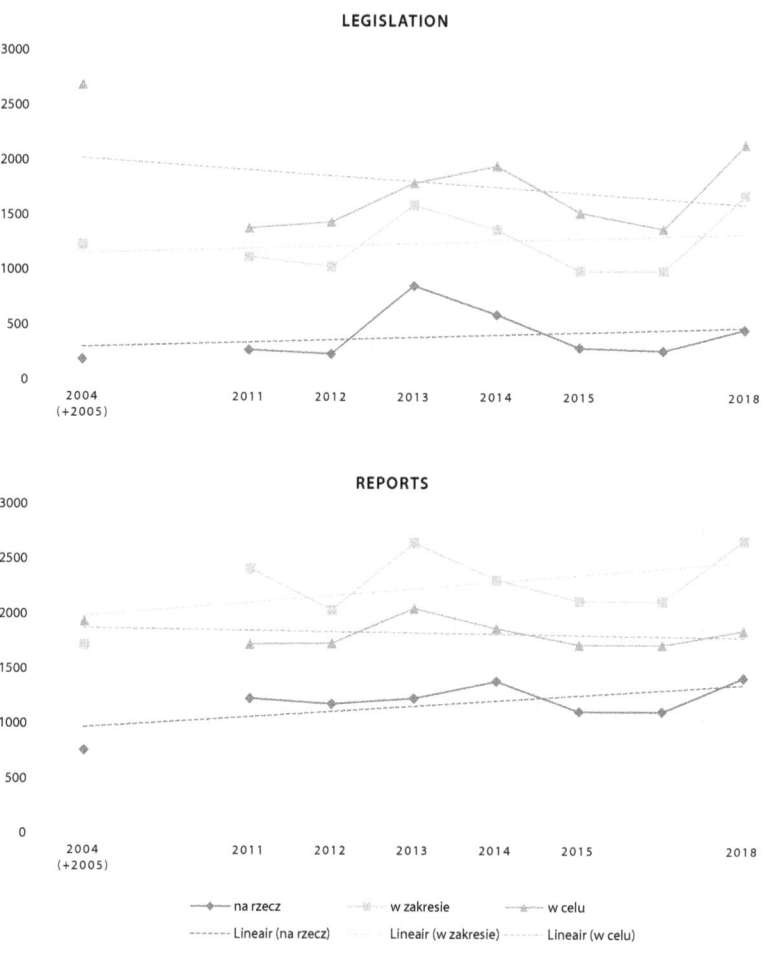

Figure 3. Problematic expressions *na rzecz* ('for'), *w zakresie* ('in the scope of') and *w celu* ('for the purpose of') in 2004–2018

Figure 4 shows the distribution of the second group of problematic expressions: *w dziedzinie* ('in the field of'), *w przypadku* ('in the case of'), *w ramach* ('within') and *w kontekście* ('in the context of'). The expressions were added to the *Vademecum* in 2016, thus only the graph for 2004–2018 is analyzed.

In the case of the second group of expressions, the higher frequency of items in the corpora of reports is not as evident as in the first group; *w przypadku* ('in the case of') is even far less common than in the corpora of legislation. The trends are upward in all but one case – the frequencies of *w dziedzinie* ('in the field of') are falling slightly in the report corpora. The differences

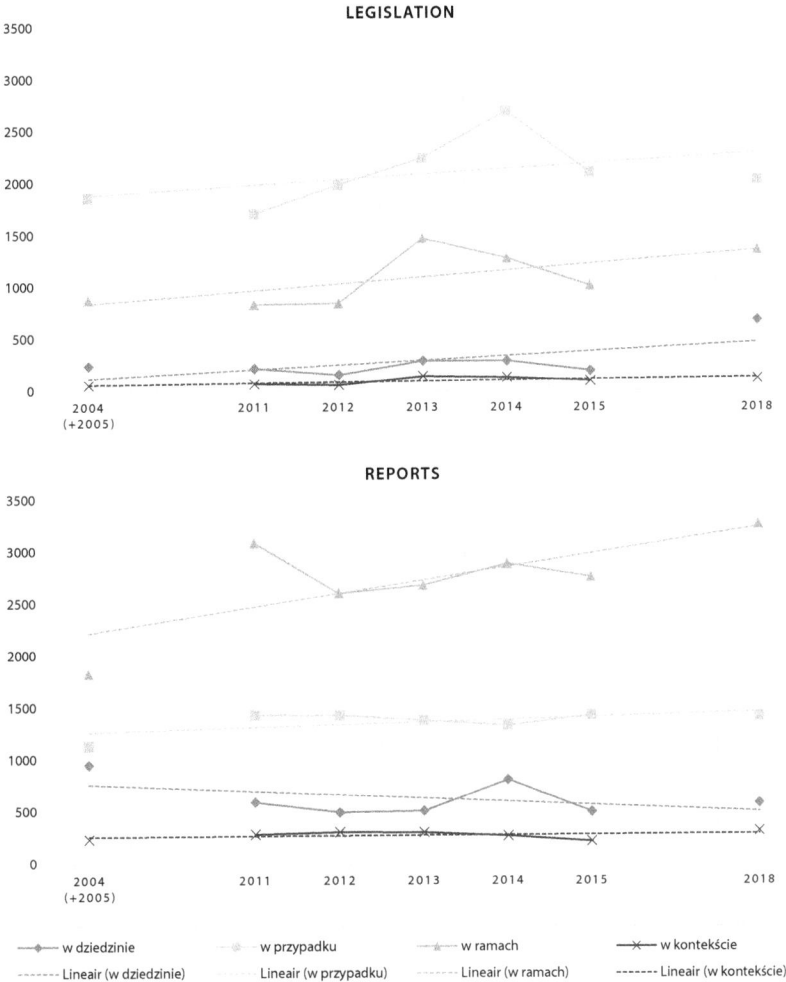

Figure 4. Problematic expressions *w dziedzinie* ('in the field of'), *w przypadku* ('in the case of'), *w ramach* ('within') and *w kontekście* ('in the context of') in 2004–2018

are generally statistically significant, but their effect size is very small, with a maximum ELL level of 0.00001.

These results suggest that the changes introduced to the *Vademecum* are not taken into consideration. The minimal values of the effect size in all cases show that there is actually little variation in the distribution of items indicated in the guidelines as undesired. It was anticipated that legislation would adhere more to the changes in the style guide than reports due to higher quality requirements for translation, including necessary compliance with the language-specific style guides. The frequency trends were expected to fall in the case of legislation, and be constant with regard to reports. Such differences between the genres are not visible. Moreover, the *Translation Quality Guidelines* instruct translators to use more idiomatic language in reports, which implies avoidance of such markers of administrative style as complex prepositions, and consequently lower frequency of these items in the corpora or reports compared to legislation. However, the results of the analysis prove otherwise.

The fact that analytical structures are frequent in both genres is not surprising, since both legislation and reports are often dealt with by the same translators. Wagner (2001, 268) notes that "translators allow the style of legislative texts to spill over into other translations", even though legislation constitutes about 40% of the translated texts. She suggests that the reason for this may be time pressure and inadequate briefing. The latter could have been true in 2001, when the paper was published, but today translators have ample guidelines on drafting and translation rules. Time pressure is always an issue (Strandvik 2017, 53), but it seems that this condition is not the only explanation.

The key factor that precludes the introduction of changes to the translations is the requirement of consistency, both within a document and across various documents, especially with regard to legislation (Stefaniak 2017, 116). Translation memories are the most necessary resource to ensure consistent translation. They contain not only pre-translated phrases and parts of legislation, which cannot be altered, but also multi-word terms and names of programs, projects and policies that often comprise complex prepositions. Translation memories are also very convenient and thus reduce any incentive for change.

Another aspect that may account for the translation choices are translators' habits and fossilized structures.[26] They are usually translators' aids, as they reduce the mental effort of the translation process – some equivalents are automatically prompted, so the translator does not focus on them in order to free the working memory for more demanding parts of texts. However, in the context of this study, they hinder the translators' adaptation to new information in the style guide.

The fact that *Vademecum* has introduced many amendments in comparison with other style guides also needs to be taken into consideration. One investigation into the scope of quality control of administrative documents carried out for the DGT found that "too many instructions can fail in their purpose and simply be ignored by drafters" (DGT 2013, 175). It is highly

---

26 Very standardized structures found frequently in a given context (see Biel 2014, 220).

probable that translators do not track changes in the style guide because they get lost in the sea of rules.

7 Conclusion

The Polish style guide is one of many translation and drafting manuals issued by the EU institutions. The numerous rules, guidelines and provisions have one goal: to ensure high-quality, consistent translation of all official EU documents. Adherence to the general principles provided in the guidelines and manuals is clearly reflected in the EU texts – the high level of standardization of the documents drafted and translated at EU institutions has been confirmed by many researchers (e.g., Koskinen 2008; Wagner et al. 2012; Schäffner et al. 2014). However, this study shows that more detailed rules are not always applied. The amendments to the Polish style guide seem to be ignored. This lack of response to the new provisions may not be attributed to the absence of information but, rather, could be explained by a combination of time pressure, required consistency, the use of translation memories, translators' habits and a high volume of instructions.

It should be kept in mind that this empirical study focuses only on a small section of translation products. The fact that the corpora do not reflect the changes introduced to the *Vademecum* does not mean that translators in general do not follow the guidelines. The macrostructure and layout indisputably show a high level of standardization and institutionalization of the texts produced. The devil, as always, is in the details.

Acknowledgement

This work was supported by the National Science Centre (NCN) under Grant 2014/14/E/HS2/00782.

References

Biel, Łucja. 2014. *Lost in the Eurofog; The Textual Fit of Translated Law*. Frankfurt am Main: Peter Lang.
———. 2016. "Mixed Corpus Design for Researching the Eurolect: A Genre-Based Comparable-Parallel Corpus in the PL EUROLECT Project." In *Polskojęzyczne korpusy równoległe. Polish-Language Parallel Corpora*, edited by Ewa Gruszczyńska

and Agnieszka Leńko-Szymańska, 197–208. Warsaw: The Institute of Applied Linguistics.

———, Dariusz Koźbiał, and Katarzyna Wasilewska. 2019. "The Formulaicity of Translations across EU Institutional Genres. A Corpus-Driven Analysis of Lexical Bundles in Translated And Non-Translated Language." *Translation Spaces* 8 (1): 67–93.

Czerwińska, Eliza. 2016. "Stylistyczne wykładniki niekomunikatywności tekstów urzędowych." *Poradnik Językowy* 6: 20–36.

De Schutter, Helder, and David Robichaud. 2015. "Van Parijsian Linguistic Justice – Context, Analysis and Critiques." *Critical Review of International Social and Political Philosophy* 18 (2): 87–112.

Directorate-General for Translation (DGT), European Commission. 2013. *Document Quality Control in Public Administrations and International Organisations*. Luxembourg: Publications Office of the European Commission.

———. European Commission. 2015. *DGT Translation Quality Guidelines*. http://ec.europa.eu/translation/maltese/guidelines/documents/dgt_translation_quality_guidelines_en.pdf.

———. Polish Language Unit, European Commission. 2016. *Vademecum tłumacza. Wskazówki redakcyjne dla tłumaczy*.

Drugan, Joanna, Ingemar Strandvik, and Erkka Vuorinen. 2018. "Translation Quality, Quality Management and Agency: Principles and Practice in the European Union Institutions." In *Translation Quality Assessment: From Principles to Practice*, edited by Joss Moorkens, Sheila Castilho, Stephen Doherty and Federico Gaspari, 39–68. Berlin: Springer.

Harvey, Anamaria. 1995. "Interaction in Public Reports." *English for Specific Purposes* 14 (3): 189–200.

How to Write Clearly. 2012. https://publications.europa.eu/en/publication-detail/-/publication/bb87884e-4cb6-4985-b796-70784ee181ce/language-en.

Interinstitutional Style Guide. http://publications.europa.eu/code/en/en-000100.htm.

Johnston, Janis E., Kenneth J. Berry, and Paul W. Mielke. 2006. "Measures of Effect Size for Chi-Squared and Likelihood-Ratio Goodness-of-Fit Tests." *Perceptual and Motor Skills* 103 (2): 412–414.

Joint Handbook for the Presentation and Drafting of Acts Subject to the Ordinary Legislative Procedure. 2018. https://www.consilium.europa.eu/media/32619/joint-handbook-en-january-2018_2018_01_25_def.pdf.

Joint Practical Guide of the European Parliament, the Council and the Commission for Persons Involved in the Drafting of European Union Legislation. 2015. 2nd ed. Luxembourg: Office for Official Publications of the EC. http://eurlex.europa.eu/content/techleg/EN-legislative-drafting-guide.pdf.

Kang, Ji-Hae. 2014. "Institutions Translated: Discourse, Identity and Power in Institutional Mediation." *Perspectives* 22 (4): 469–478.

Kołodziejek, Ewa. 2014. "Kultura komunikacji urzędowej." In *Kultura komunikacji językowej 3. Kultura języka w komunikacji zawodowej*, edited by Anna Piotrowicz, Małgorzata Witaszek-Samborska and Krzysztof Skibski, 59–66. Poznań: Wydawnictwo Poznańskiego Towarzystwa Przyjaciół Nauk.

Koskinen, Kaisa. 2008. *Translating Institutions. An Ethnographic Study of EU Translation*. London: Routledge.

———. 2014. "Institutional Translation: The Art of Government by Translation." *Perspectives* 22 (4): 479–492. https://doi.org/10.1080/0907676X.2014.948887.

Lewandowski, Marcin. 2015. "On Denominalization in Polish-English Translation. Implications for Translation Teaching." *Lebende Sprachen* 60 (1): 145–163.

Markowski, Andrzej. 2007. "Polszczyzna w dokumentach unijnych. Dylematy tłumaczy Unii Europejskiej." In *Język polski jako narzędzie komunikacji we współczesnym świecie*, edited by Jan Mazur and Małgorzata Rzeszutko-Iwan, 21–32. Lublin: Uniwersytet Marii Curie-Skłodowskiej.

Mason, Ian. 2012. "Text Parameters in Translation: Transitivity and Institutional Cultures." In *The Translation Studies Reader*, edited by Lawrence Venuti, 3rd ed., 399–410. New York: Routledge.

Nesti, Giorgia. 2010. "The Information and Communication Policy of the European Union between Institutionalisation and Legitimation." In *Public Communication in the European Union: History, Perspectives and Challenges*, edited by Giorgia Nesti and Chiara Valentini, 23–48. Newcastle upon Tyne: Cambridge Scholars Publishing.

Polish Press Agency (PAP). 2004. "Błędy w tłumaczeniach prawa unijnego." 26 July 2004. https://wiadomosci.wp.pl/bledy-w-tlumaczeniach-prawa-unijnego-6037178530505857a.

Prieto Ramos, Fernando. 2019. "Implications of Text Categorisation for Corpus-based Legal Translation Research: The Case of International Institutional Settings." In *Research Methods in Legal Translation and Interpreting: Crossing Methodological Boundaries*, edited by Łucja Biel, Jan Engberg, Rosario Martín Ruano and Vilelmini Sosoni, 29–47. London: Routledge.

Ridge, Enda, and Daniel Kudenko. 2010. "Tuning an Algorithm Using Design of Experiments." In *Experimental Methods for the Analysis of Optimization Algorithms*, edited by Thomas Bartz-Beielstein, Marco Chiarandini, Luís Paquete and Mike Preuss, 265–286. Berlin: Springer.

Robertson, Colin. 2013. "How the European Union Functions in 23 Languages." *SYNAPS* 28: 14–32.

Rzewuska, Maria. 2002. "Terminology Resources in the Context of a Major Translation Project." Proceedings from the *LREC 2002 Third International Conference on Language Resources and Evaluation*, 2145–2150. http://www.lrec-conf.org/proceedings/lrec2002/pdf/248.pdf.

Schäffner, Christina, Luciana Sabina Tcaciuc, and Wine Tesseur. 2014. "Translation Practices in Political Institutions: A Comparison of National, Supranational, and Non-Governmental Organisations." *Perspectives* 22 (4): 493–510.

Scott, Mike. 2016. *WordSmith Tools version 7*. Stroud: Lexical Analysis Software.

Stefaniak, Karolina. 2013. "Multilingual Legal Drafting, Translators' Choices and the Principle of Lesser Evil." *Meta* 58 (1): 58–65.

———. 2017. "Terminology Work in the European Commission: Ensuring High-Quality Translation in a Multilingual Environment." In *Quality Aspects in Institutional Translation*, edited by Tomáš Svoboda, Łucja Biel and Krzysztof Łoboda, 109–121. Berlin: Language Science Press.

Strandvik, Ingemar. 2017. "Towards a more Structured Approach to Quality Assurance: DGT's Quality Journey." In *Institutional Translation for International Governance: Enhancing Quality in Multilingual Legal Communication*, edited by Fernando Prieto Ramos, 51–62. London: Bloomsbury.

Svoboda, Tomáš. 2013. "Translation Manuals and Drafting Style Guides at the European Commission." *Le Bulletin du CRATIL Centre de recherche de l'ISIT* 10, 80–106.

———. 2017. "Translation Manuals and Style Guides as Quality Assurance Indicators: The Case of the European Commission's Directorate-General for Translation." In *Quality Aspects in Institutional Translation*, edited by Tomáš Svoboda, Łucja Biel and Krzysztof Łoboda, 75–107. Berlin: Language Science Press.

Temmerman, Rita. 2018. "European Union Multilingual Primary Term Creation and the Impact of its Neologisms on National Adaptations." *Parallèles* 30:1 (April): 8–20.

Uhlig, Dominik. 2005. "Błąd na błędzie w tłumaczeniach unijnych aktów." *Gazeta Wyborcza*, 9 January 2005. http://wyborcza.pl/1,75248,2485538.html?disableRedirects=true.

Van Parijs, Philippe. 2011. *Linguistic Justice for Europe and for the World*. Oxford: Oxford University Press.

Wagner, Emma. 2001. "Translation in the EU Machinery." *Perspectives* 9 (4): 263–270.

———, Svend Bech, and Jesús M. Martínez. 2012. *Translating for the European Union Institutions*. 2nd ed. Manchester: St. Jerome.

Wilkoń, Aleksander. 2000. *Typologia odmian językowych współczesnej polszczyzny*. Katowice: Wydawnictwo Uniwersytetu Śląskiego.

Institutional translation practices in South Tyrol

An exploratory study on civil servants working as 'occasional translators'

Flavia De Camillis

Abstract

While Italian is the only official language of Italy, many other languages that are spoken in the country enjoy different degrees of legal recognition and protection. Among these, three languages stand out for their legal status: French in the Aosta Valley, Slovene in Friuli-Venezia Giulia and German in South Tyrol. South Tyrolean citizens thus have the right to use Italian or German to communicate with local government entities, both in written and spoken form. Public servants must master Italian and German in order to fulfill their duties in both languages, which might also include translation assignments, according to their collective bargaining agreement. In 2017, we conducted twenty qualitative interviews with public servants from the provincial administration of South Tyrol to find out whether and how they deal with translation assignments. The interviews revealed that the interviewees have indeed experience with translating administrative documents, though none of them are professional translators, and that translating is an ancillary activity for all of them. In this contribution, we firstly describe minority languages in Italy from a linguistic and legal point of view, stressing differences in their classification and in legal recognition. Secondly, we present South Tyrol and its most important language and translation policies in government entities. Finally, we discuss the results from our pilot study as well as the institutional translation practices we were able to identify.

1 Introduction

In recent years, many scholars working in the area of translation studies have been focusing their research on institutional translation. The first scholar to identify a lack of scientific attention towards translation practices in institutions was Brian Mossop, a translator of Canada's Federal

Translation Bureau (Mossop 1988, 65), in the late 1980s. Only in the 2000s did the scientific community respond to the recommendations in his study, starting with Kaisa Koskinen who conducted an ethnographic enquiry in the European Commission (Koskinen 2008). After that, several scholars analyzed translation practices in international organizations or enterprises (Lafeber 2012; Tesseur 2014; Davier 2014) and multilingual institutions (Pym et al. 2012; Svoboda, Biel and Krzysztof 2017; Prieto Ramos 2018, 2020). Additionally, the interaction between government entities and new minorities (e.g., migratory minorities) became an object of analysis, especially verbal interactions like child language brokering (Antonini 2010; Antonini et al. 2017) and cultural mediation. Researchers showed an early interest in institutional translation for countries where different language communities co-exist (González Núñez 2014; Meylaerts 2017, 2018). This focus was the case of Spain, Ireland, South Africa and China, among others (Cruces Colado and Luna Alonso 2004; Branchadell and West 2005; Beukes 2006; O'Connell and Walsh 2006; García de Toro 2009; Pérez Ramírez 2014; Li et al. 2017).

Except for the above-mentioned studies on child language brokering and cultural mediators, Italy has not been properly analyzed in the field of institutional translation. In 2014, Flavia Vecchione did study the practices of translators within Italian ministries (Vecchione 2014) and, in 2019, Peter Sandrini published an analysis of translation policies in South Tyrol, a bilingual province (Sandrini 2019). Nonetheless, Italy is far from monolingual. This situation is true not only for South Tyrol, which will be the focus of this chapter, but for many other areas in the country as well, for which though no studies on institutional translation are available. In Section 2, we will delve into multilingualism in Italy, considering dialects and recognized minority languages, their legal treatment and historic background. Despite a constitutional[1] generic claim of protection of linguistic minorities (Constitution,[2] 6), the first and only law on the protection of linguistic minorities dates back to 1999.

Section 3 presents the special case of South Tyrol. Compared to other regions of Italy, it enjoys an extensive autonomy. Thanks to Decree No. 670/1972,[3] clear language policies regulate the multilingual existence of local institutions. However, South Tyrolean government entities have

---

1   Constitution of Italy came into force in 1948.
2   Costituzione della Repubblica italiana.
3   Decreto del Presidente della Repubblica, 31 agosto 1972. "Approvazione del testo unico delle leggi costituzionali concernenti lo statuto speciale per il Trentino – Alto Adige."

uncoordinated translation policies (Sandrini 2019, 390), as only a few aspects are defined in the laws. For example, most of the Provincial Administration's departments[4] do not have in-house translators, translation divisions or units.[5] The only exception is the Office for Language Issues, whose translators are responsible for normative texts, though not for other text types.

In order to find out how the Provincial Administration's departments meet their translation needs, in our exploratory study we started from the hypothesis that the civil servants themselves carry out translations. After presenting research questions and methodology, in Section 4 we will describe the identified translation practices of a particular type of civil servant whom we have dubbed the 'occasional translator'. Finally, in Section 5 we will draw some conclusions.

2   Multilingual Italy

According to Decree No. 670/1972, Italian is the official language of Italy (Article 99). As it occurs in a great many countries, the official language is far from being the only spoken or written language in the country (Toso 2008, 13). This is true also for Italy, which hosts a significant number of languages and dialects. Their classification differs among linguists and jurists.

2.1   Linguistic classification

Firstly, a distinction between language and dialect is necessary. As Toso puts it, the differences between a language and its dialects are mainly extra-linguistic, that is sociopolitical. Both language and dialect have phonetic, grammatical and lexical systems. While a dialect is a spontaneous and not formalized expression of a community culture, a language is an institutionalized communication system with officially recognized norms (Toso 2008, 19–20).

Loporcaro (2013, 69–72) distinguishes five groups of Latin-derived Italian dialects corresponding to their geographic distribution: northern dialects, Tuscan dialects, Friulian dialects, mid-southern dialects and Sardinian dialects. Among them, the Neapolitan-Calabrese dialect is worth mentioning.

---

4   The organizational charts of the Province of Bolzano have been analyzed during the early stage of the exploratory study, accessed 12 April 2019, https://bit.ly/2G7bJIj.
5   This statement does not refer to the local government (Giunta provinciale).

With its 5.7 million speakers,[6] according to Ethnologue,[7] it is the second most widespread language in Italy, and its use prevails in Campania (Istat 2017, 6). Furthermore, Loporcaro considers regional Italian varieties (*italiani regionali*) to be secondary dialects that consist of geographic variations of standard Italian. Finally, he calls colonial languages (*colonie linguistiche*) those languages that arrived in Italy through migration or colonization (Loporcaro 2013, 4–5). They are both of Romance (e.g., Catalan) and non-Romance origin (e.g., Albanian, German and Greek dialects).

Toso provides a different classification of minority languages in Italy, according to both linguistic and extra-linguistic aspects. He divides them into six groups: national minorities (German in South Tyrol, French in the Aosta Valley and Slovenian in Friuli-Venezia Giulia); regional languages (Sardinian, Friulian, Ladin); colonial languages (e.g., Greek, Catalan, Albanian); Franco-Provençal dialects; Italian dialects; and varieties without geographical bounds (e.g., Romani) (Toso 2008, 71–190). Neither dialects nor regional varieties have institutional recognition and for this reason they do not participate in the institutional translation scenario.

2.2 Legal classification

We shall consider now the legal classification of minority languages in Italy. Recognized language minorities in Italy are spoken by at least around 2.5 million people in total, based on the last available data (1994) (Palermo 2003, 164). According to their legal treatment and recognition, the legal doctrine splits them into three groups.

Starting from the least protected, the first group includes non-recognized minorities, which do not have any degree of protection. Among these, the Romani and Sinti communities stand out, as well as the new migratory minorities (Palermo 2003, 166). Recognized historical minorities fall into the second group. As stated in Law No. 482/1999, Art. 2, recognized minorities are the Albanian, Catalan, Germanic, Greek, Slovenian, Croatian, French, Franco-Provençal, Friulian, Ladin, Occitan and Sardinian language communities. These languages and cultures benefit from different degrees of

---

6 "Napoletano-Calabrese", Ethnologue, accessed 7 February 2019, https://bit.ly/2MSeb8s.
7 "Ethnologue: Languages of the World is a comprehensive reference work that provides information and statistics for all of the world's known living languages. Since 1951, Ethnologue has been an active research project involving hundreds of linguists and other researchers around the world. It is widely regarded as the most comprehensive source of information of its kind." https://bit.ly/2VjzXbA, accessed 24 February 2020.

protection according to the local legislation in force in each town, province or region where they are spoken. Lastly, the third group brings together minorities with a very high level of protection – so-called *superprotette* (Palici di Suni Prat 1999, 29) – such as the German-speaking minority in South Tyrol, the Slovenian-speaking community in Friuli-Venezia Giulia and the French-speaking community in Aosta Valley. They have a kin-State on the other side of the border: Austria, France and Slovenia, respectively.

These three Alpine regions, together with the islands of Sicily and Sardinia, are located along the national borders and enjoy a special autonomy status (*statuto speciale*). They enjoy greater autonomy than the other fifteen Italian regions regarding legislative, administrative and financial jurisdiction. However, language communities of the five special regions enjoy different legal benefits. The Alpine regions (Aosta Valley, Friuli-Venezia Giulia and Trentino-South Tyrol) achieved a more comprehensive autonomy and made language rights into one of their critical issues (again: French, Slovenian and German, respectively). In contrast, Sardinia and Sicily focused their autonomy on economic growth and social development rather than cultural promotion (Brigaglia and Mura 2018, 16).

2.3 The special case of Trentino-South Tyrol

Trentino-South Tyrol consists of two autonomous provinces[8] of about 500,000 inhabitants each: the Province of Trento and the Province of Bolzano/Bozen-South Tyrol.[9] They are the only two Italian autonomous provinces; as special regions, they benefit from a greater financial, administrative and legal jurisdiction than the rest of provinces. Both Trento and South Tyrol prioritize the safeguarding of linguistic rights for the minorities living within their borders. In South Tyrol, Italian and German are co-official languages, and Ladin is a historical minority language that enjoys official recognition.

3 Translating institutions in South Tyrol

Education, place names and public institutions are the three main aspects of multilingualism in South Tyrol. Focusing on public institutions, and especially

---

8   According to the Italian legal system, provinces are one of the three levels of local government: regions, provinces and communes.
9   From here on, for reason of language economy, we will use only the term 'South Tyrol'.

on administrative institutions, several decrees dictate their language policies, including what is to be published in the official languages. According to the definition of Meylaerts (Meylaerts 2018, 165), language policies encompass translation policies, as they prescribe rules of language use in and for institutions (see Section 3.1).

Despite strict language policies, translation policies of the Provincial Administration lack in some essential details. According to Sandrini, translation policies in South Tyrol are uncoordinated (Sandrini 2019, 391) and, to some extent, undefined. In this section, we will analyze the legal framework of language and translation policy for public institutions, as well as some of its deficiencies. We will then consider how the lack of detailed regulations affects translation practice.

3.1 The legal framework of translation policies

Three decrees related to language policies include some references to the translation process: Presidential Decrees No. 670/1972, No. 752/1976[10] and No. 574/1988.[11]

3.1.1 Languages of South Tyrol

The first and most important regulation for South Tyrol is the Autonomy Statute (Presidential Decree 670/1972), as it includes some important language policy keystones. Firstly, it states that Italian and German are co-official languages in the region of Trentino-South Tyrol. However, only the Italian version is legally binding for legislative acts[12] (Article 99). Secondly, it prescribes the right for German-speaking citizens to use their language with government entities and authorities within the provincial borders (Article 100), alike Italian-speaking citizens. The regional minority communities (Ladin, Cimbrian and Mòcheno) are entitled to promote and raise awareness of their cultures and traditions through local initiatives

---

10 Decreto del Presidente della Repubblica 26 luglio 1976, n. 752. "Norme di attuazione dello statuto speciale della regione Trentino – Alto Adige in materia di proporzionale negli uffici statali siti nella provincia di Bolzano e di conoscenza delle due lingue nel pubblico impiego."
11 Decreto del Presidente della Repubblica 15 luglio 1988, n. 574. "Norme di attuazione dello statuto speciale per la regione Trentino – Alto Adige in materia di uso della lingua tedesca e della lingua ladina nei rapporti con la pubblicazione amministrazione e nei procedimenti giudiziari."
12 "La lingua italiana fa testo negli atti aventi carattere legislativo e nei casi nei quali dal presente è statuto è prevista la redazione bilingue."

(Article 101). The regional and provincial[13] laws, as well as national laws and decrees of regional interest, are published in Italian and German in the Official Bulletin (Articles 57 and 58).

3.1.2 Language groups, bilingualism and translators

Decree No. 752/1976 is the first regulation almost exclusively focused on language issues. It provides the basic rules of local institutional bilingualism. The first major issue concerns the proportional hiring system. Government entities must hire employees from each language group (Italian, Germand and Ladin) according to the size of the respective group (Article 8). If the census shows that six out of ten citizens belong to the German group, three to the Italian group and one to the Ladin group, the same proportion of employees should work in government entities. To attain the required distribution, every residing citizen must declare at the courthouse or *via* census to which group they want to belong. The declaration results in a certificate, so called "certificato di appartenenza ovvero di aggregazione ad un gruppo linguistico" (Article 17).

Civil servants need also to be fluent in both official languages (Article 1), and in Ladin if the position requires it. Before applying for a public position, they must prove their language skills by passing one of the four language proficiency tests in both German and Italian, from A2 to C1 (Article 4). In this way, they acquire the 'bilingualism certificate'. They can only apply for positions that require the language level for which they are certified or lower levels. Thus, in this decree bilingualism refers to the "knowledge of Italian and German, up to the level necessary to perform the public service smoothly"[14] (Article 1). Civil servants are 'bilingual to some level'.

The bilingualism principle, as expressed in Decree No. 752/1976, sets the scene for another very important milestone of institutional bilingualism: the role of translators. As far as the *state offices* within the provincial territory are concerned – for example, Institute for social welfare, Institute for Insurance against Accidents at Work, etc. –, translators working in these facilities are not required to hold a translation degree or a degree in related topics (e.g. Linguistic, Language and Culture, etc.). They may also have a degree in Law or Economics, in addition to the common language certificate (Article 20-bis).

---

13 'Provincial' refers in this case only to the laws of the province of Bolzano.
14 "La conoscenza della lingua italiana e di quella tedesca, adeguata alle esigenze del buon andamento del servizio, costituisce requisito per le assunzioni comunque strutturate e denominate ad impieghi nelle amministrazioni dello Stato (…)."

On the contrary, according to the Collective Agreement of 8 March 2006[15] (Article 2), employees hired as translators in the Provincial Administration should have completed at least a three-year university course on a related topic and hold a C1 bilingualism certificate. However, the same Collective Agreement also states that every employee must carry out translations of texts in German, Italian and, if required, in Ladin, as a general task, with no mention of language competencies nor degrees. This inconsistency sketches two kinds of translators working in the Provincial Administration: the translators officially hired as such and the 'unofficial' translators.

3.1.3 Language use within public institutions

Decree No. 574/1988 regulates the use of German and Ladin in government entities. Most importantly, it states which acts are to be published in both official languages, that is, universal acts, individual acts for public use (e.g., identity card) and acts intended for several offices. Versions in Italian and German are to be published side by side, with the same font and text size, and must contain the official terminology, that is, those terms approved by the Terminology Commission (Article 6). The Terminology Commission was established to draw up "complete and consistent legal and administrative terminology in German[,] that would faithfully convey the concepts of the Italian legal system" (Chiocchetti et al. 2013, 10). It operated from 1994 until 2012 and approved around 7,400 pairs of terms. Ladin translations usually come after Italian and German versions (Article 32). Moreover, the decree consistently defines who is responsible for translating the acts to be published in the Official Bulletin (Article 5, par. 7), but does not do so for other texts, leaving many aspects on translation procedures open to interpretation (Sandrini 2019, 370).

3.2 The Provincial Administration and its translating institutions

The Administration of the Province of Bolzano numbers some 12,000 employees (ASTAT 2019, 2) divided into five large sections. In this chapter, we will focus only on one section, that is, the Provincial Administration *sensu stricto*.[16] This is the administrative core of the local government, as it

---

15 Contratto collettivo 8 marzo 2006. "Contratto collettivo di comparto sull'individuazione ed ascrizione dei profili professionali del personale provinciale."
16 Its name is precisely "Amministrazione provincial in senso stretto / Landesverwaltung im engeren Sinne."

manages its most important financial and legal issues. Its structure works on four levels: government bureaus, departments, divisions, offices.

The Office for Language Issues belongs to the Government Legal Service[17] and is the main language consultant for the Provincial Administration. Here, twelve individuals work as professional translators; they provide assistance to the Administration offices and departments in matters of language and terminology, as well as in drafting administrative acts. They translate or, as is more often the case, proofread provincial laws, bills and administrative provisions (i.e., from the provincial legislative body), and other relevant documents for the entire community. In recent years, the Office workload has registered an increase of revisions requests and a consequent decrease of translation assignments.[18] They also translate the most important national laws, released exclusively in Italian by the National Parliament (e.g., the Traffic Code, Privacy Code)[19] into German. In addition, there is a Ladin team, which consists of three employees. They translate usually normative texts and, rarely, informative texts from German and Italian into one of two Ladin dialects, alternatively Badiot and Gherdëina. Only in the case of highly relevant communications do they translate documents into both language varieties.[20] Some employees tasked with Ladin translations develop legal and administrative terminology and store it in the online accessible information system, *bistro*.[21] To some extent, the Office is a central translation bureau, similar to the Central Language Services of the Swiss Federal Chancellery. However, its translators generally deal with legally binding acts, though not with those acts without executive and executory character (called *meri atti amministrativi*, administrative measures) (Ferrari 2008, 104–107) or with informative texts. For this last type of text, local language policies do not foresee specific translation procedures.

When drafting and translating an administrative act or an informative text related to a specific area of expertise, civil servants do not usually seek the help of the Office for Language Issues[22] or of other internal offices. Among them, there are rarely any official translators, as shown in the organizational charts (see Section 1). Therefore, we can assume that civil servants manage

17   Avvocatura della Provincia / Anwaltschaft des Landes
18   Interview No. 1 (We have anonymized all interviewees and sorted the interviews in numerical order).
19   "Ufficio Questioni linguistiche", Amministrazione Provincia Bolzano, accessed 21 February 2019, https://bit.ly/2SSFB4k.
20   Interview No. 2.
21   "*bistro*", accessed 21 February 2019, http://bistro.eurac.edu/.
22   Interview No. 1.

to translate administrative or informative documents either internally or by outsourcing the job. This research looks at how the translation process for this type of text takes place.

4 Civil servants as occasional translators

Among civil servants, translation has been the subject of disputes and discontent.[23] Over the course of the last decade, it gained the attention of the General Direction of the Province, which launched an initiative in 2014, aimed at facilitating language management and using internal resources more efficiently. Until 2017, no enquiry had started to analyze the extent of the internal translation role.

We started from the assumption that translations are either managed externally to the institution, or internally (however, not by in-house translators) or both. Since translation is a general, mandatory task in the Administration (see Section 3.1.2), we formulated the following hypothesis: civil servants translate texts and, when necessary, outsource them to translation service providers. Our research question aims at finding out how civil servants manage their translation tasks without being formal translators. In our exploratory study, we aimed to figure out what they translate, how much, how often and which tools they use. A partnership with the General Direction of the Province helped fund the study and facilitated communication between the researchers and the civil servants. The following sections will focus on the development and results of this exploratory study.

4.1 Methodology and research questions

For this exploratory study, we applied the social research and ethnography technique of qualitative, semi-structured interviews.[24] Qualitative social research usually facilitates the understanding of little-investigated entities through exploratory communication concerning the object studied. This situation is the case with public employees and their experience related to translating. Furthermore, the interview technique is particularly suited for

---

23 Interviews No. 1, 2, 6.
24 Our exploratory study is the preliminary stage of a PhD project, in which we combine qualitative and quantitative techniques to delve into institutional translation processes in the Provincial Administration.

exploratory studies, as it can later be combined with quantitative research tools (Corbetta 2014, 109).

We selected participants from eight divisions (see Section 3.2). By doing so, we considered different expertise areas, numerical distribution of German- and Italian-speaking staff, as well as commonly used text types (e.g., informative, performative, etc.). The directors of the divisions shared with us information on their collaborators who usually translate texts (e.g., their mother tongue, work experience, and internal role). The sample consisted of twenty civil servants, all working in different offices and with a balanced number of men and women, as well as a balanced amount of German and Italian native speakers. Our final aim was to outline the internal translation activity in the Provincial Administration and, if possible, sketch a 'translator profile'. We asked the interviewees to describe their translating activity, that is, which texts they translate; how, how much and how often they do it; what training they received for this task; and how they feel about translating. In what follows, we present the results.

4.2 Translation process

The amount of translated texts and the typologies vary considerably among the divisions. Nine respondents say they usually translate just brief texts, whereas the other eleven also translate longer documents. Many of them translate only occasionally, some of them translate more regularly, a few of them even on a daily basis. All interviewed employees usually translate administrative texts, including resolutions, decrees, regulations, circulars, forms, and so on. Nine of them also translate legal texts, that is, laws or bills. Eleven employees usually translate communications or general correspondence (letters, e-mails) as well as informative texts, such as user manuals for new software. Our results show that civil servants thus translate a wide range of text types.

Delving into the translation procedure, we asked about terminology management, language tools and resources they use and about translation strategy, directionality and process. We also tried to find out how they experience the translation task, that is, to what extent they struggle when translating. All told, we were able to uncover some shared practices, although translation workflow of the employees varies greatly. Firstly, only few of the interviewees systematically collect frequently used terms or terms related to their domains. Three people out of twenty participated in drawing up glossaries in the past, that is, term-to-term lists. In general, respondents do not report the urge to record in a database, a catalogue or in a glossary the recurring technical terms they encounter. They often convey 'to have everything in mind' or to see the terminology collection as a waste of time:

> Inzwischen benutze ich die nicht mehr. Weil es eben immer die gleichen Begriffe sind, die wiederkehren und die ich einfach inzwischen… [kenne].[25] Und dann denke ich mir, bevor ich da irgendwie dann rumsuchen muss, weil wenn ich so ein Glossar… also, wenn er [das Glossar] nur kurz ist und überschaubar, ok, dann… wenn [es] zwanzig Worte umfasst, dann ist [es] ok, aber sobald's über zwanzig [sind], dann muss ich mir ja schon überlegen, wie lege ich [das] Glossar an, wie find ich den Begriff, weil sonst, wenn ich da suchen muss, nein… Also, das mache ich nicht.[26]

> (I don't use [glossaries] anymore, because it's always the same terms that keep coming up, which in the meantime I'm just familiar with… And then I think to myself, before I have to be searching around there, because, if I have such a glossary… well, if [it] the glossary is just short and manageable, ok, then… if it contains twenty words, then [it] is ok, but as soon as there [are] over twenty, then I have to consider how do I create [the] glossary, how do I find the term, because otherwise, if I have to search there, no… Well, I don't do that.)

This attitude could depend on the translation topic. Employees typically translate texts written within their own offices, that is, related to topics with which they are familiar and whose recurrent terms they perfectly manage. While translating, interviewees most frequently use bilingual dictionaries, in both digital and paper versions. Only a few interviewees use monolingual or specialized dictionaries. Other resources frequently consulted include the local multilingual legal database, LexBrowser (twelve out of twenty) and the local search system of legal terminology, *bistro* (seven out of twenty), although less frequently. Many interviewees use Google or 'the Internet' to resolve terminological queries. It seems that they do not feel the need for internal termbases nor freely available institutional termbases (for example IATE, Interactive Terminology for Europe, or TERMDAT, the Federal (Swiss) Administration's terminology database).

Translation directionality seems to be often double. More than half of the interviewees translate in both directions, that is, both from their mother tongue to the second language (inverse translation) and vice versa (direct

---

25   Interview No. 18. Translations are the author's unless otherwise indicated.
26   Interview No. 5.

translation). Only five employees translate mostly into their mother tongue and three into their second language. During the translation phase, three of them report to translate literally and according to the original text style, while eight others prefer to sound idiomatic and to simplify the message whenever possible. The cause for a recurrent literal strategy may lie in the publication requirements. Italian and German versions of local legal texts (e.g., laws) must be published side by side and have identical typographical layout and length. This requirement could be why civil servants tend to see a translated text as a mirror for the original one: "Ich arbeite wirklich den Text einfach von Satz zu Satz durch [...]. [I]ch erschließe mir den Text einfach, in dem ich mal durchgehe und ich nehme einen Absatz her und versuche den zu übersetzen." ("I really just work through the text from sentence to sentence [...]. I catch the meaning of the text by going through it, then I take a paragraph and try to translate it.")[27]

The employees who translate more idiomatically claim to be concerned about simple and clear institutional communication and usually reformulate the content before translating it. They pay attention to the meaning of each message and prefer idiomatic translations: "[M]agari la prima traduzione che facevo, la facevo parola per parola. Poi rileggendo il testo non capivo un tubo, al che ho dovuto ripensarci… è ovvio che se non lo fai spesso, o non l'hai mai fatto perché a studiare [...] non ti serviva la traduzione, poi inizi un po' a cambiare la tua tecnica." ("I was used to doing the first translation draft by proceeding word for word. Then, when I proofread it, I didn't quite understand. So, I had to replan my method… It's obvious that if you don't translate often, or if you've never done it because you didn't need translating to study [...]. But after some time, you start to change your technique a bit.")[28]

There seems not to be any common translation process outline or general translation guidelines. Rather, employees report to have developed their "own process" with time. Taking as a standard the translation process presented in the ISO 17100:2015 "Translation services – Requirements for translation services", we know that at least four steps in the production process are necessary to accomplish a professional translation. These are: translation, check, revision, final verification and release. Furthermore, both translation theorists and practitioners (Scarpa 2008; Osimo 2001; ISO 2015) agree that a translation without revision is an incomplete translation. Revision – understood as a check carried out by a person other than the translator to ensure the absence of translation errors and the translation's suitability for purpose

---

27   Interview No. 7.
28   Interview No. 19.

(ISO 2015, Section 5.3.3) – is an essential step necessary to ensure a quality standard. Generally, it looks like there is no standard translation process among our interviewees. They report different approaches and experiences. A few of them often simply adjust old translations of similar texts and add new information, rather than translate them from scratch: "[M]an startet nicht bei Null […], man hat gewisse Vorlage[n], gewisse Muster, gewisse Formulierungen wiederholen sich, und dann übernimmt man schon einiges, was es schon gibt, und dann meistens, übersetzt, übersetzt man nicht alles komplett von Neu an […]. Da sind nur gewisse Absätze neu zu schreiben." ("You don't start from zero […], you have templates, patterns, some formulations repeat themselves, and then you adopt some things that already exist. Mostly, you don't translate everything completely from scratch […]. Only certain paragraphs have to be rewritten.")[29]

Only three interviewees report a more systematic translation process, which brings to light a smart way of exploiting internal competencies. In this case, one employee translates the text and another proofreads it. The 'translator' knows the given field very well and the 'proofreader' is usually a native speaker. In this way, they guarantee both terminological precision and linguistic accuracy, while making sure that at least two people always read every text. However, in general the revision phase seems to be occasional and discretionary among the interviewees. Nine of them report to perform or request a revision only by terminological doubts or by reverse translations.

Finally, some interviewees use machine translation. Although the majority of them affirm their dislike of it, two of them appreciate it, as they can start their work having a pre-translated text. They certainly correct it, although they make no mention of quality assessment of the machine-translated output or of standardized procedures for post-editing. Lastly, outsourcing seems not to be used as an alternative to internal translation. The interviewees report to have rarely outsourced translations during their career, and most of them remember very few occasions.

4.3 Occasional translators' profile

The interviewees educational background is quite heterogeneous. Eleven of them hold a university degree, four of whom are specialized in a language-related field, five in law and the rest in a technical field. The other nine have a high school diploma. These results suggest that the institution considers

---

29 Interview No. 4.

a high school diploma sufficient to carry out daily translation tasks. If we compare their average education to the education requirements for official provincial translators presented in Section 3.1.2, we notice how they diverge. It seems that the legislator considered a degree in linguistics necessary only for in-house translators. However, no specific education requirements seem necessary for small, daily translation tasks. If we take a closer look at the Collective Agreement, we find that in-house translators should, among other things: a) translate legal provisions, administrative acts and technical texts; b) revise translations drawn up by third parties; c) provide advice on the translation of technical terms and stylistic issues. The interviewees as well carry out these activities, even though none of them is an in-house translator nor has attended courses on Translation while working at the Provincial Administration. Only three out of twenty employees have attended a course on drafting administrative texts.

Finally, with regard to their personal opinions on translation, sixteen employees out of twenty express a positive opinion on the translation task *per se* and accept it with pleasure: "A me piace anche tradurre, non è che mi dispiace [...]. È una cosa che mi piace, anche che mi dà soddisfazione" ("I do like translating, I cannot say I dislike it [...]. It is something that I like and that gives me satisfaction.)"[30]; "Mir macht das Übersetzen sehr viel Spaß." ("I enjoy translating very much.")[31]

On the contrary, translation as part of the Provincial Administration's day-to-day operations is perceived as a rather arduous and cumbersome task. The cause for discontent seems not to be the task itself but, rather, the fact that nobody and yet everybody seems to be responsible for it. For some of them it becomes a restraint for professional development: "[E]s ist für mich hier jetzt [...] nicht interessant mir noch mehr Übersetzungen herzuholen, weil das hier eine Sackgasse wäre für die berufliche Entwicklung. [...] wir sind meistens das letzte Glied in der Kette und... da muss es dann oft sehr schnell gehen." ("It is not interesting for me here [...] to get more translations to do, because this would be a dead end for my professional development. [...] [Translations] are usually the last link in the chain and... then it often has to happen very quickly.")[32]

Language proficiency seems to be one crucial factor: the higher the language competencies, the more enjoyable the translation assignments. Depending on that, some civil servants might end up with an overload compared to their

---

30   Interview No. 6.
31   Interview No. 18.
32   Interview No. 8.

colleagues: "Ho anche sempre cercato di far capire: sì, ma non sono qui per fare la traduttrice, solo perché sono più bilingue di altri." ("I've always tried to make it clear: I'm not here to work as a translator, just because I'm more bilingual than others.")[33]

It seems, rather, that the employees accept the task with pleasure only in small amounts and in low frequency. Otherwise, they feel overwhelmed by it:

> Diciamo che quello delle traduzioni è sempre stato un problema all'interno della ripartizione. [...] [S]e glielo fai fare sporadicamente [...] lo sopportano, e invece eh... se devi fare sempre e solo quello o devi far tutto tu... [...] è pesante, è percepito come pesante, sì.[34] Tutti brontolano quando si parla di traduzione, perché la cosa... Anche se è un peccato perché è un bel lavoro, però qua la considerano una perdita di tempo [...].[35]

> (Let us say that translation has always been a problem within the Division. [...] If you let the employees do it only once in a while [...] they go through it, but, eh... if they have to deal with it always, or if they have to do it all... [...] it becomes a burden, they experience it as a burden. Everyone grumbles when it comes to translation, because... That's a pity, because it's a nice job, but here everybody considers it a waste of time.)

5 Conclusion

The aim of this chapter was to outline the translation practices in a multilingual institution in South Tyrol. We started by contextualizing language policies in Italy and its different multilingual scenarios. We presented the special rights of minority language communities in Italy and compared them to language minorities in South Tyrol. Institutional multilingualism in South Tyrol has a solid foundation. Local regulations foresee that German- and Italian-speaking citizens can interact with government entities in their own language. Ladin-speaking citizens can do the same in the Ladin-speaking areas. Civil servants must be proficient in German and Italian, as well as in Ladin if necessary. Through a Collective Agreement, the institution pointed out clear requirements and tasks for in-house translators, but it did not regulate as clearly the profile of what we called 'occasional translators'. According to the

---

33 Interview No. 19.
34 Interview No. 12.
35 Interview No. 6.

agreement, translation is not only a task for in-house professional translators; it is also a general task for each civil servant regardless of education, language proficiency and specific competencies. The Provincial Administration has no clue as to which and how many of its collaborators actually translate texts. Before our exploratory study, there had been no systematic, internal enquiries on this matter. The lack of central regulation led to spontaneous self-organization in each office. The exploratory study presented in this chapter took place in 2017, and describes the phenomenon of 'occasional translation' by non-professional translators within an institutional setting. The interviewees described different internal translation scenarios. This can help increase awareness of successful translation practices as well as of practices in need of review. Our research showed that the institutional occasional translators come from a broad spectrum of educational backgrounds, ranging from high school diplomas to university graduates and from technical studies to the humanities. How much each of them translates texts depends in many cases on the availability of colleagues who translate as well. If a civil servant is the only 'occasional translator' in their office, they may translate a lot. The frequency varies greatly from rare to daily translation assignments, with the majority of interviewees translating occasionally.

As for the translation process itself, no translation guidelines were ever mentioned by the interviewees. Some of them translate more systematically, dividing the task into steps (e.g., translation by an expert, revision by a mother-tongue collaborator), while others described a quicker process where they edit old texts or start from machine translation outputs. To almost all of them, revision is not a mandatory step of the process. In addition, we have seen that, despite the official 'bilingualism certificate', language competencies cannot be taken for granted. The collective agreement does not specify any language requirement for the general task of translation. This means that also employees with relatively low language competencies could carry out translations. Furthermore, the interviewees often reported to translate into their second language, which professional translators generally do not do, as language skills are only rarely equal between working languages. Many scholars argue that only translation into the mother tongue can be accurate and effective, though not all beliefs related to L2-translations are corroborated by empirical evidences (Beeby Lonsdale 2009; Whyatt 2019).

Our interviews with twenty civil servants working as occasional translators showed us that the translation of documents in the daily functioning of the Provincial Administration lacks regulation. The employees organize the translation task however they see fit and not without difficulties. Communication between institution and citizens certainly flows, but the translation duty seems to lack standardization and a general regulation on time, competencies and phases, especially where revision is concerned. Translation appears to have a subsidiary role in the administrative procedure, that is, "the last link in the chain" as one interviewee put it.[36] If documents are translated in a rush, without quality assurance, possibly without proper competencies, the communication quality can turn out to be poor. Some interviewees wonder why they have such a responsibility, given that they are not translators: "[S]econdo me un testo giuridico lo deve fare un giurista, un piano per una casa lo deve fare un architetto e non un cuoco. Io sono il cuoco che deve costruire una casa, questo è per me il problema, no?" ("In my opinion, a laywer should write a legal text, an architect should make a plan for a house, and not a cook. Here I am like a cook trying to build a house: that is the problem for me, do you understand?")[37]

In a multilingual region with a strong linguistic identity and solid language policies, we have found not equally solid institutional translation policies. As Sandrini points out, a greater awareness of translation planning and management is needed in South Tyrol to achieve a proper translation policy (Sandrini 2019, 409). To attain greater control over the translation task and its management, the Provincial Administration of Bolzano might benefit from a comprehensive set of institutional rules and guidelines. The first step would be to acknowledge translation as one of many necessary phases of the administrative process, each of them requiring time, specific competencies and rules. Each step contributes to the proper functioning of the institution. The translation task in particular ensures that all citizens can interact with government entities in their language, which is an essential right especially for minorities. We believe that more awareness from the institution itself towards internal translation practices would lead to a greater control over the task and reinforce institutional multilingualism. In late 2017, we started a PhD project to gain a deeper understanding of institutional translation practices in the South Tyrolean local administration.

---

36 Interview No. 8.
37 Interview No. 7.

References

Antonini, Rachele. 2010. "The Study of Child Language Brokering: Past, Current and Emerging Research." *mediAzioni* 10: 1–23.

Antonini, Rachele, Letizia Cirillo, Linda Rossato, and Ira Torresi, eds. 2017. *Non-Professional Interpreting and Translation*. Amsterdam: John Benjamins.

ASTAT. 2019. "Dipendenti pubblici. 2018." *Astat Info* 69: 1–24.

Beeby Lonsdale, Allison. 2009. "Directionality." In *Routledge Encyclopedia of Translation Studies,* edited by Mona Baker and Gabriela Saldanha, 2nd ed., 84–88. London: Routledge.

Beukes, Anne-Marie. 2006. "Translation in South Africa: The Politics of Transmission." *Southern African Linguistics and Applied Language Studies* 24 (1): 1–6.

Branchadell, Albert, and Lovell Margaret West, eds. 2005. *Less Translated Languages*. Amsterdam: John Benjamins.

Brigaglia, Manlio, and Salvatore Mura. 2018. *Storia dell'autonomia Sarda: 1847–2018. Antologia*. Sassari: Carlo Delfino Editore.

Chiocchetti, Elena, Natascia Ralli, and Isabella Stanizzi. 2013. "When Language Becomes Law: The Methodology and Criteria Adopted by the South Tyrolean Terminology Commission for the Standardisation of German and Italian Translation Equivalents." *Linguistica* 53 (2): 9–23.

Corbetta, Piergiorgio. 2014. *La ricerca sociale: metodologia e tecniche*. Bologna: Mulino.

Cruces Colado, Susana, and Ana Luna Alonso, eds. 2004. *La traducción en el ámbito institucional: autonómico, estatal y europeo*. Vigo: Universidade de Vigo.

Davier, Lucile. 2014. "The Paradoxical Invisibility of Translation in the Highly Multilingual Context of News Agencies." *Global Media and Communication* 10 (1): 53–72.

Ferrari, Giuseppe Franco, ed. 2008. *Introduction to Italian Public Law*. Milan: Giuffrè.

García de Toro, Cristina. 2009. *La traducción entre lenguas en contacto. Catalán y Español*. Bern: Peter Lang.

González Núñez, Gabriel. 2014. "Translating for Linguistic Minorities: Translation Policy in the United Kingdom." PhD diss., Universitat Rovira i Virgili.

ISO (International Organization for Standardization). 2015. Translation Services – Requirements for Translation Services. ISO 17100:2015. https://www.iso.org/standard/59149.html.

Istat (Istituto nazionale di statistica). 2017. "L'uso della lingua Italiana, dei dialetti o delle lingue straniere." Statistical Report. http://www4.istat.it/it/files/2017/12/Report_Uso-italiano_dialetti_altrelingue_2015.pdf?title=Lingua+italiana,+dialetti+e+altre+lingue+-+27/dic/2017+-+Report_Uso+italiano_dialetti_altrelingue_2015.pdf.

Koskinen, Kaisa. 2008. *Translating Institutions: An Ethnographic Study of EU Translation*. Manchester: St. Jerome.

Lafeber, Anne. 2012. "Translation at Inter-Governmental Organizations: The Set of Skills and Knowledge Required and the Implications for Recruitment Testing." PhD diss., Universitat Rovira i Virgili.

Li, Shuang, Duoxiu Qian, and Reine Meylaerts. 2017. "China's Minority Language Translation Policies (1949–Present)." *Perspectives* 25 (4): 540–555.

Loporcaro, Michele. 2013. *Profilo linguistico dei dialetti italiani*. Rome: Laterza.

Meylaerts, Reine. 2017. "Studying Language and Translation Policies in Belgium: What Can We Learn from a Complexity Theory Approach?" *Parallèles* 29 (1): 45–59.

———. 2018. "The Politics of Translation in Multilingual States." In *The Routledge Handbook of Translation and Politics*, edited by Fruela Fernández and Jonathan Evans, 1st ed., 221–237. London: Routledge.

Mossop, Brian. 1988. "Translating Institutions: A Missing Factor in Translation Theory." *TTR : Traduction, Terminologie, Rédaction* 1 (2): 65–71. https://doi.org/10.7202/037019ar.

O'Connell, Eithne, and John Walsh. 2006. "Translation and Language Planning in Ireland: Challenges and Opportunities." *Administration: Journal of the Institute of Public Administration of Ireland* 54: 22–43.

Osimo, Bruno. 2001. *Traduzione e nuove tecnologie: Informatica e internet per traduttori*. Milan: Hoepli.

Palermo, Francesco. 2003. "La tutela delle minoranze nell'ordinamento italiano: Un sistema complesso tra asimmetria, decentramento, uguaglianza e promozione delle diversità." In *Valorizzare Le Diversità: Tutela Delle Minoranze Ed Europa Multiculturale*, edited by Eva Pföstl, 163–207. Rome: Apes.

Palici di Suni Prat, Elisabetta. 1999. *Intorno alle minoranze*. Turin: G. Giappichelli Editore.

Pérez Ramírez, Irati. 2014. "Lenguas minoritarias y cooficiales de España y su traducción en los servicios públicos." Master thesis, Universidad de Alcalá.

Prieto Ramos, Fernando, ed. 2018. *Institutional Translation for International Governance. Enhancing Quality in Multilingual Legal Communication*. London: Bloomsbury.

———, ed. 2020. *Institutional Translation and Interpreting: Assessing Practices and Managing for Quality*. London: Routledge.

Pym, Anthony, François Grin, Claudio Sfreddo, and Andy L. J. Chan, eds. 2012. *The Status of the Translation Profession in the European Union: Final Report*. Luxembourg: European Union.

Sandrini, Peter. 2019. *Translationspolitik für Regional-oder Minderheitensprachen: unter besonderer Berücksichtigung einer Strategie der Offenheit.* TransÜD, vol. 99. Berlin: Frank & Timme.
Scarpa, Federica. 2008. *La traduzione specializzata: Un approccio didattico professionale.* Milano: Hoepli.
Svoboda, Tomáš, Łucja Biel, and Łoboda Krzysztof, eds. 2017. *Quality Aspects in Institutional Translation.* Berlin: Language Science Press.
Tesseur, Wine. 2014. "Transformation through Translation: Translation Policies at Amnesty International." PhD diss., Aston University.
Toso, Fiorenzo. 2008. *Le minoranze linguistiche in Italia.* Bologna: Il Mulino.
Vecchione, Flavia. 2014. "Tradurre per le istituzioni: Panoramica dei traduttori che operano nelle principali istituzioni governative italiane e della loro attività." *mediAzioni* 16: 1–33.
Whyatt, Bogusława. 2019. "In Search of Directionality Effects in the Translation Process and in the End Product." *Translation, Cognition & Behavior* 2 (1): 79–100.

Judicial review of translation policy
The case of bilingual Catalonia in monolingual Spain

Albert Branchadell

Abstract
This chapter aims to reflect on the nature of egalitarian translation policies in multilingual settings by exploring a relatively new venue of research. We look at what case law on translation and interpreting can tell us about the equal treatment of languages in multilingual polities. In the first place, we argue the relevance of the Spanish case to elaborate current overviews of translation regimes. Unlike multilingual federal states such as Belgium or Switzerland, which combine institutional monolingualism at the local level and institutional multilingualism at the federal level (Meylaerts 2011c), Spain is a state in which certain 'regional' or 'minority languages' enjoy official status at the regional level – alongside Spanish – but are not official languages of the state as a whole. The focus of this chapter is on how translation is organized in such settings, which are more frequent across European states than might be imagined. In the second place, we argue the relevance of case law in the study of translation policies. A shift in focus from the judiciary as a setting where translation policies are implemented to the judiciary as a policy-maker that shapes translation policies is suggested. In the third place, we describe and analyze a selection of decisions made by the Spanish Constitutional Court. They involve areas as relevant as the authenticity of legislative texts published in more than one language; the use of regional or minority languages before public authorities within the territorial unit where those languages are official (with emphasis on the judiciary); and the use of regional or minority languages outside that territorial unit. On the basis of our analysis, we offer some tentative conclusions on the contribution of translation policies to the equal treatment of languages in legal and institutional domains.

1   Introduction

This chapter reflects on the nature of egalitarian translation policies in multilingual settings by exploring a relatively new venue of research. We are interested in what case law can tell us about the equal treatment of languages in multilingual polities as far as translation and interpreting are concerned.

In the first section, we argue the relevance of the Spanish case to elaborate current overviews of translation regimes. Unlike multilingual federal states such as Belgium or Switzerland, which combine institutional monolingualism at the local level and institutional multilingualism at the federal level (Meylaerts 2011c), Spain is a state in which certain 'regional' or 'minority languages' (Basque, Catalan, Galician) enjoy official status at the regional level – alongside Spanish – but are not official languages of the state as a whole. This chapter focuses on how translation is organized in such settings, which are more frequent across EU member states than might be imagined. Cases comparable to that of Spain are Denmark (Faroese in the Faroe Islands), Italy (German in South Tyrol and French in the Aosta Valley), the Netherlands (Frisian in Friesland), and the United Kingdom (Welsh in Wales). This chapter explicitly compares the situation in Spain (vis-à-vis Catalan in Catalonia) and Italy (German in South Tyrol).

In the second section, we argue the relevance of case law in the study of translation policies. In previous research (e.g., González Núñez 2013), the judiciary has been studied as a setting for translation policies. In this chapter, we suggest a shift in focus: from the judiciary as a setting where translation policies are implemented to the judiciary as a policy-maker that shapes translation policies as it does other kinds of public policy.

In the third section, we describe and analyze a selection of decisions made by the Spanish Constitutional Court in the light of the focus of this volume on the legal and institutional domains. We concentrate on translation in relevant areas, such as the authenticity of legislative texts published in more than one language; language use before public authorities within the territorial unit where regional or minority languages are official, with emphasis on the judiciary; and language use outside the territorial unit where regional or minority languages are official. On the basis of our analysis, we offer some tentative conclusions on the contribution of translation policies to the equal treatment of languages.

2 The relevance of the Spanish case in a typology of translation regimes

This is a study on the judicial review of translation policy in Spain. Spain represents a type of polity that is somewhat overlooked in the literature on translation policy. In her classic typology of translation regimes, Meylaerts (2011c, 745) discussed four 'prototypical regimes' in terms of how authorities communicate with their citizens:

1. Complete institutional multilingualism with obligatory multidirectional translation in all languages for all
2. Complete institutional monolingualism and non-translation
3. Institutional monolingualism and translation into the minority languages
4. Institutional monolingualism [at the local level] combined with institutional multilingualism [at the superior level]

In earlier versions of this typology, Meylaerts (2009, 15; 2010, 229; 2011b, 128) included Spain in type 4. However, Spain is the *opposite* of type 4: it is a case of institutional monolingualism at the 'superior' level combined with institutional multilingualism at the local level.

Koskinen (2014, 487) conveniently filled the gap left by Meylaerts. Commenting on Meylaerts's four prototypical options, she pointed out that "option (4) can also exist in an opposing manner, together with option (1): monolingual state level governance can be combined with local level multilingualism, providing extensive translation and interpreting for public services but keeping the higher level administration monolingual." Later on, Meylaerts (2017, 6) amended her typology by adding "or vice versa" to her earlier formulation: "monolingualism at the lower, local level and multilingualism at the superior (e.g., federal) level *or vice versa*." By way of example she mentioned the United Kingdom government, "which is largely monolingual, while co-existing with Wales, which is bilingual." Drawing on Meylaerts's expanded definition, De Camillis (2021, 60) underlined that Italy is another example of "monolinguismo nazionale combinato con il multilinguismo locale" ("national monolingualism combined with local multilingualism"), as far as South Tyrol is concerned.[1]

A second, related typology of translation policies is that of Diaz Fouces (2010). According to this typology, in multilingual contexts administrations can adopt one of two main strategies, which are the two ends of a continuum:

---

1 For a study on non-professional translation by bilingual civil servants in South Tyrol, see De Camillis, this volume.

institutional monolingualism or institutional multilingualism. At the multilingual end of the spectrum, the administration communicates with its citizens "in their own language(s) or the language(s) of their choice" and the resulting translation policy roughly corresponds to Meylaerts's type 1. At the monolingual end of the spectrum, the administration communicates with its citizens exclusively in the language granted official status, thus corresponding to Meylaerts's type 2. Between the two ends of the spectrum we find monolingualism with supportive translation for minorities (close to Meylaerts's type 3) and multilingualism with official – not multidirectional – translation, a category in which Diaz Fouces places Belgium, where federal institutions always make translations available in French and Dutch but not in German. Córdoba & Diaz Fouces (2018) combined Diaz Fouces's (2010) classification of translation policies with two different conceptualizations of translation, namely, translation as an accommodation right (subsidiary to other rights) vs. translation as a right in itself.

Let us now describe the Spanish model of "bilingual institutional islands under a monolingual umbrella", to rephrase Meylaerts's (2011a, 752) well-known metaphor. In 1978, the new democratic Spanish Constitution designated Spanish the official language of the state. It declared the languages of Spain other than Spanish official as well, within their respective autonomous regions.

Article 3 of the Spanish Constitution provides that (English translation supplied by the Spanish Parliament):

1. El castellano es la lengua española oficial del Estado. Todos los españoles tienen el deber de conocerla y el derecho a usarla.
   (Castilian [Spanish] is the official Spanish language of the State. All Spaniards have the duty to know it and the right to use it.)
2. Las demás lenguas españolas serán también oficiales en las respectivas Comunidades Autónomas de acuerdo con sus Estatutos.
   (The other Spanish languages shall also be official in the respective Autonomous Communities in accordance with their Statutes.)
3. La riqueza de las distintas modalidades lingüísticas de España es un patrimonio cultural que será objeto de especial respeto y protección.
   (The wealth of the different language modalities of Spain is a cultural heritage which shall be the object of special respect and protection.)

In the Spanish context, elevating Catalan and the other languages to official status was a tool for overcoming past inequalities. Yet what exactly does 'official' status mean? The Spanish Constitutional Court provided its own definition: "es oficial una lengua, independientemente de su realidad y peso como fenómeno social, cuando es reconocida por los poderes públicos como medio normal de comunicación en y entre ellos y en su relación con los sujetos privados, con plena validez y efectos jurídicos." ("Regardless of its situation and standing in society, a language is official when it is recognized by public authorities as a normal means of communication within and between them and in their relationship with private subjects, with full validity and legal effects.")[2]

It follows from the above definition that Spain does *not* have a minority rights regime of type 3 in Meylaerts's typology. What Spain has is an *official* language regime in which co-official languages have full validity and legal effects in their designated territories. In terms of Córdoba and Diaz Fouces's conceptualizations, translation in Spain is not to be seen as an accommodation right (subsidiary to other rights) but rather as a right in itself. As we will see below, in Spain's bilingual regions citizens have the right to choose the official language they want to use in their dealings with public authorities, "regardless of its situation and standing in society". In certain situations, this free choice requires the administration to engage in translation or interpreting.

Spain's official language regime is governed by the territoriality principle. In the decision quoted above, the Spanish Constitutional Court declared that:

> la [...] cooficialidad lo es con respecto a todos los poderes públicos radicados en el territorio autonómico, sin exclusión de los órganos dependientes de la Administración central y de otras instituciones estatales en sentido estricto, siendo, por tanto, el criterio delimitador de la oficialidad del castellano y de la cooficialidad de otras lenguas españolas el territorio, independientemente del carácter estatal (en sentido estricto), autonómico o local de los distintos poderes públicos.

> (co-official status [of languages] applies to all public authorities located in the autonomous territory, without excluding the subsidiary entities of the Central Administration and other state institutions in the strict sense; territory is therefore the defining criterion of the official and co-official status of languages, regardless of whether the different government entities are state (in the strict sense), regional or local entities.)

As mentioned in the introduction, Spain is not alone in holding a constellation of "bilingual institutional islands under a monolingual umbrella"; in that respect, it is comparable to the UK, Italy, the Netherlands and Denmark.

---

2   Sentencia del Tribunal Constitucional (Constitutional Court Judgment) 82/1986, 26 June.

All the states in question are officially monolingual but contain territories in which one or more languages other than the state language enjoy official status (Welsh in Wales; German in South Tyrol, French in the Aosta Valley; Frisian in Friesland; and Faroese in the Faroe Islands).

3   The relevance of case law in the analysis of translation policies

In standard fields of political science (political theory, political institutions, law and politics, public policy), courts have been identified as a powerful political actor in contemporary democracies – there has even been discussion of a trend towards the 'judicialization of politics' and 'juristocracy' (e.g., Hirschl 2004, 2008 and, on the specific case of Southern Europe, Magalhães et al. 2006). In contrast, coverage of the active role of courts in translation policy is noticeably lacking in the relevant literature, as reviewed below.

Meylaerts (2011b, 744) defined language policy as "a set of legal rules that regulate language use for purposes of education and communication, the latter covering the language of legal affairs, of political institutions, of the media, and of administration." Additionally, Meylaerts (2011a, 165) defined translation policy as "a set of legal rules that regulate translation in the public domain: in education, in legal affairs, in political institutions, in administration, in the media."

'Legal rules', in various shapes and forms, are indeed the medium through which translation policy is delivered. However, 'legal rules' can be interpreted and even modified by the judiciary. This condition is what is absent from Meylaerts's early formulations of translation policy and the subsequent development of the concept by González Núñez (2016).

González Núñez (2016) endeavored to find inspiration in the field of language policy. After noticing that definitions are no less messy in the field in question, he followed Spolsky (2004) to develop a concept of translation policy encompassing translation management, translation practice and translation beliefs which has gained wide acceptance. In terms of political actors, translation management includes "people who have the authority to decide the use or non-use of translation within a domain", which means "anyone from legislators to local site managers, so that the decision may be made from outside the domain as well as inside" (González Núñez 2016, 92). Translation practices are the area of 'a given community', whose members go – or do not go – by the rules established by translation management decisions. In this way, translation policy can helpfully be understood as more than 'a set of legal rules' that bear on the use of translation, which would amount to identifying 'translation policy' with 'translation management'.

González Núñez did remark on the 'tension' between translation management and translation practice, but did not mention any tension *within* the sphere of translation management itself. Four types of 'internal' tensions that have so far not been seriously tackled come to mind. First, there might be tension between competing alternatives open to political actors. Second, there might be tension between translation policies chosen by central and local (i.e., devolved) authorities. Third, there might be inconsistencies between policies chosen by the *same* authority for *different* domains. Our main focus in this chapter is a tension of a fourth type: the tension between translation policies selected by legislators and the review of those policies by judicial bodies. Meylaerts (2011a) observed that "[the key role of] translation policies [for the implementation of citizens' linguistic rights] remain[s] a blind spot in the literature on language rights and language policies." Rephrasing Meylaerts, we could say that the role of judicial review as an integral component of translation management in multilingual regions remains a blind spot in the literature on translation policy.

In the European context, European Court of Human Rights (ECtHR) case law on the right to an interpreter in criminal proceedings (when the defendant does not speak the language of the court) has been extensively dealt with (e.g. Brannan 2010; Magaldi 2012; Open Society Justice Initiative 2013). In contrast, we are not aware of ECtHR decisions regarding translation (or interpreting) and regional or minority languages. In this European context there are also very few contributions on *domestic* case law related to translation policy, especially in the settings we are interested in. Where Italy is concerned, there are some works on case law related to the protection of linguistic minorities which mention translation in passing. Vacca (2016), for example, examined some Italian Constitutional Court judgments on minority languages and focused on Judgment 159 of 2009, whereby the Italian Constitutional Court ruled that six articles contained in Friuli-Venezia Giulia's Regional Law 29 of 17 December 2007 – one of them regarding translation – were "constitutionally illegitimate". However, we are not aware of any work specifically focused on translation policy. As for Spain, Milian (2011) dealt with case law on language matters, which does include translation, but no specific work seems to exist on case law regarding translation management decisions.

4 Selected domains

In this section we approach translation management by identifying and describing policy decisions as codified through laws by the Spanish Parliament and the Catalan Parliament in three domains (legislation, public administration in general and the judicial system in particular). We focus explicitly on the contribution of translation to the equal treatment of languages.

4.1 Translation of legislation

In Catalonia, regional statutes are published in the two official languages, Catalan and Spanish. Article 6 of the Law on Language Normalization (English translation supplied by the Catalan government, see Webber and Strubell 1991) provided that:

> Les lleis que aprova el Parlament de Catalunya s'han de publicar en edicions simultànies, en llengua catalana i en llengua castellana, en el *Diari Oficial de la Generalitat*. El Parlament n'ha de fer la versió oficial castellana. En cas d'interpretació dubtosa, el text català serà l'autèntic. Quant a la seva publicació en el *Boletín Oficial del Estado*, hom s'ha d'atenir al que disposa la norma legal corresponent.

> Laws approved by the Parliament of Catalonia must be published simultaneously in Catalan and Castilian [Spanish] editions, in the *Diari Oficial de la Generalitat* [Catalan Official Gazette]. The Parliament is responsible for drawing up the official version in Castilian. Should there by any doubts in interpretation, the Catalan version shall be considered valid. With regard to their publication in the *Boletín Oficial del Estado* [Spanish Official Gazette], the corresponding legal norms must be abided by.[3]

Article 8 of the Law on Language Policy reworded the above (English translation supplied by the Catalan government): "Les lleis que aprova el Parlament de Catalunya es publiquen, en edicions simultànies en català i en castellà, en el *Diari Oficial de la Generalitat de Catalunya*. Correspon al Parlament de fer-ne la versió oficial castellana." ("Bills enacted by the Parliament of Catalonia are published, in simultaneous editions, in Catalan and Castilian, in the

---

3 Llei de normalització lingüística a Catalunya (Law on Language Normalization in Catalonia) 7/1983, 18 April.

Diari Oficial de la Generalitat de Catalunya. The Parliament is responsible for preparing the official version in Castilian.")[4]

It is worth noting that statutes are published in two official languages in other autonomous regions of Spain, but Catalonia is the only one in which the authenticity of the regional official language (in the case of dubious interpretation) has been explicitly stated.

In 1983, the Spanish government filed a plea of unconstitutionality against two articles of the Law on Language Normalization. With regard to Article 6.1, the State Attorney argued that to attribute an interpretive pre-eminence to the Catalan text over the official Spanish version "contradicts the principle of co-official status set out in § 3.2 of the Spanish Constitution and § 3.2 of the Catalan Statute of Autonomy", and "entails an impingement on the state competence over the rules regarding the application and efficacy of legal norms outlined in Article 149.1.8 of the Constitution."

In its allegations, the Catalan Parliament considered that there was no violation of the Constitution either in formal or in material terms. On the formal side, the Parliament argued that Article 6.1 gave a "technical solution" to a problem created by co-official status, namely "texts clashing as a result of translation". On the material side, the Parliament made an interesting argument on equality: "The Constitution and the Statute of Autonomy do not guarantee equality between the co-official languages, but equality between citizens, equality that should be understood to mean non-discrimination but not absolutely identical treatment, as derived both from the case law of the Constitutional Court and from that of the European Court of Human Rights."

According to the Catalan Parliament, "distinction in treatment must be reasonably justified." In the case at hand, the justification was the simple fact that "so far, and without exception, all the acts passed by the Catalan Parliament have been passed in their Catalan version, and the official Spanish version is produced *later*, in such a way that there is an original version, the Catalan one, and a Spanish translation" (italics added). In this argument, then, the Catalan Parliament acknowledged that the Catalan and Spanish *languages* were not treated equally, but it considered that this treatment was legitimate as long as it did not discriminate between *citizens*.

In its allegations, the Catalan Government responded in the same vein. It stated that 'authentic' has the meaning of 'authoritative', a qualification corresponding to the Catalan version "inasmuch as the Catalan Parliament carries out the parliamentary procedure of any law in the Catalan language."

---

4   Llei de política lingüística (Law on Language Policy) 1/1998, 7 January.

In its decision, the Spanish Constitutional Court declared the two articles that had been challenged unconstitutional.[5] With regard to Article 6.1, the Court stated that the fact that acts are written in Catalan does not entail the prioritization or 'authenticity' of the Catalan text in the case of doubt or of conflict with the Spanish text. Furthermore, the Court found an additional, somewhat unexpected problem: it felt that Article 6.1 could impair legal security as envisaged in Article 9.3 of the Constitution, with respect to those able to claim ignorance of the language considered a priority in Article 6.1, and also to the fundamental right to effective judicial protection. In other words, in the view of the Constitutional Court each language version is considered to be equally authentic.

The approach taken by the Spanish Constitutional Court brings the Catalan case more into line with EU standards on this matter. As is well-known, under the multilingualism policy, EU legislation is adopted in twenty-four official languages. According to the principle of equal authenticity (Šarčević 1997, 64), all twenty-four language versions are equally valid from the legal point of view. Both in the EU and in Catalonia, the policy of linguistic equality presupposes equivalence of all language versions.

Comparatively speaking, the status of Catalan resulting from the Constitutional Court decision is still more advantageous than that of other languages in comparable bilingual regions. A case in point is that of South Tyrol. Article 99 of the Special Statute for Trentino-Alto Adige provided that in the region in question the German language is "made equal" to the Italian language, yet then stated that the Italian version of legislation is the authoritative one.

In this case, then, one could say that the Spanish model – as reviewed by the Constitutional Court – is more egalitarian than the Italian one.

4.2 The use of (official) languages in court

In the previous section, we saw a law in which the Catalan legislator tried to give preference to Catalan over Spanish, until the Spanish Constitutional Court forbade this asymmetry and ruled that the Catalan and Spanish versions of statutes are to be considered equal. In the present section, we will see a law in which the Spanish legislator gave preference to Spanish over Catalan, a move that was *validated* by the Court. In the judiciary, Catalonia has two official languages; in practice, however, they do not both enjoy the same protection.

---

5   Sentencia del Tribunal Constitucional (Constitutional Court Judgment) 83/1986, 26 June.

Spain's Law on the Judiciary governs the use of official languages in court. Article 231 provides that (English translation supplied by the Spanish government):

1. En todas las actuaciones judiciales, los Jueces, Magistrados, Fiscales, Secretarios y demás funcionarios de Juzgados y Tribunales usarán el castellano, lengua oficial del Estado.
   (In all judicial proceedings, Judges, Magistrates, Prosecutors, Secretaries and other officials of Courts and Tribunals shall use Spanish, the official language of the State.)

2. Los Jueces, Magistrados, Fiscales, Secretarios y demás funcionarios de Juzgados y Tribunales podrán usar también la lengua oficial propia de la Comunidad Autónoma, si ninguna de las partes se opusiere, alegando desconocimiento de ella que pudiere producir indefensión.
   (Judges, Magistrates, Prosecutors, Secretaries and other officials of Courts and Tribunals may also use the official language of the Autonomous Community, if neither party objects, alleging ignorance of it that could lead to defenselessness.)

3. Las partes, sus representantes y quienes les dirijan, así como los testigos y peritos, podrán utilizar la lengua que sea también oficial en la Comunidad Autónoma en cuyo territorio tengan lugar las actuaciones judiciales, tanto en manifestaciones orales como escritas.
   (Parties, their representatives and those guiding them, in addition to witnesses and experts, may employ the official language of the Autonomous Region in which the judicial proceedings take place, in both written and verbal statements.)

4. Las actuaciones judiciales realizadas y los documentos presentados en el idioma oficial de una Comunidad Autónoma tendrán, sin necesidad de traducción al castellano, plena validez y eficacia. De oficio se procederá a su traducción cuando deban surtir efectos fuera de la jurisdicción de los órganos judiciales sitos en la Comunidad Autónoma, salvo, en este último caso, si se trata de Comunidades Autónomas con lengua oficial propia coincidente, o por mandato del Juez o a instancia de parte que alegue indefensión.
   (Judicial proceedings that are carried out in the official language of an Autonomous Region and documents presented in this language will have full validity and efficacy, without the need for their translation into Spanish. *Sua sponte*, they will be translated where they are to have an effect outside the jurisdiction of the judicial bodies based in the Autonomous Region, unless the official language is the same in the Autonomous

Regions in question, or by order of the Judge or at the behest of a party alleging defenselessness.)
5. En las actuaciones orales, el Juez o Tribunal podrá habilitar como intérprete a cualquier persona conocedora de la lengua empleada, previo juramento o promesa de aquélla.[6]
(In oral proceedings, the Judge or Court may authorize as an interpreter any person with knowledge of the language used, after swearing or promising.)

Article 231 gives anyone appearing before a court the right to use the official language of his or her choice. The nature of this right raises a number of points.

First, the unconditional right to use the official language of one's choice can trigger the use of an interpreter when the judge does not understand the language chosen by the party. It is important to bear in mind a fundamental distinction between the right of anyone appearing before a court to use the official language of his or her choice, which may entail the use of an interpreter, and the right of the accused to the free assistance of an interpreter, which is enshrined in international law. The latter only applies when the accused cannot understand or speak the language used in court (Article 6 of the European Convention on Human Rights (ECHR) and Article 14 of the International Covenant on Civil and Political Rights (ICCPR)). The case law of both the ECtHR and the Human Rights Committee has stressed that neither the ECHR nor the ICCPR guarantees the right of the accused to speak in a language of his or her choice (Brannan 2010; Magaldi 2012; Open Society Justice Initiative 2013). In the Spanish context, what triggers the use of an interpreter is the combination of free choice of (official) language by parties and lack of proficiency in the language chosen on the part of judges. In international law, it is the combination of no-choice and lack of proficiency in the language used in court on the part of the accused.

Second, it is clear that the right to use an official language other than Spanish provided for by Article 231 does not entail parties' right to be (directly) understood in that language by the court. Such a 'right to be understood' has no basis in the Constitution.

Third, the right to address the court in the official language of one's choice in accordance with Article 231 is available to "parties, their representatives and those guiding them, in addition to witnesses and experts" – not just "the accused".

---

6   Ley Orgánica del Poder Judicial (Organic Law on the Judiciary), 6/1985, 1 July.

Fourth, freedom of choice entails both a right to translation (interpretation) of oral statements and a right to non-translation of written documents.

Spain's Law on the Judiciary was challenged on a number of grounds by the Catalan Parliament and the Basque, Catalan and Galician autonomous governments.[7] The Catalan Parliament disputed paragraphs 1 and 2 of Article 231. It claimed that designating Spanish the language of the judiciary and relegating the use of Catalan to a "mere possibility" violated the co-official status of Catalan as provided for in the Spanish Constitution and the Catalan Statute of Autonomy. More specifically, it violated the equality of the two languages.

Similarly, the Basque government considered that Article 231 failed to meet the requirements of the Spanish Constitution and the Basque Statute of Autonomy, in that it made the use of Basque a "mere possibility", thereby establishing a "residual and second-rate official status".

The Galician government questioned not only paragraphs 1 and 2 but also 3 and 4. It claimed that paragraph 1 imposed a single language, which excluded Galician, also an official language in Galicia. Paragraphs 2 and 4, it said, impinged on the power of the Galician autonomous region to regulate the use of Galician. Paragraph 3, meanwhile, allegedly also impinged on the region's power and implied "a tacit exclusion [of Galician] that entails unequal treatment".

In sum, what all these actors agreed on was that the provisions of Article 231 of the law governing language in court did not guarantee the equal treatment of official languages as allegedly provided for by the Spanish Constitution and the regional statutes of autonomy.

In its decision on this case, the Spanish Constitutional Court found no evidence of unconstitutionality and rejected the claim that Article 231 relegates languages other than Spanish to a 'residual' or 'second-rate' official status.[8] The Court considered paragraph 1 to stem from the constitutional status of Spanish as the state's official language, and that paragraphs 2 and 3, which recognize the right to use regional co-official languages, "presuppose, in principle, a position of equality for the two official languages within the corresponding Autonomous Communities." According to the Court, the mandatory use of Spanish at the request of one of the parties, as established in paragraph 2, and the mandatory translation envisaged in paragraph 4 are "fully consistent with co-official language status as it has been constitutionally

---

7   The following quotations are taken from the text of the Constitutional Court Judgment referenced below.
8   Sentencia del Tribunal Constitucional (Constitutional Court Judgment) 56/1990, 29 March.

designed." The rationale behind the Court's argument is similar to that of the Catalan government when it was defending the pre-eminence of Catalan over Spanish in the previous case by arguing that "the Constitution and the Statute of Autonomy do not guarantee equality between the co-official languages, but equality between citizens."

This obvious asymmetry between Spanish and Catalan as official languages is not *prima facie* very different from the asymmetry that governs EU multilingualism. As Gibová (2009, 146) put it, "even though all the EU languages are officially supposed to be equal, this equality is to a considerable extent only an illusion because some languages are in fact used much more than the others." If we investigate a little more thoroughly, though, it is possible to argue that the Spanish situation is *contrary* to European standards as regards equality between citizens.

Milian is one prominent Catalan scholar who criticized the Constitutional Court judgment we are reviewing here for its failure to acknowledge the inconsistency between the rules contained in Article 231 of the Law on the Judiciary and co-official status.

Milian (2011, 150f) claimed that the rule for determining the language of proceedings established in paragraph 2 of Article 231 is a far cry from the "inexcusable balance" that must exist between the two official languages. He opined that a "more equitable" rule would be to grant the acting party (or, in penal proceedings, the accused) the right to choose which of the two official languages should be the language of the proceedings (see Section 3.3 below on Law 30/1992). In the event of Catalan being chosen and any party not understanding it, the danger of defenselessness could be easily overcome through the use of interpreters working from Catalan into Spanish. In his view, "it is not necessary to sacrifice, as the Court does, the use of official languages other than Spanish in order to guarantee the higher value of effective judicial protection" (Milian 2011, 153).

Milian's proposal regarding the right to choose the language of proceedings is in line with the provisions of the European Charter for Regional or Minority Languages, which Spain has ratified. In Article 9 of the Charter, its signatories undertake "to provide that the courts, at the request of one of the parties, shall conduct the proceedings in the regional or minority languages" in the case of criminal and civil proceedings and proceedings before courts concerning administrative matters.

Milian asserted that the rule established in Article 231.2 is part of a biased pro-Spanish language policy decision that the Court seeks to disguise with legal criteria. This language policy decision includes the principle that judges posted to courts in Catalonia are not required to understand Catalan despite its co-official status. According to Milian, we should question whether such a lack of knowledge "excessively conditions" the exercise of the formally unconditioned right to use Catalan provided for in paragraph 3. The formal guarantees provided for in paragraph 3 notwithstanding, it could be argued that Catalan speakers receive judicial services that are inferior to those received by the Spanish-speaking population.

With no apparent relation to the 1990 case, paragraph 4 of Article 231 was amended in 1994. The new wording provided that (difference with previous text underlined):[9]

4. Las actuaciones judiciales realizadas y los documentos presentados en el idioma oficial de una Comunidad Autónoma tendrán, sin necesidad de traducción al castellano, plena validez y eficacia. De oficio se procederá a su traducción cuando deban surtir efecto fuera de la jurisdicción de los órganos judiciales sitos en la Comunidad Autónoma, salvo si se trata de Comunidades Autónomas con lengua oficial propia coincidente. También se procederá a su traducción cuando así lo dispongan las leyes o a instancia de parte que alegue indefensión.
(Judicial proceedings that are carried out in the official language of an Autonomous Region and documents presented in this language will have full validity and efficacy, without the need for their translation into Spanish. *Sua sponte*, they will be translated where they are to have an effect outside the jurisdiction of the judicial bodies based in the Autonomous Region, unless the official language is the same in the Autonomous Regions in question. Translation will also be employed <u>where it is legally stipulated</u> or at the behest of a party alleging defenselessness.)

This change was contested by the People's Party, the major right-wing party in Spain. In its appeal, the PP claimed that the amendment in paragraph 4 of Article 231 – making translation mandatory "where it is legally stipulated" instead of "by order of the Judge" – amounted to an unlawful obligation for judges and magistrates to master the co-official language of the autonomous region in which they are posted.

The Catalan government disagreed. It argued that the new wording of paragraph 4 did not eliminate the right and duty of judges to obtain the translation of documents that they are not able to understand, but rather prevented the "unwarranted" exercise of the power in question.

---

9   Ley Orgánica por la que se reforma la Ley Orgánica del Poder Judicial (Organic Law to reform the Organic Law on the Judiciary) 16/1994, 8 November.

In its decision on this case, the Spanish Constitutional Court sided with the Catalan government to reject the claim that the new wording of Article 231.4 entailed the obligation for judges and magistrates to master the co-official language of the autonomous region in which they are posted.[10] The Court found that this new wording did not prevent judges and magistrates from ordering the translation of documents when necessary to fulfill the jurisdictional function.

If the goal was to ensure equality between Catalan and Spanish, the Spanish regulations are clearly less appropriate than those of comparable settings. Take the case of South Tyrol again. Article 100 of the Statute of Autonomy provides that German-speaking citizens of the province of Bolzano may use their own language in dealings with the judicial offices, and that those offices shall use the language of the applicant. The measures for the application of this principle were established sixteen years later in a decree.[11] According to Article 1 of the Decree, the German language is made equal in the region to the Italian language, the official language of the state, for dealings with the judicial offices and all kinds of courts. Article 13 provides that, in dealings with the citizens of the province of Bolzano, all judicial offices and bodies must use the language used by the applicant.

Unlike in the case of Spain, in South Tyrol's fully bilingual judiciary regime there is no default language for proceedings. In criminal proceedings, the mother tongue of the accused is the basic principle according to which the language of proceedings is established. In civil proceedings, each party has the right to choose in which one of the regional official languages it draws its case file. If both parties use the same language, the process is conducted in it. Otherwise, the process becomes bilingual and each party uses the language it desires.

Note that in the Italian context not all regional official languages are treated alike. In the Aosta Valley, Italian and French are on a level playing field apart from Italian being the only official language in the judiciary. Article 38 of the Regional Statute provides that public documents may be in either language, "with the exception of the acts of the judicial authority, which are established in Italian."[12]

In this particular regard, there are regional differences in the UK as well. Pursuant to the Welsh Language Act 1993, any participant in legal

---

10   Sentencia del Tribunal Constitucional (Constitutional Court Judgment) 105/2000, 13 April.
11   Decreto del Presidente de la Repubblica (Decree of the President of the Republic) 15 July 1988, n. 574.
12   Legge costituzionale Statuto Speciale per la Valle d'Aosta (Constitutional Law Special Statute of the Aosta Valley) 26 February 1948, n. 4.

proceedings has the right to use Welsh in them, be they criminal, civil or administrative proceedings (Vacca 2013). In contrast, the Administration of Justice (Language) Act (Ireland) of 1737 requires that, in Northern Ireland, all court proceedings and associated documents be in English.

4.3 The right to use (official) language(s) before public authorities

In this section, we address the right of citizens to use Catalan when dealing with public authorities and the relationship of that right to translation. In light of the official status of the language, the right to use Catalan when dealing with public authorities is unconditionally acknowledged, with no limitations. This is in sharp contrast with other settings across Europe in which the right to use minority languages when dealing with public authorities is either not recognized (e.g., France or Greece) or severely restricted (e.g., Estonia or Slovakia). The case we examine in this section is that of *state* public authorities, bearing in mind that Spanish is the only state language according to the Spanish constitution.

Article 36 of the Law on Public Administrations provides that:[13]

1. La lengua de los procedimientos tramitados por la Administración General del Estado será el castellano. No obstante lo anterior, los interesados que se dirijan a los órganos de la Administración General del Estado con sede en el territorio de una Comunidad Autónoma podrán utilizar también la lengua que sea cooficial en ella.
    En este caso, el procedimiento se tramitará en la lengua elegida por el interesado. Si concurrieran varios interesados en el procedimiento, y existiera discrepancia en cuanto a la lengua, el procedimiento se tramitará en castellano, si bien los documentos o testimonios que requieran los interesados se expedirán en la lengua elegida por los mismos.
    (The language of the procedures conducted by the General State Administration will be Spanish. Notwithstanding the above, interested parties who address the bodies of the General State Administration based in the territory of an Autonomous Community may also use any language with co-official status there.

---

13   Ley de Régimen Jurídico de las Administraciones Públicas y del Procedimiento Administrativo Común (Law on the Legal Regime of Public Administrations and the Common Administrative Procedure) 30/1992, 26 November.

In such cases, the procedure will be conducted in the language chosen by the interested party. If the procedure involves various interested parties and there is disagreement regarding the language to be used, the procedure will be conducted in Spanish, although the documents and testimonies required by the interested parties will be issued in their chosen language.)

2. En los procedimientos tramitados por las Administraciones de las Comunidades Autónomas y de las Entidades Locales, el uso de la lengua se ajustará a lo previsto en la legislación autonómica correspondiente.

En cualquier caso, deberán traducirse al castellano los documentos que deban surtir efectos fuera del territorio de la Comunidad Autónoma y los dirigidos a los interesados que así lo soliciten expresamente.

(In the procedures conducted by Autonomous Community and Local Administration Entities, the use of language will be as specified in the corresponding Autonomous Community legislation.

In any case, documents must be translated into Spanish if they are to have effect outside the territory of the Autonomous Community or are addressed to interested parties who expressly request such translation.)

3. Los expedientes o las partes de los mismos redactados en una lengua cooficial distinta del castellano, cuando vayan a surtir efectos fuera del territorio de la Comunidad Autónoma, deberán ser traducidos al castellano por la Administración Pública instructora.

(Files or parts of files written in a co-official language other than Spanish must be translated into Spanish by the Public Administration Body conducting the procedure if they are to have effect outside the territory of the Autonomous Community.)

This law is substantially different from the previous one regarding the judiciary. Spanish is the default language of both the judiciary and bodies of state administration (including those located in bilingual regions), but in the latter case interested parties are given a power that they do not enjoy in the former: "the procedure will be conducted in the language chosen by the interested party." A second difference, regarding translation, was the topic of Judgments 56/1990 and 105/2000 reviewed above.

The Catalan government filed a plea of unconstitutionality against the second half of paragraph 2 and paragraph 3 of Article 36. It did not object to the principle of Spanish as the default language, nor did it challenge mandatory translation per se. Its argument was that documents written in a regional official language should *not* be translated into Spanish when they are intended to have effect in another autonomous region with the same regional official language; otherwise, the official status of that language would not be "respected".

In its decision on this case, the Spanish Constitutional Court upheld the wording of Article 36 but interpreted it to agree with the Catalan government.[14]

The Court pointed out that Article 36 had very recently been amended through Law 4/1999, which provided that translation is not necessary when documents written in a regional official language are intended to have effect in another autonomous region with the same regional official language.[15] But since the Law on Public Administrations was still in force, the Constitutional Court was constrained to deliver a judgment on the constitutionality of Article 36 in its original wording. The Court acknowledged that the official status of the language of an autonomous region "does not stop at the boundaries of its territory". It noted that the Catalan government was "right" in claiming that to mandate translations into Spanish for documents that, originating in one region, should have effect in another region with the same co-official language "would be an attack on the official status of the language in question". However, it did not declare the disputed paragraphs of the Law on Public Administrations null and void. Instead, it declared them not unconstitutional provided that the mandatory translation into Spanish referred to therein does not include cases in which documents written in an official language other than Spanish are to take effect in the territory of another autonomous community in which the language in question is also official.

Although the Court did not mention it, the issue of documents written in Catalan taking effect in other autonomous regions where Catalan is also co-official had already been settled in the case of the judiciary. Remember what Article 231.4 of the Law on the Judiciary (reviewed above) established from the outset: judicial proceedings carried out in the official language of an autonomous region will be translated where they are to have an effect outside the jurisdiction of the judicial bodies based in that region, "unless the official language is the same in the Autonomous Regions in question."

In comparison to its regulations on the judiciary, Spain's law on administrative matters is closer to that of South Tyrol. As far as the state administration is concerned, Article 7 of DPR 574/1988 is similar in spirit to Article 36 of

---

14 Sentencia del Tribunal Constitucional (Constitutional Court Judgment) 50/1999, 6 April.
15 Ley de modificación de la Ley 30/1992, de 26 de noviembre, de Régimen Jurídico de las Administraciones Públicas y del Procedimiento Administrativo Común (Law to reform Law 30/1992 on the Legal Regime of Public Administrations and the Common Administrative Procedure), 4/1999, 13 January.

the Spanish Law on Public Administrations: all administrative bodies are required to communicate "in the language used by the applicant." There is also similarity as regards translation from a regional official language into the state language. DPR 574/1988 specifies that the administrative body (not the citizen) is responsible for providing translations from German into Italian.

Since South Tyrol is the only Italian region where German enjoys official status, the Italian context does not provide any insight into what happens when a document written in a regional official language is intended to have effect in another region with the same regional official language.

5   Conclusion

In multilingual settings, translation policy decisions can be assessed in terms of how equally languages are treated. In this chapter we have chosen a very particular – and, in translation policy studies, quite under-researched – multilingual setting, namely that of bilingual regions in monolingual states, represented by the case of Catalonia within Spain. More specifically, we have investigated the role of case law in shaping translation policy decisions taken by legislative bodies.

In the first case examined (translation of legislation), we found that the Catalan legislator had attributed pre-eminence to Catalan – the regional co-official language – over Spanish – the sole state language. The Spanish Constitutional Court overturned this decision and ruled that both language versions of laws are equally authoritative. This judgment confirmed the strict equality of Catalan and Spanish, which still placed the former in a more favorable position than German in South Tyrol, where only the *Italian* version of a law is authoritative.

In the second case examined (use before judicial authorities), the Spanish legislator had attributed pre-eminence to Spanish – the sole state language – over Catalan – the regional co-official language – but at the same time gave citizens the unconditional right to use Catalan and the associated right to be assisted by an interpreter working into Spanish. The Catalan government challenged the imbalance in the positions of the languages in this domain, but the Spanish Constitutional Court ruled them to be in a "position of equality" as long as citizens have the right to use either when addressing a court. While quite egalitarian on paper, it is clear that Spanish and Catalan do not have equal standing in practice. There is a serious discrepancy between the right to use the official language of one's choice and the practical implications of choosing Spanish or Catalan.

In this particular case, German in South Tyrol enjoys more equal treatment than Catalan in Catalonia. In South Tyrol too, citizens have the right to use the official language of their choice before a court. This right has a different consequence, however: instead of just giving rise to the right to an interpreter (when the court does not understand the chosen language), in South Tyrol the citizen's choice determines the language in which all the proceedings are to be conducted.

In the third case examined (use before *state* administrative authorities), the Spanish legislator attributed pre-eminence to Spanish over Catalan, yet also gave citizens the unconditional right to use Catalan and the administration the associated duty to conduct the administrative process in Catalan. This is egalitarian enough and places Catalan on a par with German in South Tyrol. The Catalan government challenged the law, though not because of the pre-eminence of Spanish or the obligation to translate documents into Spanish per se. Its objection was to mandatory translation – a direct consequence of the "bilingual region-monolingual state" arrangement – in the specific case of documents intended to have effect in other autonomous regions where Catalan also enjoys official status. The Spanish Constitutional Court did not amend the wording of the law but admitted that the Catalan government was right and interpreted the law in a way that made translation from Catalan into Spanish unnecessary when documents are intended to have effect in another autonomous region where Catalan is also official. In this regard, comparison with South Tyrol is impossible. What is relevant in both cases is this: the administration (not the citizen) is responsible for translating documents into the state language. Of course, the most egalitarian scenario for Catalan and German would be one of no translation at all: documents written in Catalan would have effect anywhere in Spain and documents written in German would have effect anywhere in Italy. Such a move – which would surely place an excessive burden on people who do not speak Catalan in Spain or German in Italy – would go beyond the "bilingual region-monolingual state" arrangement that we are dealing with. Whether fully equal treatment of languages requires that regional official languages be official languages of their respective states is a topic for separate research.

To summarize, then, in this chapter we have selected and analyzed a number of judgments that show how judicial review has contributed to the delineation of translation policies in bilingual Catalonia and helped to define their position with respect to the equal treatment of Catalan and Spanish. While we have compared the situation of Catalan in Catalonia with that of German in South Tyrol, the insights that have emerged from our analysis could provide further guidance for approaches to other bilingual regions in monolingual states across the world. When legal texts in a bilingual region are written in two languages, are both versions equally authoritative? What is the contribution of translation (and interpreting) to the equal treatment of (official) languages in court? What happens when a text written in a regional official language is to have effect outside the relevant region? These questions belong to a larger checklist that could be used to describe translation policies – and their relation to the equal treatment of languages – in many places. If properly handled, they could contribute to an empirically based theory of translational justice as well.

References

Alber, Elisabeth, and Carolin Zwilling. 2014. "Continuity and Change in South Tyrol's Ethnic Governance." In *Autonomy Arrangements around the World: A Collection of Well and Lesser Known Cases*, edited by Levente Salat et al., 33–66. Institul pentru Studierea Problemelor Minorităților Naționale: Cluj-Napoca.

Brannan, James. 2010. "ECHR Case-Law on the Right to Language Assistance in Criminal Proceedings and the EU Response." Unpublished manuscript.

Córdoba, María-Sierra, and Oscar Diaz Fouces. 2018. "Building a Field: Translation Policies and Minority Languages." *International Journal of the Sociology of Language* 251: 1–17.

De Camillis, Flavia. 2021. "La traduzione non professionale nelle istituzioni pubbliche dei territori di lingua minoritaria: il caso di studio dell'amministrazione della Provincia autonoma di Bolzano." PhD diss., Università di Bologna.

Diaz Fouces, Oscar. 2010. "(Eco)linguistic Planning and Language-Exchange Management." *MonTI: Monografías de Traducción e Interpretación* 2: 283–313.

Gibová, Klaudia. 2009. "EU Translation as the Language of a Reunited Europe Reconsidered." In *Language, Literature and Culture in a Changing Transatlantic World: International Conference Proceedings*, 145–153. Prešov: Prešov University.

González Núñez, Gabriel. 2013. "Translating for Linguistic Minorities in Northern Ireland: A Look at Translation Policy in the Judiciary, Healthcare, and Local Government." *Current Issues in Language Planning* 14 (3–4): 474–489.

———. 2016. "On Translation Policy." *Target* 28: 87–109.

Hirschl, Ran. 2004. *Towards Juristocracy: The Origins and Consequences of the New Constitutionalism*. Cambridge: Harvard University Press.

———. 2008. "The Judicialization of Politics." In *The Oxford Handbook of Law and Politics*, edited by Gregory A. Caldeira, R. Daniel Kelemen and Keith E. Whittington. Oxford: Oxford University Press.

Koskinen, Kaisa. 2014. "Institutional Translation: The Art of Government by Translation." *Perspectives* 22 (4): 479–492. https://doi.org/10.1080/0907676X.2014.948887.

Magaldi, Núria. 2012. "Els drets lingüístics a la jurisprudència del Tribunal Europeu de Drets Humans." *Revista de Llengua i Dret* 57: 123–162.

Magalhães, Pedro C., Carlo Guarnieri, and Yorgos Kaminis. 2006. "Democratic Consolidation, Judicial Reform, and the Judicialization of Politics in Southern Europe." In *Democracy and the State in the New Southern Europe*, edited by Richard Gunther, P. Nikiforos Diamandouros, and Dimitri A. Sotiropoulos. Oxford: Oxford University Press.

Meylaerts, Reine. 2009. "« Et pour les Flamands, la même chose »: quelle politique de traduction pour quelles minorités linguistiques?" *Meta* 54 (1): 7–21.

———. 2010. "Multilingualism and Translation." In *Handbook of Translation Studies*, vol. 1, edited by Yves Gambier and Luc van Doorslaer, 227–230. Amsterdam: John Benjamins.

———. 2011a. "Translation Policy." In *Handbook of Translation Studies*, vol. 2, edited by Yves Gambier and Luc van Doorslaer, 163–168. Amsterdam: John Benjamins.

———. 2011b. "Taal, vertaling en beleid in de XXIe eeuw." In *Lessen voor de eenentwintigste eeuw*, edited by Bart Raeymaekers, 141–160. Leuven: Leuven University Press.

———. 2011c. "Translational Justice in a Multilingual World: An Overview of Translational Regimes." *Meta* 56 (4): 743–757.

———. 2013. "Multilingualism as a Challenge for Translation Studies." In *The Routledge Handbook of Translation Studies*, edited by Carmen Millán and Francesca Bartrina, 519–533. London: Routledge.

———. 2017. "The Politics of Translation in Multilingual States." Paper delivered at the Workshop on Linguistic Diversity and Democratic Politics, KU Leuven, December 2017.

Milian, Antoni. 2011. "Principis i criteris en la jurisprudència del Tribunal Constitucional espanyol en matèria lingüística." In *Jurisprudències constitucionals en matèria lingüística: principis i criteris*, edited by Antoni Milian, 129–174. Barcelona: Generalitat de Catalunya. Institut d'Estudis Autonòmics.

Open Society Justice Initiative. 2013. *European Standards on Criminal Defence Rights: ECtHR Jurisprudence*.

Šarčević, Susan. 1977. *New Approach to Legal Translation*. The Hague: Kluwer.

Spolsky, Bernard. 2004. *Language Policy*. Cambridge: Cambridge University Press.

Vacca, Alessia. 2013. "Protection of Minority Languages in the UK Public Administration: A Comparative Study of Wales and Scotland." *Revista de Llengua i Dret* 60: 50–90.

———. 2016. "The Italian Constitution, Constitutional Court Judgments and the Distribution of Competences on Minority Languages." *Revista de Llengua i Dret* 65: 149–158.

Webber, Jude, and Miquel Strubell. 1991. *The Catalan Language. Progress towards Normalisation*. Sheffield: Sheffield Academic Press.

Investigating the status of Italian as an 'official minority language' within the Swiss multilingual institutional system

Paolo Canavese

Abstract

Switzerland is a multilingual country in which three languages are granted the same legal status, as unequivocally stated in Article 70 of the Federal Constitution: "[t]he official languages of the Confederation are German, French and Italian." This chapter analyzes the level of equality between these languages, taking into account their representation within the federal institutions and focusing in particular on Italian. Italian is not only an official but also a minority language. A historical overview will shed light on how the status of Italian has evolved over the last two centuries. The narrative will start from the foundation of the modern Confederation in 1803 and will cover the three language regimes (of 1848, 1917 and 1974). It will illustrate the most important events and milestones that led from the absence of Italian within the federal institutions to its *de jure* equality to German and French. However, the struggle to reach a *de facto* equality is still not over, as shown for example by the fact that Italian is (almost systematically) a translation language and that some institutional texts are not available in the 'third language'. Will a fully trilingual institutional system ever become a reality? In order to answer this question, a reflection on the strengths, weaknesses, opportunities and threats (SWOT) of such a system will be presented, thus depicting a potential future scenario in which the three official languages of Switzerland may in reality enjoy the same status.

1   Introduction

Switzerland is often taken as an upstanding example of a multilingual[16] country.[17] This status may be promoted by the fact that it is a *Willensnation* (a nation created by its own will, see, e.g., Kreis 2011), in other words, that it is made up of different linguistic and cultural communities that have decided to be together and pursue a common interest by being a united federal country. This idea is so strong that multilingualism can be considered to be an integral part of the Swiss identity.[18] All this combined with the stereotypical image that Switzerland enjoys abroad – its natural beauty, its neutrality, the fact that it is home to different international organizations – may project the image of absolute perfection.[19]

If one investigates more thoroughly and takes into account the linguistic functioning of the federal institutions, by adopting, for instance, the viewpoint of a minority language like Italian,[20] one will soon discover that the reality

---

16   The choice of 'multilingual' over 'plurilingual' demanded some reflection. It is widely acknowledged that 'multilingualism' refers to "the presence of [more] languages in a given geographical area", whereas 'plurilingualism' is to be understood as a "speaker's competence" (Beacco 2007, 10). The Federal Act on the National Languages and Understanding between the Linguistic Communities of 5 October 2007 (status as of 1 January 2017, CC *441.1*, henceforth referred to as 'Languages Act'), which is also translated into English, systematically uses the term 'plurilingualism' to refer to the 'multilingual' nature of Switzerland. The author, however, has decided to retain these two terms as commonly used in the literature throughout this chapter.

17   In this respect, Umberto Eco once argued that "(…) la Svizzera costituisce sinora l'unico modello (sia pure limitato a sole quattro lingue) di una comunità politica e culturale che è riuscita a realizzarsi attraverso l'istituzionalizzazione del plurilinguismo" ("To date, Switzerland is the only model – albeit limited to only four languages – of a political and cultural community that has succeeded by institutionalizing its plurilingualism.") (1991, 73). The Italian philosopher and semiotician explained that not only Switzerland was able to bring together four languages and cultures without compromising its unity and national identity, but that, on the contrary, it also made its diversity an "element of strength". He concluded that the Swiss multilingualism model could serve as an example for Europe: "L'Europa delle lingue potrebbe essere possibile perché, almeno una volta nella storia, e per sette secoli, è stata possibile una Svizzera delle lingue" ("The Europe of languages could be possible because, at least once in history, and for seven centuries, a Switzerland of languages has been possible.") (ibid.).

18   See for example Borghi (2005, 4) and Mader (2005), as well as Article 2 letter a of the Languages Act (fn. 1).

19   While on the one hand, these stereotypes are quite widespread (Eco 1991, 86), on the other, as Steinberg (2015, 5) noted, "[t]he oddest thing about Switzerland is how little most foreigners know about it." Institutional multilingualism might be one of the aspects that fall into this grey area.

20   This may prove to be a difficult task, as most of the literature about the status of Italian within the Swiss institutional system is available in Italian only, thus making it quite inaccessible for a wider international public. A quick look at the reference list at the end of this chapter will confirm this.

is not as perfect as it may seem. The aim of this chapter is not to confute the idyllic scenario described above but, rather, to shed light on some inequalities that still exist today between the Swiss official languages. To this end, after this brief introduction (Section 1), this chapter will adopt a diachronic perspective and describe the evolution of the status of Italian from 1803 to the present day (Section 2). It will then discuss its status today (Section 3) and present potential future scenarios (Section 4), before drawing some concluding remarks (Section 5).

Before delving into some salient historical aspects that characterize the use of Italian in Switzerland, a few fundamental facts are presented in this introduction, which should help the reader to better understand the linguistic context of Switzerland. First, what does 'multilingualism' mean in the Swiss context? As clearly shown in Figure 1, Switzerland can be divided into four linguistic regions: the German, the French, the Italian and the Romansh regions.

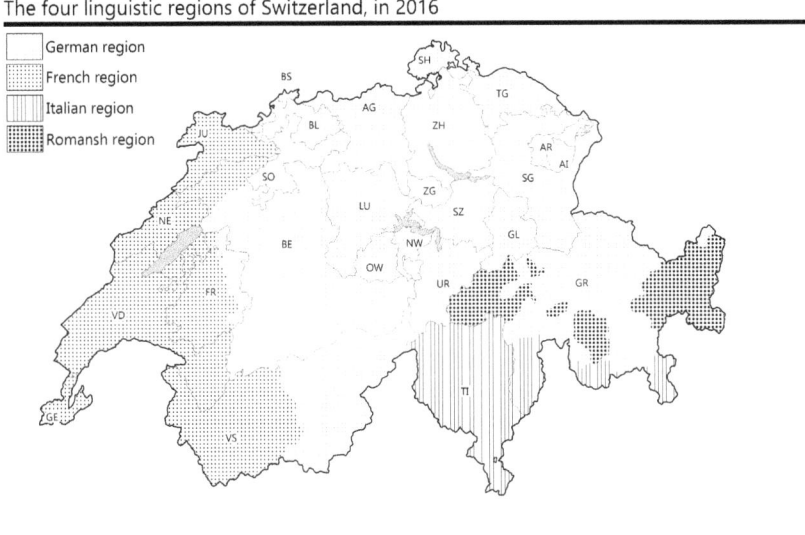

Source: Federal Statistical Office - Structural Survey

Figure 1. The four linguistic regions of Switzerland[21]

---

21 This map was created by the Federal Statistical Office based on the structural survey of 2016, see the web page "Les 4 régions linguistiques de la Suisse par commune" (https://www.bfs.admin.ch/bfs/fr/home/statistiques/catalogues-banques-donnees/cartes.assetdetail.2543293.html, last accessed 29 January 2019).

German is the official language of 17 monolingual cantons, French of four and Italian of one (Ticino). Moreover, three cantons (Bern, Fribourg and Valais) are bilingual (German and French) and one canton (Graubünden) is trilingual (German, Italian and Romansh). More details about the linguistic landscape of Switzerland are displayed in Table 1.

Table 1. Languages used in Switzerland, legal status and number of speakers[22]

Language	Status		Speakers	Speakers (in %)
	national language	official language		
German	✓	✓	4,459,323	63.4 %
French	✓	✓	1,607,865	22.9 %
Italian	✓	✓	593,205	8.4 %
Romansh	✓	✗	40,444	0.6 %
Other languages	✗	✗	1,715,479	24.4 %

At the federal level, three out of four national languages have the status of 'official languages'.[23] By number of speakers, German is the first official language, French the second and Italian the third. In the literature, *terza lingua ufficiale* has almost become a fixed collocation used to refer to Swiss Italian.[24] Unfortunately, as it should become clear throughout the chapter,

---

22 For the column 'status', Article 4 and Article 70 of the Swiss Constitution of 18 April 1999 (status as of 1 January 2020, CC *101*) can be consulted. The number of speakers is provided by the structural survey of 2017, carried out by the Federal Statistical Office (see the document "Population résidante permanente de 15 ans et plus, selon les langues principales", https://www.bfs.admin.ch/bfs/fr/home/statistiques/population/langues-religions/langues.assetdetail.7226743.html, last accessed 29 January 2019). The author has calculated the percentages. The sum of the percentages is greater than 100 because the respondents could indicate more than one 'main language'.
23 The difference between official and national language is crucial. While all four national languages shall be treated equally (Article 3 Languages Act, fn. 1), some important differences can be identified when it comes, for example, to the official publications. The Federal Gazette, the Official Compilation of Federal Legislation and the Classified Compilation of Federal Legislation are published simultaneously in the three official languages (Article 14 of the Federal Act on the Compilations of Federal Legislation and the Federal Gazette of 18 June 2004, status as of 26 November 2018, CC *170.512*) and the enactments are equally binding in the three versions. Only texts of particular importance and documents related to federal elections are available in Romansh as well (Article 11, Languages Act).
24 See for instance Egger et al. (2013, 13); Moretti (2004, 2005); Terzoli and Di Bisceglia (2014).

'third' does not only refer to the ranking by numbers of speakers, as shown above, but also to a broader 'ranking by importance'.

Stating that 8.4% of the Swiss population uses what is referred to as 'Swiss Italian' is correct, but further details should be provided at this point to clarify the different contexts in which Italian is used in Switzerland. Schmid (2002), among others, proposes a very clear classification of 'Swiss Italian', which is:
- the main language used in Ticino and in some territories of Graubünden;
- the mother tongue of Italian speakers living in non-italophone cantons (both Swiss from Ticino and Graubünden and Italians);
- a second language for Swiss nationals and foreigners living in Switzerland;
- the variety of Italian used by the institutions, also called *italiano federale* ('federal Italian') or *italiano elvetico* ('Helvetic Italian').[25]

For the sake of precision, this last category could also be split in different subcategories. Federal Italian is the (mostly written) language used in all the contexts in which the Italian text is the result of a translation from German or French, produced in the vast majority of cases in the non-italophone part of Switzerland, above all in Bern. Federal Italian is used not only by the federal institutions, but also by big companies such as banks, insurance companies and business chains that offer their products and services throughout the country (Moretti 2011, 1436).

Referring to Lüdi's classification of multilingualism (2013), one could state that the first category corresponds to the 'territorial', the second and third to the 'individual' and the fourth to 'institutional multilingualism'. In order to provide a complete overview of the linguistic landscape of Switzerland, all four categories should be defined. However, the analysis of the first three goes beyond the scope of this chapter, the aim of which is to paint a picture of the status of Swiss Italian at the federal level, in the context of institutional multilingualism.

---

25 The first definition is by Biscossa (1968), the second by Berruto (1984). Pandolfi (2009) proposes a similar definition, that is, *italiano statale* (State Italian). However, it has a broader meaning compared to Biscossa's and Berruto's terms; it focuses instead on the polycentric nature of Italian, which has different autonomous varieties (one being, of course, the Swiss one) in addition to the one used in Italy.

2 The status of Italian from a historical perspective[26]

As stated by Dullion (2018, 397), "[a] historical approach to legal translation can (...) help to understand current institutional policies and practices and put them in perspective (...)." It is in this spirit that this section has been compiled. Ideally, this brief historical overview would go back to 1803, when the modern Confederation was founded and Ticino and Graubünden officially joined it. As far as the old Confederation (from 1291 until 1798) is concerned, suffice it to say that it was monolingual German (Lüdi 2013). During the Helvetic Republic (from 1798 until 1803), on the contrary, all federal acts were available in German, French and Italian. However, this was a short-lived experience and the Act of Mediation of 1803 did not recognize Italian as a national language. The first forty-five years of this historical overview were therefore characterized by the exclusive use of German by the federal institutions; all federal publications had to be translated into French and Italian by the Cantons concerned.

2.1 First language regime (1848–1916)

It was not until the adoption of a new Swiss constitution in 1848 that Italian was recognized as a national language: "Art. 109. Le tre lingue principali della Svizzera, la tedesca, la francese e l'italiana sono lingue nazionali della Confederazione." ("The three main languages of Switzerland, German, French and Italian, are the national languages of the Swiss Confederation.") From a formal point of view, this legal recognition of the multi- (and pluri-)lingual nature of Switzerland was an important step. Indeed, 1848 is considered to be the beginning of the 'first language regime'. At that time, the term 'official language' was still not used. It was introduced later on in the Constitution of 1938, which first distinguished between 'national' and 'official' language.

---

26 For a more comprehensive historical overview, see Pini (2017), who first proposed the division into 'first, second and third language regime' and offers in his book an in-depth description of these three periods. This section of the present chapter was compiled also thanks to the work of Snozzi (1996, 2005) and Pedrazzini (1952). In order to offer an intelligible and fluid narrative of the most important events that determined the evolution of the status of Italian as a Swiss institutional language, the author decided to avoid specifying the reference for every single event. This applies especially to the period before 1990, for which a limited number of works is available. Readers who are interested in learning more can turn to the preceding four sources named here. For the period after 1990, there is more literature available and, consequently, more references. This development also demonstrates how the academic interest in the status of the third official language of Switzerland has only emerged quite recently.

However, the recognition of Italian as a 'main' and 'national' language in 1848, alongside German and French, marked its institutionalization and opened up the (long) path towards the equalization of Switzerland's three main languages. At the beginning of this institutional trilingualism, the use of Italian within the federal institutions was very limited, both in the legislative and executive branch.[27] In parliament, Italian was excluded from the legislative procedure. The Official Compilation of Federal Legislation was available in the three national languages, but the federal acts were only translated after adoption. This 'legal fiction' (Snozzi 1996, 24) would last until the third regime. In government, the status of Italian was not very different: the most important decisions adopted by the Federal Council were translated, but the official journal of the Swiss government, the Federal Gazette, was not issued in Italian.

2.2   Second language regime (1917–1973)

At the beginning of the twentieth century, the idea of providing an adequate translation into Italian of the federal legislation started to spread. The new act on the relationships between the two Councils of 1902, for instance, laid down the necessity of assuring the equivalence of Italian legislative acts to its German and French counterparts. Moreover, it instituted a parliamentary commission in charge of the Italian version of legal texts. The ground was fertile for the beginning of the 'second language regime', which formally dates back to 5 October 1917. On that day, two important events took place.

Firstly, Motta, the head of the Federal Department of Finance and Customs at the time, wrote a circular to the federal departments, in which he pointed to the appalling quality of the federal institutional texts in Italian. He demanded that more attention be paid and a centralized supervision be organized. This request was fully accepted and a *Segretariato di lingua italiana* was created within the Federal Chancellery to ensure that the federal institutions speak (or rather, write) in good Italian. Secondly, the Department of Justice of Ticino demanded the publication of the Federal Gazette in Italian. This

---

27   The executive branch was not taken into account in this chapter. As explained by Dullion (2017, 74), "[w]hereas Swiss legislation is enacted in three official languages, judgments are usually passed in only one language, depending on the geographical origin of the case." Translation of judgments is carried out within a *régime de traduction privée* ('private translation regime', ibid., 76) with the aim of disseminating case law and allowing for a coherent interpretation of legislation throughout the country. As this type of translation is non-official, it will not be considered within the scope of this chapter.

request also received a positive response: the Swiss government started to publish its official journal in Italian as well, although not in full. The status of Italian in parliament, on the contrary, did not change in any significant way.

2.3 Third language regime (1974–present)

For another forty to fifty years, the status of Italian did not improve either in government or in parliament. From the 1960s onward, the most important achievements were the result of intensive activity at the political level. Several procedural requests were addressed by parliamentarians to the Federal Council, and two motions in particular led to the beginning of a new language regime. Thanks to a motion submitted by Maspoli in 1962, the content of the Italian version of the Federal Gazette was expanded upon the following year. Five years later, Franzoni demanded that all federal acts be voted on and adopted in their Italian version as well. This request came into force in 1972. Moreover, in 1974, the Italian version of the Federal Gazette was fully equalized to the German and French versions. Since 1974, Italian has enjoyed a more equitable treatment both in the legislative and executive branch, and this change marked the beginning of the (still ongoing?) 'third language regime'.

2.4 Towards a fourth language regime?

To state that, since 1974, Italian has been fully equalized to the two main languages of Switzerland would be both optimistic and misleading. Maspoli's motion was an important step that led to the beginning of a new language regime, but one should add that it contained a subsidiary request, that is, that the Italian language be represented during the entire legislative process. This request was only partially accepted at the time, and only since the beginning of the twenty-first century have all documents produced during the legislative process been translated into Italian as well. Moreover, the decision to publish a fully trilingual Federal Gazette is undoubtedly very positive, but it should also be mentioned that the simultaneous publication of the three language versions would only become a reality in the 1990s.

To fully understand the status of Italian within the Swiss institutional system, one should bear in mind its position as a 'translation language' (more on this in the next section). In particular, from the 1990s onwards, several initiatives were adopted to improve translation into Italian and to attain full equalization to the first and second official languages. First, clear structures, processes and competences were defined within (and between) the different translation services of the federal institutions (Offices, Departments and Central Language Services of the Federal Chancellery). This reorganization towards a greater centralization allowed their trilingual voice to rely on a more modern and effective translation sector (Pini 2017, 115–116). In the same spirit, between 1991 and 2002, a massive program was organized to expand on translation into Italian. It originally aimed to employ forty-five more translators so that a greater amount of institutional texts could be translated into Italian (ibid., 121–122).

In addition to these 'quantitative efforts' aimed at structuring and strengthening the workforce within federal translation services, some 'qualitative measures' were adopted as well. After all, expanding the number of institutional texts translated into Italian would not have sufficed, had they been of poor quality. To avoid this, some initiatives were taken, designed not only to improve the products, that is, institutional texts in Italian, but also the qualifications for the actors involved as well as the context of production. With regard to the context, one example is the decision of the Federal Chancellery (and, more precisely, of the Italian Division of its Central Language Services) to become a member of the *Rete per l'eccellenza dell'italiano istituzionale* (REI), the network for excellence in institutional Italian. The REI was founded in 2005 by different representatives of Italian-speaking institutional contexts (European Union (EU), Italy, Croatia, etc.) with the aim of sharing best practices and improving the quality of State-to-citizen communication.[28] The measures involving the actors and products were not limited to Italian but concerned institutional communication in general, including German and French. Official actors, in particular federal translators, were offered different training courses, namely, *ad hoc* seminars and courses on legistics and terminology, which are still organized on a yearly basis in the three official languages.[29] A clear intent to improve the quality of the product is demonstrated by several guidelines that were created on the drafting of normative acts and, more generally, institutional texts (see Egger 2011; Bruno 2013). The publication of *LeGes*, a journal for the quality of legislation, which first appeared in 1990, takes a similar approach.[30]

---

28 One of the most influential works done by the REI is the "Manifesto for a quality institutional Italian" (reported, e.g., in Egger 2010), which is a reference point for clear, accessible and comprehensible institutional communication.

29 For an overview of the different training programs offered, see the website of the Federal Chancellery: https://www.bk.admin.ch/bk/fr/home/documentation/seminaires-et-cours.html (last accessed 31 January 2019).

30 See the website of the Swiss society for legislation (SGG) http://www.sagw.ch/fr/sgg/LeGes.html (last accessed 31 January 2019). All the issues of *LeGes* are available online.

One final element remains in order to complete this overview: the measures taken to preserve, promote and strengthen Switzerland's quadrilingualism and its minority languages. The most significant step in this sense was the adoption of the Languages Act in 2007. It established the equal treatment of the four national languages by federal institutions, thus constituting a strong legal basis for the promotion of a *de facto* equalization of Italian to French and German.

Unlike the first and the second language regimes, the third is quite a dynamic one. From 1974 until now, many things have changed, and one might wonder if a fourth language regime has already begun or is yet to begin. Maybe a few years from now, a larger temporal distance will allow for a clearer and more objective evaluation of these events, and the adoption of the Languages Act (or any other event presented in this section) could be considered to be the milestone marking the beginning of a fourth language regime.

3 The status of Italian today

The historical evolution presented in the previous section suggests that, today, Italian is granted full equality, at least *de jure*. This status is confirmed by the new Swiss constitution of 1999, which mentions the four national languages in its "General Provisions", thus underlying that the multilingual nature of Switzerland is one of its fundamental values: "Art. 4 National languages. The National Languages are German, French, Italian, and Romansh."

Article 70 further regulates specific questions related to the languages of Switzerland, such as the status of the federal and cantonal official languages, the protection and promotion of minority languages at the local level and the understanding and exchange between the four linguistic communities. It exemplifies how the central State pays attention to all languages used in Switzerland, a principle that has recently been reprised in the Languages Act of 2007:

Art. 3 Principles
[1] In fulfilling its tasks, the Confederation shall observe the following principles in particular:
a. it shall ensure that it treats the four national Swiss languages equally.
b. it shall guarantee and apply linguistic freedom in all its areas of activity.
c. it shall take account of the traditional linguistic composition of Switzerland's regions.
d. it shall promote understanding between the linguistic communities.

However, praxis should be presented alongside theory. Having discussed the legal foundation for equality between the three official languages, this chapter will now address the implementation of these provisions within the institutions. In this Section, some select examples are used to illustrate to what extent a *de facto* equality is far from being reality.[31]

The first one concerns legislation. As already mentioned in Section 2, even though today the Federal Gazette and the Official Compilation of Federal Legislation are made available simultaneously in all three official languages, Italian remains a translation language (Borghi 2011, 326; Egger 2015, 164; Snozzi 2005, 321). A federal normative act is rarely drafted in Italian and then translated into German and French. A study conducted by Grüter (2015) focused on 199 legislative projects for which a consultation was carried out between 2010–2012. Her findings show that approximately 83% of them were carried out in one language, 17% in more than one language (i.e., co-drafted) and, among the former, none was carried out in Italian. These results are in line with the ones reported by Zwicky and Kübler (2018, 17–21), which are based on all normative acts passed between 1998 and 2015. Only around 1% of them were originally drafted in Italian. However, as shown by Kübler (2010, 25), in most cases these acts are either bilateral agreements between Switzerland and Italy or directly concern the Italian-speaking part of Switzerland. In short, Italian is not used as a source language for normative acts with national relevance. This statement has no critical purpose; some authors even underline the privileged position of the Italian version, which can be drafted on the basis of the German and French ones.[32] However, the existence of a systematic translation direction, DE (+FR) > IT, is quite telling about the asymmetry and power relationship between the three official languages.

---

[31] The extent to which full equality is reasonable or appropriate will not be discussed here, as this would require much broader, interdisciplinary reflections that include language policy and planning, law, politics and philosophy. As stated in the introduction, this chapter is based on the premise that Switzerland is a *Willensnation*, which decided to be united in its cultural and linguistic diversity to pursue a common interest. Another element that is taken into account here is the strong societal and political interest described above, which aims at promoting full equality between the official languages. It has allowed the status of Italian to significantly improve throughout the last two centuries until this ambitious goal was enshrined in law and reiterated in different legal sources. In other words, the aim of this section is to discuss, from a positive point of view, whether or not the legal provisions that lay down full equality of the three official languages are abided by.

[32] See, for instance, Egger and Grandi (2013, 215) and Schweizer et al. (2011, 32). Relying on two language versions helps to better understand the sense of a norm and to express it in a clear manner in the target text.

The second example more broadly concerns institutional communication and makes the unequal treatment of Italian even clearer. While legislation, in the end, is published in Italian as well (albeit as the result of translation), other texts written by the federal institutions are not available to Swiss citizens whose mother tongue is Italian. This is the case, for instance, of full reports on the activities of federal departments and offices, as well as websites. The Internet inarguably plays an important role in State-to-citizen communication. A quick look at some randomly selected web pages of the federal authorities, however, reveals a worrisome situation: several pages are not available in Italian. Figures 2 and 3 exemplify this situation by presenting two interesting cases.

The first one is a page of the Federal Tax Administration that provides information on tax burden in Switzerland. On the top right-hand side of the page (circled), users can find the language selector and choose from German, French and English. The page is not available in Italian. Offering institutional websites in English is a praiseworthy effort as it makes relevant content available, for instance, to foreign residents with a low proficiency in the official languages and, more broadly, to anyone looking for information about Switzerland from abroad. Van Parijs (2011) welcomes the use of a *lingua franca* in multilingual institutional systems, such as the EU, and argues that his proposal might be applicable to other contexts as well. Switzerland might be one of them. However, the Swiss (national) case differs significantly from the EU (supranational) one, since English is neither an official language of Switzerland nor an established *lingua franca*, as it is in the EU. Moreover, one should bear in mind that every Swiss national should be able to access institutional information online, regardless of the linguistic community they belong to, as laid down in article 12 of the Languages Act of 2007.

> Art. 12 Communications, signs and identity documents
> [1] The federal authorities shall use the local official language for public communications.
> [2] The federal authorities shall communicate with the public in the four official languages, in particular in the design:
> a. of its printed matter;
> b. of its internet home pages;
> c. in signs in its buildings.

In light of this, the priority given to a non-national language over Italian might not be the most equitable way of ensuring accessibility.

INVESTIGATING THE STATUS OF SWISS ITALIAN AS AN 'OFFICIAL MINORITY LANGUAGE' 145

Figure 2. Website of the Federal Tax Administration[33]

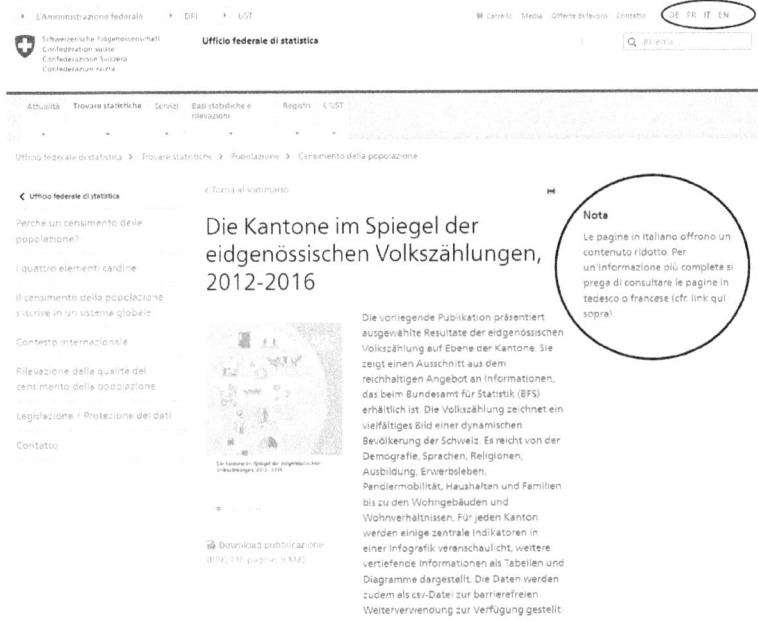

Figure 3. Website of the Federal Statistical Office[34]

33 Source: https://www.estv.admin.ch/estv/de/home/allgemein/steuerstatistiken/fachinformationen/steuerbelastungen.html (last accessed 7 December 2018). This page was checked again on 31 August 2021 and a translation in Italian is now available. The same applies for Figure 3.
34 Source: https://www.bfs.admin.ch/bfs/it/home/statistiche/popolazione.html (last accessed 18 December 2018).

Figure 3 provides another telling example, this time from the website of the Federal Statistical Office. In this case, the section "Look for statistics" is available in the four national languages plus English (see circled language selector). However, some pages contained in this section have not been translated. Moreover, a side note (also circled) informs users that the content displayed in the Italian page is not complete. The same note pops up when browsing the English page: "Remark. Our English pages offer only a limited range of information on our statistical production. For our full range please consult our pages in French and German (top right-hand screen)." However, whereas this limitation is fully justified as far as the English version of the website is concerned, finding the same note on the Italian page provides food for thought: italophone citizens are not given the same access to public information compared to their French and German-speaking compatriots.

The final example concerns university law programs offered in Switzerland. In the whole country, there is not a single faculty in which one can study Swiss law in Italian. Italian-speakers must attend a Swiss-German or Swiss-French university to get a degree in law (Borghi 2011, 322). This is quite surprising, especially in light of the consubstantial nature of language and law widely recognized in the literature. Some Swiss universities (Lucerne and Bern, for instance) offer some courses in Italian, but it is far from being a whole curriculum in Italian. Another option is to study in Italy at the Università degli Studi dell'Insubria, where a 'Swiss curriculum' can be chosen within the law degree. The target of this curriculum, however, seems to be an Italian rather than a Swiss-Italian public.[35] This situation is another example of the inequalities that still exist between the official languages and, more generally, of how the linguistic communities of Switzerland are treated differently.

After this short review, the current status of Italian can be described by drawing on Egger, Ferrari and Lala (2013b, 13), who state that Italian-speaking citizens still struggle to assert their rights. In other words, this section has confirmed that for now equality is *de jure*, though not yet *de facto*.[36]

---

35 See the description on the welcome page for the degree coursework: https://www.uninsubria.it/offertaformativa/giurisprudenza-sede-di-como (last accessed 20 December 2018).
36 On this topic, Egger and Grandi (2013, 213–214) also use the metaphor 'front' to describe a twofold battle, the first to enhance the status of Italian as an official language and the second to achieve a high-quality, Swiss-institutional Italian.

4   The status of Italian tomorrow

In the first language regime, Italian was nearly absent in the institutional context, in the second it got a formal recognition, in the third it was equalized, at least *de jure*, to German and French. The aim of this section is to evaluate a new potential language regime characterized by a *de facto* equality. To this end, this study draws on a model from the field of business economics and, more specifically, of strategic management: the SWOT analysis. SWOT stands for 'strengths', 'weaknesses', 'opportunities' and 'threats' of a strategic option in business planning.[37] Strengths and weaknesses refer to internal factors, opportunities and threats to external factors, all of which are to be evaluated. In order to compile the SWOT matrix, an in-depth literature review has been carried out. However, this analysis does not aim at exhaustiveness; in future studies, further elements could be included in each of the four quadrants. Here, only the most relevant ones are discussed. The compiled matrix is presented here and is followed by an explanation of each aspect in greater detail:

Table 2. SWOT analysis of a new language regime characterized by a *de facto* equality of the three official languages

Strengths	Weaknesses
- spirit of Swiss plurilingualism - equal treatment of the different linguistic communities - quality of federal Italian - quality of institutional texts	- underrepresentation of Italian speakers - few German translators - systemic barriers
Opportunities	**Threats**
- legal provisions - growing awareness of inequalities between the official languages - actions to promote a full equalization - exchange of best practices with other multilingual institutional systems - translation technologies	- organizational efforts - reluctance at the political level - improper use of translation technologies

Strengths
Undoubtedly, such an institutional system has significant strengths. In the first place, it would embody the spirit of Swiss multilingualism and guarantee equal treatment of the different linguistic communities, as provided for in the law (see Sections 2.4 and 3 for more details). Moreover, Italian would

---

37   For more details about the SWOT analysis, see, for example, Lynch (2006, chapter 13).

stop systematically being a translation language and would take on the role of a source language as well. This change would have a number of positive outcomes. A few linguists complain that some Swiss institutional texts in federal Italian do not always "sound" Italian because of the influence of the source language. This observation is, for instance, the conclusion of a study conducted by Ferrari (2013) on a corpus of press releases issued by the federal institutions. The new language regime would partially solve this problem, as part of the documents produced by Swiss institutions would directly be written in (a presumably high-quality) 'federal Italian'.

More broadly, this change is likely to enhance the overall quality of institutional texts, regardless of the language version. Indeed, several authors agree on the fact that, in many cases, translation helps to improve the source and the target text (Berther 2011, 272; Egger 2012, 430; Schnyder 2001, 43–45). In fact, translators often detect problems in the source texts and draw drafters' attention to them. In this way, not only translated texts but also original versions can be improved. If translation is carried out in multiple translation directions, enrichment between the three linguistic versions becomes reciprocal.

Weaknesses

A crucial weakness often mentioned in the literature is the lack of qualified civil servants that such an institutional system demands. On the one hand, Italian speakers are underrepresented within the federal institutions (Borghi 2011, 332; Bruno 2013, 136–137; Snozzi 1996, 23), particularly when it comes to servants at managerial levels (Andrey and Kübler 2008; Federal Delegate for Plurilingualism 2015; Zwicky and Kübler 2018). This deficiency reduces the possibilities of drafting texts in Italian. As far as normative acts are concerned, a further analogous difficulty arises: the lack of external domain experts whose mother tongue is Italian, and who can provide consultation on legislative projects, both in terms of content and language (Egger and Grandi 2008, 37).

On the other hand, even if the institutions found a way of writing a larger quantity of texts in Italian, the linguistic services of the different departments and offices would lack internal translators who could take on the task of translating them into German and French. In particular, there are a limited number of translators into German, as suggested by the distribution of the federal translators by their A language, as reported in Pini (2017, 218). In short, the major weakness of this new language regime lies in systemic barriers, which may be difficult to overcome due to the external threats that will be discussed below.

Opportunities
At the same time, the external context offers very promising opportunities. As stated several times in this chapter, strong, already extant legal provisions can be brought into play in order to claim a *de facto* trilingualism within the federal institutions. Although there is space for improvement,[38] they are an invaluable reference point. It should also be mentioned that, starting from the 2000s, a growing awareness of the inequalities between the three official languages began to spread, and different actions were taken. For instance, more research started aiming to promote the equality of the official languages, to enhance the status of the minority language and to improve the linguistic quality of institutional texts (e.g., the volumes edited by Borghi 2005a; Schweizer and Borghi 2011; Egger et al. 2013a; and the monograph by Egger (2019), to mention just four of them).

More generally, Swiss institutions started to collaborate with other (monolingual and multilingual) institutional systems, with whom they began an exchange of good practices. In Section 2.4, the network for excellence in institutional Italian, REI, has already been presented. One practical outcome of these efforts is an attempt to reach terminological harmonization with other italophone legal and institutional systems, above all the Italian and European systems (Egger and Grandi 2013, 232). This makes Swiss Italian less isolated and more motivated to strive for quality and clarity. As far as German is concerned, in 2011, an exchange program was organized involving two legislative drafters from the German Section of the Central Language Services of the Federal Chancellery in Bern and the *Redaktionsstab Rechtssprache* of the Ministry of Justice in Berlin. The aim of this program was for each service to learn from the other's quality assurance practices in legislative drafting.[39]

Last but not least, translation technologies, such as machine translation, are making great strides and represent an opportunity for Swiss multilingualism, as has been the case for other institutions (e.g., Pasteur 2013, 293–297, who

---

38 See, for instance, Borghi (2011, 325–326). A striking example is the legislation on federal administration personnel. It provides for a fair representation of the four linguistic communities within the personnel. However, it does not lay down that this representation be achieved in all salary classes. This explains the underrepresentation of italophone civil servants in managerial positions mentioned above in the subsection 'Weaknesses'. Furthermore, the fact that the percentage of italophone civil servants currently active in the federal administration is distorted by a high number of italophone translators is not taken into account. Indeed, their numbers are justified by the very lack of employees who can produce institutional texts in Italian.
39 See Raff and Schiedt (2012) for a report of this experience.

describes the implementation of a statistical machine translation system[40] at the World Trade Organization). Machine translation could help increase the efficiency of the linguistic services; in the future, it may be possible to offer also an Italian version of those texts that, likely due to a lack of resources, are currently only available in German and French (see Section 3).

Threats
The major threat connected to this change of paradigm concerns organizational aspects and, of course, its financial impact. Any decision that leads to a deep restructuring of translation services would require a great deal of effort. In this regard, recall the 1990 decision to reorganize translation services for greater centralization (see Section 2.4), which required five years of intense activity from an *ad hoc* interdepartmental work group (Pini 2017, 115–116).

Even before reorganization, however, a political willingness to give birth to a new language regime is required. As already mentioned in the concluding remarks of Section 3, some work still needs to be done at the political level to ensure effective equal treatment of the three official languages. The great number of procedural requests in the last few years that have been directed to the Federal Council by different members of Parliament asking to strengthen Swiss multilingualism (Federal Delegate for Plurilingualism 2015, 5–7) demonstrates that work still needs to be done in this direction.

The aforementioned translation technologies are an invaluable opportunity that, at the same time, can turn into a threat if they are not used properly. It must be stressed that these technologies should be used exclusively by the translation services of the institutions, which are constituted by highly qualified translators who are specifically trained to use them. As Pasteur (2013, 298) himself points out, translators should maintain a central role; technologies are of great help to improve speed and quantity, but the gatekeeper of quality remains the translator.

The result of this SWOT analysis is very clear. Strengths and opportunities show that a potential new language regime characterized by *de facto* equality between the three official languages has fertile ground on which it could grow. At the same time, weaknesses and threats reveal some barriers within the

---

40 Statistical machine translation (SMT) is a type of machine translation that builds "(…) probabilistic models of faithfulness and fluency and then combin[es] these models to choose the most probable translation." (Jurafsky 2014, 893). Another promising (and more recent) alternative is neural machine translation (NMT), which is based on machine learning. Swiss institutions have recently tested such a system, as explained in this press release: https://www.admin.ch/gov/de/start/dokumentation/medienmitteilungen.msg-id-77610.html (last accessed 28 December 2019). A report on this test is available (in German only!) on the same web page.

institutions as well as at the political level, which would have to be removed in order to attain a fully trilingual system. From the recognition of Italian as a national language in 1848 until today, the status of the third language has followed an upward trend. This evolution suggests that the new language regime described in this section may become a reality in the near or far future.

5 Conclusion

The aim of this chapter was to demonstrate the peculiarity of Swiss institutional trilingualism. It adopted the perspective of the 'third language', Italian, and presented the evolution of its status from 1803 until today. From its absence within the institutions at their origins, it gradually (and constantly) gained in importance. Today, full equality has still not been reached but seems to at least be in sight. Switzerland is undoubtedly a case of 'government by translation' (Koskinen 2014); without an extensive translation practice, the State could not successfully represent its different linguistic communities. In order to summarize the peculiarities of this institutional system, one can turn to the classification of translation policies in multilingual settings proposed by Meylaerts (2013). Switzerland fits into the third category: the local level is monolingual, and the superior level is multilingual with obligatory multidirectional translations.[41]

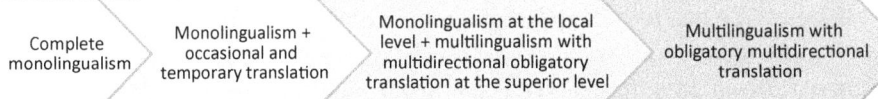

Figure 4. Switzerland in Meylaerts's classification of translation policies in multilingual settings (2013, 526–527)

At the superior (i.e., federal) level, however, the concept of 'multidirectional translations' must be downsized. In Switzerland, three different translation directions exist, that is, DE>FR/IT, FR>DE/IT and IT>DE/FR, but the first one is overrepresented, the second occurs less frequently, and the third is

---

41 The four categories are not to be understood as watertight, but allow for options in between. For example, one could argue that in Switzerland, there are some bi- and trilingual Cantons and Municipalities, and that consequently, it is not completely correct to state that the local level is monolingual.

quite rare. Moreover, the first direction is characterized by a clear asymmetry between the subdirections DE>FR and DE>IT on a quantitative level, as well as partially on a qualitative level. This is one argument – among others presented in this chapter – for the inequalities that still exist between the three official languages. At the same time, analyzing the main strengths and weaknesses of a potential trilingual institutional system and comparing and contrasting them with the most relevant external opportunities and threats has revealed a trend towards a full equalization of Italian to German and French. In other words, Italian still holds the third place on the 'language podium' (Bruno 2014, 552), to be sure. However, a review of the past and present status of Italian has presented the picture of a future, near or far, in which the 'third language' might no longer need to be qualified using an ordinal number. More broadly, it is hoped that the three official languages will one day all share the first position on a level podium.

References

Andrey, Stéphanie, and Kübler Daniel. 2008. "L'italiano all'amministrazione federale svizzera: proporzioni linguistiche e conseguenze per l'italianità." *Dati – Statistiche e società* VIII (4): 93–106.

Beacco, Jean-Claude, ed. 2007. *From Linguistic Diversity to Plurilingual Education: Guide for the Development of Language Education Policies in Europe*. Strasbourg: Council of Europe.

Berruto, Gaetano. 1984. "Appunti sull'italiano elvetico." *Studi linguistici italiani* 10: 76–108.

Berther, Arno. 2011. "Elements d'in nov linguatg giuridic rumantsch." In *Mehrsprachige Gesetzgebung in der Schweiz: Juristisch-linguistische Untersuchungen von mehrsprachigen Rechtstexten des Bundes und der Kantone*, edited by Rainer J. Schweizer and Marco Borghi, 239–276. Zurich: Dike.

Biscossa, Giuseppe. 1968. "Evoluzione della lingua italiana nel Ticino." *Il Veltro* 6: 497–541.

Borghi, Marco, ed. 2005a. *Lingua e diritto: La presenza della lingua italiana nel diritto svizzero*. Basel: Helbing & Lichtenhahn.

———. 2005b. "Ev- Inv(?)oluzione della lingua italiana nel linguaggio giuridico in uso nel Canton Ticino." In *Lingua e diritto: La presenza della lingua italiana nel diritto svizzero*, edited by Marco Borghi, 3–16. Basel: Helbing & Lichtenhahn.

———. 2011. "Riflessioni sull'uso dell'italiano nella legislazione svizzera." In *Mehrsprachige Gesetzgebung in der Schweiz. Juristisch-linguistische Untersuchungen von mehrsprachigen Rechtstexten des Bundes und der Kantone*, edited by Rainer J. Schweizer and Marco Borghi, 319–334. Zurich: Dike.

Bruno, Giovanni. 2013. "Lo strumento «Omnia»: quando e come normare la scrittura amministrativa?" In *Le forme linguistiche dell'ufficialità: L'italiano giuridico e amministrativo della Confederazione Svizzera*, edited by Jean-Luc Egger, Angela Ferrari and Letizia Lala, 135–150. Bellinzona: Casagrande.

———. 2014. Review of *Il mondo in italiano: Varietà e usi internazionali della lingua*, by Barbara Turchetta. *LeGes* 26 (1): 549–552.

Dullion, Valérie. 2017. "La traduction des décisions de justice dans les revues juridiques suisses : développement d'un régime de traduction privée (1853–1912)." *Parallèles* 29 (1): 74–89. https://doi.org/10.17462/para.2017.01.07.

———. 2018. "Legal History." In *A History of Modern Translation Knowledge: Sources, Concepts, Effects*, edited by Lieven D'hulst and Yves Gambier, 397–400. Amsterdam: John Benjamins. https://doi.org/10.1075/btl.142.55dul.

Eco, Umberto. 1991. "Sulla lingua svizzera." In *Svizzera e Italia, per sette secoli: In occasione del settecentesimo anniversario della fondazione della Confederazione Elvetica*, edited by Flavio Cotti and Francesco Cossiga, 68–73. Rome: Presidenza del Consiglio dei Ministri, Dipartimento per l'Informazione e l'Editoria.

Egger, Jean-Luc. 2010. "Un manifesto per l'italiano istituzionale." *LeGes* 21 (2): 275–280.

———. 2011. "Le regole per la redazione dei testi ufficiali in italiano." In *Il linguaggio e la qualità delle leggi*, edited by Raffaele Libertini, 41–50. Padua: CLEUP.

———. 2012. "Elementi per un paradigma della traduzione istituzionale." *LeGes* 23 (3): 429–435.

———. 2015. "25 anni di legislazione federale in lingua italiana: alcuni spunti di riflessione." *LeGes* 26 (1): 151–171.

———. 2019. *A norma di (chi) legge: Peculiarità dell'italiano federale*. Milan: Giuffrè.

Egger, Jean-Luc, and Filippo Grandi. 2008. "Il nuovo Codice di procedura penale: un cantiere anche linguistico." *LeGes* 19 (1): 31–72.

———. 2013. "Italiano giuridico federale: un dispaccio dal fronte." In *Le forme linguistiche dell'ufficialità. L'italiano giuridico e amministrativo della Confederazione Svizzera*, edited by Jean-Luc Egger, Angela Ferrari and Letizia Lala, 213–242. Bellinzona: Casagrande.

Egger, Jean-Luc, Angela Ferrari, and Letizia Lala, eds. 2013a. *Le forme linguistiche dell'ufficialità: L'italiano giuridico e amministrativo della Confederazione Svizzera*. Bellinzona: Casagrande.

———. 2013b. "Introduzione." In *Le forme linguistiche dell'ufficialità: L'italiano giuridico e amministrativo della Confederazione Svizzera*, edited by Jean-Luc Egger, Angela Ferrari and Letizia Lala, 11–15. Bellinzona: Casagrande.

Federal Delegate for Plurilingualism. 2015. *Promozione del plurilinguismo: Rapporto di valutazione a destinazione del Consiglio federale e raccomandazioni sulla politica del plurilinguismo (art. 8d. cpv. 4. OLing): Evoluzione 2008–2014: Prospettive per il periodo 2015–2019*. Bern: Federal Department of Finance.

Ferrari, Angela. 2013. "La versione italiana dei comunicati stampa dell'Amministrazione federale, tra tedesco, francese e italiano d'Italia." In *Le forme linguistiche dell'ufficialità. L'italiano giuridico e amministrativo della Confederazione Svizzera*, edited by Jean-Luc Egger, Angela Ferrari and Letizia Lala, 17–41. Bellinzona: Casagrande.

Grüter, Barbara. 2015. "In welcher Sprache entstehen die Gesetze des Bundes?" *LeGes* 26 (2): 351–366.

Jurafsky, Daniel, and James H. Martin. 2014. *Speech and Language Processing: An Introduction to Natural Language Processing, Computational Linguistics and Speech Recognition*. 2nd ed. Harlow: Pearson.

Koskinen, Kaisa. 2014. "Institutional Translation: The Art of Government by Translation." *Perspectives* 22 (4): 479–492. https://doi.org/10.1080/0907676X.2014.948887.

Kreis, Georg. 2011. Nation. In *Historisches Lexikon der Schweiz*. https://hls-dhs-dss.ch/de/articles/017437/2011-04-26/.

Kübler, Daniel. 2010. "L'italiano nell'amministrazione federale." In *Come può il Ticino contare di più a Berna? Atti del convegno*, edited by Oscar Mazzoleni and Andrea Planta, 21–30. Poschiavo: Menghini.

Lüdi, Georges. 2013. Mehrsprachigkeit. In *Historisches Lexikon der Schweiz*. https://hls-dhs-dss.ch/de/articles/024596/2013-07-18/.

Lynch, Richard. 2006. *Corporate Strategy*. 4th ed. Upper Saddle River: Prentice Hall.

Mader, Luzius. 2005. "La nouvelle loi fédérale sur les langues : une loi en devenir – loi d'avenir?" In *Lingua e diritto: La presenza della lingua italiana nel diritto svizzero*, edited by Marco Borghi, 331–342. Basel: Helbing & Lichtenhahn.

Meylaerts, Reine 2013. "Multilingualism as a Challenge for Translation Studies." In *The Routledge Handbook of Translation Studies*, edited by Carmen Millán and Francesca Bartrina, 519–533. London: Routledge.

Moretti, Bruno, ed. 2004. *La terza lingua: Volume primo, norma e varietà di lingua in Ticino*. Locarno: Dadò.

———, ed. 2005. *La terza lingua: Volume secondo, dati statistici e «varietà dinamiche»*. Locarno: Dadò.

———. 2011. "Svizzera, italiano di." In *Enciclopedia dell'italiano*, edited by Raffaele Simone, 1435–1438. Rome: Il Vocabolario Treccani.

Pandolfi, Elena Maria. 2009. *LIPSI: Lessico di frequenza dell'italiano parlato nella Svizzera italiana*. Bellinzona: Osservatorio Linguistico della Svizzera Italiana.

Pasteur, Olivier. 2013. "Technology at the Service of Specialized Translators at International Organizations." In *Legal Translation in Context: Professional Issues and Prospects*, edited by Fernando Prieto Ramos and Anabel Borja Albi, 283–297. Bern: Peter Lang.

Pedrazzini, Mario Michelangelo. 1952. *La lingua italiana nel diritto federale svizzero*. Locarno: Tipografia Pedrazzini.

Pini, Verio. 2017. *Anche in italiano! 100 anni di lingua italiana nella cultura politica svizzera*. Bellinzona: Casagrande.

Raff, Gudrun, and Margaret Schiedt. 2012. "Der Redaktionsstab Rechtssprache beim Bundesministerium der Justiz – Ein Situations- und Erfahrungsbericht." *LeGes* 23 (1): 61–74.

Schmid, Stephan. 2002. "La rilevanza sociolinguistica della comunità italofona e il legame fra comunità immigrate e italofonia nella Confederazione elvetica." In *L'umanesimo latino in Svizzera: aspetti storici, linguistici, culturali*, edited by Luciano Trincia, 99–113. Treviso: Fondazione Cassamarca.

Schnyder, Bernhard. 2001. "Zur Mehrsprachigkeit der schweizerischen Gesetzgebung im Allgemeinen." *LeGes* 12 (3): 33–48.

Schweizer, Rainer J., Jérôme Baumann, and Jan Scheffler. 2011. "Grundlagen und Verfahren der mehrsprachigen Rechtsetzung im Bund." In *Mehrsprachige Gesetzgebung in der Schweiz: Juristisch-linguistische Untersuchungen von mehrsprachigen Rechtstexten des Bundes und der Kantone*, edited by Rainer J. Schweizer and Marco Borghi, 13–46. Zurich: Dike.

Schweizer, Rainer J., and Marco Borghi, eds. 2011. *Mehrsprachige Gesetzgebung in der Schweiz: Juristisch-linguistische Untersuchungen von mehrsprachigen Rechtstexten des Bundes und der Kantone*. Zurich: Dike.

Snozzi, Alfredo. 1996. "L'italiano, lingua ufficiale della Confederazione: un caso tipico per la (dis)parità tra le lingue ufficiali." *Babylonia* 1996 (4): 23–30.

———. 2005. "L'italiano nella legislazione federale svizzera." In *Lingua e diritto: La presenza della lingua italiana nel diritto svizzero*, edited by Marco Borghi, 317–329. Basel: Helbing & Lichtenhahn.

Steinberg, Jonathan. 2015. *Why Switzerland*. 3rd ed. Cambridge: Cambridge University Press.

Terzoli, Maria Antonietta, and Carlo Alberto Di Bisceglia, eds. 2014. *L'italiano in Svizzera: lusso o necessità? Riflessioni giuridiche, culturali e sociali sul ruolo della terza lingua nazionale*. Bellinzona: Casagrande.

Van Parijs, Philippe. 2011. *Linguistic Justice for Europe and for the World*. Oxford: Oxford University Press.

Zwicky, Roman, and Daniel Kübler. 2018. *Topkader und Mehrsprachigkeit in der Bundesverwaltung, Studienberichte des Zentrums für Demokratie Aarau*. Aarau: ZDA.

Translation, interpreting and institutional routines

The case of Slovakia

Marketa Štefková & Helena Tužinská

Abstract

Public service translation and interpreting (PSIT) is crucial for the interaction between a government and citizens belonging to national minorities, non-natives and citizens with special needs. Through these language services, such citizens gain improved access to information about legal proceedings, social security applications and inclusion rights. This chapter focuses on two aspects of the provision of institutional translation and public service interpreting in Slovakia: (1) the translation policy towards target groups of institutional translation: labor migrants, asylum applicants, refugees and members of language minorities; (2) the quality of the translation and interpreting services provided. We describe the way in which language services are provided in the institutional sector, by defining the target groups and the legal framework for the provision of PSIT. We outline the historical development of the provision of language services to non-native populations in the framework of language rights and the provision of PSIT for labor migrants. The chapter also considers the most recent target group of public service translation and interpreting: asylum applicants and refugees. In conclusion, we make recommendations for the introduction of systematic and standardized measures of institutional translation and interpreting in Slovakia.

1 Introduction

Institutional interpreting and translation are crucial for the interaction between a government and citizens belonging to national minorities, non-natives and citizens with special needs. Through these language services, such citizens have access to information on areas of law, social security and integration. This access gives them the opportunity to express themselves fully in a range of critical situations, such as court cases, in connection with the public prosecution office, and when dealing with the police and the migration office. In this context, this chapter focuses on two aspects of the provision of institutional translation and public service interpreting in Slovakia: (1) the translation policy towards three target groups of institutional translation: labor migrants, asylum applicants and refugees and language minorities; (2) the quality of the translation and interpreting services provided.

We analyze the translation and interpreting services provided by institutions against Koskinen's definition (2014, 479): "the core function of institutions as regulatory organizational systems is to govern, and in a multilingual environment they can and often do employ translation in performing their governing function. In that case, they govern by translation."

We understand translation policy as defined by Meylaerts (2011), that is, as legal rules that regulate translation in the public domain. As Meylaerts (2011, 165) states: "By means of its translation policy, a government thus regulates people's access to or exclusion from public life and services (...) Translation policies are instrumental in furthering (or hindering) the right to communicate with the authorities (...) They are an integral part of languages policies, which regulate language use in the public domain." This definition of institutional translation and interpreting partly overlaps with parallel concepts such as community, social, liaison and public service translation and interpreting (PSIT). The specific delineation of these concepts depends on the differences in translation and interpreting policy and legislation in particular countries. Since the 1990s, community interpreting has been established as an independent sub-discipline within translation studies and has focused on a range of research domains: interpreting for the police, in hospitals, in asylum procedures, as well as sign-language interpreting.

As a follow-up to this, several governmental and professional organizations developed strategies for the professionalization and standardization of the provision of language services to non-native speakers. In Canada, based on the initiatives of professional organizations, the National Standard Guide for Community Interpreting Services[1] was developed. Similar programs have also been created in Australia, the United States and later on in some European countries among a variety of groups of labor immigrants and asylum seekers. An important step in the standardization of community and public service interpreting was ISO 13611: 2014 Interpreting – Guidelines for Community Interpreting.[2]

---

1   http://www.saludycultura.uji.es/archivos/HIN_National_Standard_Guide_for_CI_(Canada).pdf.
2   https://www.iso.org/standard/54082.html.

The high demand for interpreting and translation in criminal proceedings in the European Union (EU) with a wide variety of standards and quality of service, and the need to support the interests and concerns of national associations, led to the foundation of the European Legal Interpreters and Translators Association (EULITA) in 2007. In 2010, this association was involved in the formulation of a directive of the European Parliament and the Council on the right to interpreting and translation in criminal proceedings.[3] The directive encompasses key recommendations regarding the right to interpreting and translation of essential documents and regarding the quality of that interpreting and translation. Those recommendations are very relevant and influential for other legal and institutional settings where translation and interpreting are required. One of the initiatives of EULITA is the formulation of a new ISO-norm on legal translation and interpreting which will clearly establish and delineate legal and community translators and interpreters.[4] Following these developments in the field, it was a logical next step to start formulating recommendations for the European Commission concerning a common European legislation and financing policy for translation and interpreting in the public service sector. Therefore, in 2014, the Belgian organization Junction Migration-Integration initiated the establishment of the European network for Public Service and Translation (ENPSIT).[5] ENPSIT encourages relevant stakeholders to work towards a unified European framework of institutional interpreting and translation.

The guarantee of language services for diverse groups in society speaking a language other than the official state language is the subject of a broad spectrum of interdisciplinary research. It moves from the examination of language rights of citizens in the public sector, to the scope, manner and quality of the provision of translation and interpreting services in the individual sectors of public services, through to the analysis of completed translations. Attention is also paid to the asymmetry of power, the person of the interpreter and translator, the method and opportunities for lifelong learning of interpreters and translators, and the extent and effectiveness of the use of accessible language technology in this communication sector. Also crucial are the ethical aspects of this type of communication.[6]

---

3   See Directive 2010/64/EU of the European Parliament and of the Council of 20 October: https://eur-lex.europa.eu/legal-content/EN/ALL/?uri=CELEX%3A32010L0064.
4   On the initiative of developing ISO standard on Legal translation and interpreting: https://www.iso.org/standard/69032.html.
5   See the ENPSIT website to consult the history at http://www.enpsit.org/.
6   See for instance Hale (2004, 2007); see also Wadensjö (1996); Mikkelson (2000); Hertog and van der Veer 2006, Kadrić (2008); Kainz, Prunč, and Schogler (2011).

In what follows, and in line with D'hulst, O'Sullivan, and Schreiber (2016, 15), we outline translation policy in the institutional environments in Slovakia by explaining two aspects of translation policy: (1) the objectives, principles and procedures established by the state entities to regulate the translation practices of the language communities in Slovakia and (2) the actual translation practice.

2 Translation policy and the target groups of institutional translation and interpreting in Slovakia

Slovakia, as a small and traditionally multilingual country, has conducted wide-ranging discussions regarding language policy, the use of state languages, of languages of national minorities and of the languages of labor migrants and refugees. The concept of public service translation and interpreting is relatively unknown and underdeveloped in Slovakia. In the practical provision of translation and interpreting services by state authorities, only translators and interpreters registered by the Ministry of Justice are employed. The commonly used term for this language service provider is 'court translator/interpreter'. However, the contexts in which the registered interpreters and translators are employed fall within the legal, social and community sectors.

In the next section, we describe the way in which language services are provided in the institutional sector, mainly for state institutions, by defining the target groups and the legal framework for the provision of institutional translation and interpreting. We also mention the historical development of the provision of language services to non-native populations. We briefly outline the evolution of language rights and language services for minorities and subsequently compare the position of three national minorities in Slovakia, that is, the Czechs, Hungarians and Roma. We describe the provision of translation and interpreting for labor migrants and the most recent target group of public service translation and interpreting: asylum applicants and refugees in Slovakia.

2.1 Target groups

Slovakia is one of the smallest countries in the EU with an estimated 5.5 million inhabitants. Due to its geographical location and history, Slovakia has always been a multilingual country, where nine recognized national minorities are currently living. Originally, the territories of the Slovak Republic belonged to and were ruled by the Dual Monarchy of Austria-Hungary. After its dissolution and after the Second World War, the second Czechoslovak Republic came into being, establishing Slovak as the official language of the Slovak part and Czech as that of the Czech part of the Republic (the former kingdom of Bohemia and Moravia). The Czech and Slovak languages were mutually comprehensible to the citizens of the Czechoslovak Republic because of their similarity and the intensive contact between the two language groups. Since the division of Czechoslovakia and the creation of the independent Slovak Republic in 1993, the use of languages in the Slovak Republic has been regulated by legislation on the state language of the Slovak Republic.[7] This law is the primary text establishing the use of languages within the territory of the Slovak Republic and stipulating the use of the state language, as well as the rules for the use of national minority languages.

Based on legislation on the use of languages of **national minorities**, there are nine national minority languages: Bulgarian, Czech, Croatian, Hungarian, German, Polish, Romani, Ruthenian and Ukrainian. This law allows citizens of the Slovak Republic belonging to national minorities to use their language in contacts with the official state authorities. It also sets the rules for the use of the minority language in municipalities, where the proportion of citizens belonging to a national minority reaches 20%.

These national minorities are guaranteed the right to disseminate and receive information in their native language, the right to education in their language, and the right to use their language in official contacts, as a result of international provisions (such as the Framework Convention for the Protection of National Minorities and the European Charter for Regional or Minority Languages). Therefore, state institutions are obliged to provide translation and interpreting for these citizens.[8] As an example, the Slovak Republic recently published translations of some relevant laws in Ukrainian, Ruthenian, German and Romani.[9] The report on the use of national minority languages (2014) states that there are significant differences in the use of minority languages in connection with public authorities. The report mentions for example that in 56% of the municipalities with a Hungarian national minority, citizens communicate with the local institutions in Hungarian. However, in municipalities with other national minorities, inquiries into

---

7   Act No. 270/1995 Coll., English version: https://www.scribd.com/document/19267068/Act-of-the-National-Council-of-the-Slovak-Republic-No-270-1995-Coll-on-the-state-language-of-the-Slovak-Republic. International legal framework for use of languages of national minorities is contained in the European Charter of Regional or Minority Languages, Framework Convention for the Protection of National Minorities.
8   https://www.narodnostnemensiny.gov.sk//pouzivanie-jazykov-narodnostnych-mensin/.
9   The full text of the translated legislation can be found at www.slov-lex.sk

communication in the language of the national minority are limited or do not appear at all.[10]

In our research, similar discrepancies in the use of minority languages were also noted in the number of translation and interpreting tasks carried out by the translators and interpreters registered by the Ministry of Justice in Slovakia between 2010 and 2014.[11] It pointed out that the extent of interpreting in the Hungarian language in the legal and institutional context is many times higher than the number of interpreting tasks in other languages. Figure 1 shows that from among the official national minority languages in Slovakia, Hungarian is the most frequent used language in the interpreting tasks, occurring more frequently than Russian, German and English.

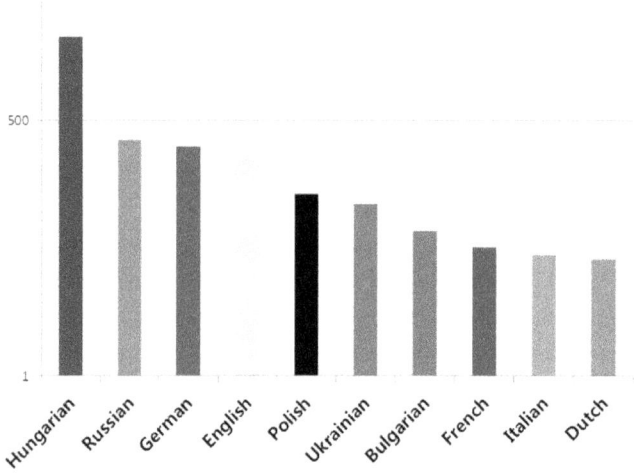

Figure 1. The ten most frequent languages regarding the number of interpreting tasks provided by interpreters registered by the Ministry of Justice in Slovakia in 2010 (Rakšányiová et al. 2015)

---

10   The English version of the report which includes results of a survey on the situation of the use of languages of national minorities on the level of territorial self-government authorities: https://www.narodnostnemensiny.gov.sk/data/files/5422_sprava_en.pdf.

11   As part of the research for the TRANSIUS scientific project ("From conventions to norms in the legal discourse", 2014–2017), we have carried out a thorough, practice-oriented analysis of public service translation and interpreting focusing among other things on the scope of translation and interpreting assignments for the individual languages, the number of translators per language, clients, use of translation processes, interpreting techniques, computer assisted translation tools, LL of translators and interpreters and the degree of standardization and conventionalization of the translation and interpreting process. (Project number: APVV-0226-12, https://fphil.uniba.sk/Transius).

Regarding the number of official translations and interpreting assignments, the situation with the Czech language is quite different. The reasons are the affinity between the Czech and Slovak languages, the traditionally positive relations between these linguistic communities, and the fact that translations of official documents from Czech to Slovak are not required, because the Slovak government institutions accept documents in Czech. Only in 2018 was the Roma language included in the list of languages in which translators or interpreters can be accredited by the Ministry of Justice.[12] To date, no registered interpreter or translator for this language has been registered on the list. An unofficial statement from the Ministry said that no state institution had reported a need for a certified interpreter in the Roma language. We assume that the demand for translation and interpreting services on the part of minorities has a direct impact on the provision of translation and interpreting services by the state, based on the fact that for the smallest minority language, Ruthenian, there is no actual possibility to be certified as a court translator and interpreter.

In addition to national minorities, public service interpreting and translation are provided in Slovakia to migrants, asylum seekers and refugees. The most notable groups of immigrants that arrived after World War II are the now already mostly integrated Vietnamese and Chinese communities, who were invited and settled in the era of socialism. The fact that the provision of translation services to these two language groups of migrants was and is underdeveloped is highlighted by the fact that there are only five certified interpreters for these languages registered at the Ministry of Justice.

Since Slovakia's accession to the EU, the number of labor migrants from EU Member States has grown due to the strong development of the automotive industry. An intensive migration of laborers has taken place from beyond the borders of the EU, mainly from Ukraine (more than 20%), Serbia, Russia, China and Korea.[13] The number of migrants with resident permits in Slovakia is 150,012 (2020). In 2020, Slovakia registered 1,295 irregular migrants and 282 asylum applications but only granted asylum to 11 persons.

---

12 See the list of languages in which the interpreters and translators can be accredited on: https://www.justice.gov.sk/Stranky/Nase-sluzby/Civilne-pravo/Tlmocnici-a-prekladatelia/Zoznam-tlmo%C4%8Dn%C3%ADckych-a-prekladate%C4%BEsk%C3%BDch-odborov-pod%C4%BEa-jazykov.aspx.
13 For concrete numbers of migrants in Slovakia, see: https://www.iom.sk/sk/migracia/migracia-na-slovensku.html.

The state institutions are not developing a systematic translation policy that could respond to the growing numbers of migrants. Slovakia has not yet developed an institutionalized and functioning model of PSIT that would be inclusive. The right to use their language only relates to these communities for communication in some legal settings such as criminal proceedings and, in the case of refugees, in asylum procedures. Compulsory language services are provided in schools to a limited extent, but PSIT in hospitals remains at a preliminary stage.

2.2 Certification and registration of translators and interpreters

Interpreting and translation services for foreign-speaking citizens in the Slovak Republic are officially provided by the State through interpreters and translators registered on the list of the Ministry of Justice. These translators and interpreters are registered under the current legislation after passing an exam organized by the Interpreting Institutes and the Ministry after meeting the administrative conditions prescribed by law.[14]

The register listing the current information about interpreters and translators is publicly accessible on the Ministry's web page.[15] The Register lists some 250 interpreters and 850 translators of thirty-six languages. In some countries of Central Europe, such as the Czech Republic, sworn translation and interpreting is united under one concept. However, in the Slovak Republic, interpreting and translation are separated. In practice, the professions of sworn interpreter and translator are complementary. Depending on the procedural circumstances, the interpreter is asked to provide, in addition to interpreting or translation, a written or oral summary of the source communication or to prepare an assessment report on the performance of a colleague.

As a result of previously mentioned labor migration, widening of business activities and development of cooperation, the demand for translation from and into languages such as Dutch, Chinese, Turkish, Finnish, Vietnamese, Hebrew, Japanese and other non-Central European languages is increasing. Market research concerning translation services in Central

---

14   The activities performed by interpreters and translators in Slovakia are regulated by Act No. 308/2007 Z.z. and its implementation regulations amended by Act No. 65/2018, Decree No. 490/2004 Z.z. regulating the performance of Act. No. 382/2004 Z.z. on expert witnesses, interpreters and translators and on amending certain laws, and Decree No. 491/2004 Z.z., on remuneration, compensation of expenses, and compensation for lost time of expert witnesses, interpreters and translators.
15   See: https://obcan.justice.sk/infosud-registre/-/isu-registre/zoznam/tlmocnik.

Europe, specifically in the Czech and Slovak Republics, has shown that the intensification of trade contacts and labor migration within the EU has led to the highest demand for translation and interpreting services, particularly in the field of institutional and legal interpreting. This tendency may not be reflected in the number of qualified translators and interpreters. There is only a very limited number of qualified interpreters and trained language specialists available on the market in this field. The lack of qualified sworn interpreters and translators has a direct impact on the actions of investigative bodies, the public prosecutor's office, the courts, social services, as well as on the quality of healthcare, where no translation or interpreting services are provided. This significantly complicates the working and living conditions of labor workers and migrants (Rakšányiová et al. 2015).

The lack of professional interpreters for the above-mentioned languages is also due to the fact that no educational institution in Slovakia offers specialized courses for legal or community interpreters, namely, for those who have not studied translation and interpreting but specialize in a different discipline and at the same time have a good knowledge of a foreign language. Interpreting for government bodies, such as courts, the police and the migration office, is carried out under specific conditions, which, apart from consecutive interpreting, require the use of other interpreting techniques. These include chuchotage, sight-reading, interpreting and summarizing the contents of a document, interpreting via a third language, videoconference interpreting and interpreting by telephone.

The special circumstances of interpreting for asylum seekers and migrants is given insufficient state attention.[16] Interpreters do not receive special training or guidance, and they often work ad hoc. Some governmental authorities provide interpreting within the framework of project cooperation with partner institutions abroad via videoconferences and in a third language. Existing legislation needs to be amended in order to meet the needs of the present situation in the public sector and to improve the quality of the performance of individual translators and interpreters. Moreover, there is a lack of lifelong education, insufficient supervision of the performance of translators and interpreters and a shortfall in the commissioning of translators and interpreters who are not listed in the register.

---

16   Relevant results from field research on interpreting in asylum procedures in Slovakia can be found in Tužinská (2011, 2017, 2020).

3 Quality of the services provided – observations from the asylum procedure

This study integrates analytical insights from anthropological and sociolinguistic studies on communication in legal settings (Wadensjö 1996; Pöllabauer 2004; Maryns 2006; Good 2007; Eades 2008; Gill and Good 2019). Research data come from first-hand participant observation of the asylum hearings at the Regional Court in Bratislava and from ethnographic interviews conducted in 2006–2008 and 2016–2019 with asylum applicants, their legal representatives, interpreters, as well as with decision makers from the Migration Office of the Ministry of Interior of the Slovak Republic.[17] The interviews were semi-structured, focusing on the context of communication, specifically on the role of interpreters in the asylum process. Standards of interpreting were observed in three main state entities dealing with asylum applicants: the foreign police, the migration office and the regional courts.

Regarding the complexity of problems with interpreting in the asylum field, we discuss the observed routines in three areas: (1) availability of interpreters, (2) the process of language identification, (3) communicating rights to asylum applicants.

3.1 Availability of interpreters

Institutions dealing with asylum applicants have a range of attitudes towards interpreting standards, dependent on their executive power and their role in the civil service. The lack of qualified interpreters in civic/legal proceedings and constraints resulting from this unavailability pose a double challenge: overcoming linguistic and cultural challenges are not given sufficient priority. All stakeholders are under pressure to accept "at least someone willing to arrive". This contributes to an applicant's vulnerability and increases his or her possible dependency on the interpreter.

---

17 This study also refers to data from interviews with legal representatives of asylum applicants from nongovernmental organizations in the Central European region in the project "Communication with Foreigners: Legal Implications of Interpreting. A Comparison of Practices in the V4 Countries (Poland, Hungary, Czech Republic and Slovakia) and the Ukraine" in 2010–2011. The project was initiated by the Human Rights League in association with the Polish Helsinki Foundation for Human Rights, the Hungarian Helsinki Committee, the Czech Organization for Aid to Refugees and the Ukrainian Caritas. The repeated semi-structured qualitative interviews were carried out individually and in focus groups during project meetings with legal representatives of each above-mentioned country and with sworn interpreters in Slovakia.

Although there is a publicly available list of court interpreters, passing the exams and paying the compulsory fees represent an additional administrative burden. The state entities are not required to exclusively contract court interpreters and may appoint an interpreter ad hoc. People having a command of rarely accessible languages in the region are on the internal lists of agencies, police, migration office and the courts. Employing interpreters who have not undergone professional training is generally highly problematic for comprehension. Pöllabauer explains how miscommunication also happens due to a lack of shared backgrounds and linguistic resources. Unequal sociocultural backgrounds and disparities in the educational level of the interactants represent a particular challenge: "Apparently 'simple' explanations do not always produce better understanding" (Pöllabauer 2004, 171).

In the case of asylum applicants, when first in contact with the police, interpreting might be conducted by one of the migrants from the group under scrutiny. In such circumstances, ad hoc interpreters, upon whom the applicants might be dependent later on, thereby gain access to the applicants' personal data. There are cases in which the interpreter belongs to the party from which the applicant has fled or is of a religious or political affiliation involved in the former persecution of the applicant. Some of the applicants reported that they minimalized their testimony out of fear of the consequences of revealing sensitive data. If the essential facts are distorted or omitted, the trustworthiness of applicants is later in doubt. Moreover, the asylum seekers fear that proceedings might be discontinued, or the application rejected, if they report dissatisfaction with the services of the state from which they seek refuge.

With regard to the location and time of the interviews (Tužinská 2020), limited numbers of interpreters are likely to be willing to come to police stations or detention centers on demand, at irregular times and to less accessible places. Therefore, it is not unusual for ad hoc interpreters to be only accessible via mobile phone. Even though for interviews in the migration office and for court hearings the time allocated for finding an interpreter is longer than at the state borders, it may not increase the chances for the appointment of a professional. As a police officer concludes:

> There is the question of whether he agrees to the interpreting of that, whether he fully understands it. Basically, that's about it, otherwise it could not be interpreted in any institution, because there are not so many interpreters with that stamp with the state emblem of the court interpreters so, unfortunately, we have to take such interpreters too, but that's a minor percentage. The ministry now has a contract with such an agency that provides these interpreting services, and they primarily contact only court interpreters.

Court interpreters, however, view this situation differently (Tužinská 2020): "The agency cuts down the prices and prefers those who cooperate with the ministry." Asylum applicants add: "Such interpreters are often in foreign police. Terrible friends with the cops, they have them on Facebook as friends, and now they bring the cakes to them. As soon as they arrive, they say Ciao!" The same might apply vice versa, when the interpreter arbitrarily speaks with the applicant during the proceedings and is unaware of the negative consequences. Simultaneously, "forging alliances with the officers, however, does not necessarily mean that they show uncooperative behavi[or] to the asylum-seekers" (Pöllabauer 2004, 175). However, the over-cooperative behavior with the state entity is an ambiguous signal to the applicant.

Our long-term observation is that objections of asylum applicants raised at appeal courts are usually of two types. Firstly, the interpreters might not fully understand what was said; secondly, the report could be incomplete or may contain inaccurate translations of particular statements. Over the course of time, the applicants claim to have discovered that the interpreters also expressed to the third party their personal attitudes, evaluating speech of applicants as insubstantial or incomprehensible (Tužinská 2020).

3.2 Process of language identification

Even if authorities declare that ensuring correct interpreting is the cornerstone of successful and fair communication, it does not correspond to what asylum applicants and their legal representatives report later on. If officials in the asylum applicants' presence communicate with the interpreter in the state language, that is, a language which the applicant does not know, they cast doubt upon their own impartiality; the same occurs when an interpreter communicates with applicants in the language of interpreting in the officials' presence. The following passage from an interview with a legal representative illustrates the point (Tužinská 2020). She was called to a detention center by a person who intended to apply for asylum.

> Imagine the interpreter as he interprets the instructions and the client just stares at me. Nothing. "Continue," the policeman tells him. Well, he goes on and then I say, "Maybe we could make sure he understands it." And then the interpreter asked in Urdu, and I did in English – he only shook his head, that he did not understand. And the policeman said, "Well, interesting! Before you came, he understood." I ask, "When before?" "Before you came, we were talking with him already."

The legal representative claimed that the applicant could speak Pashtu, "a little English" and perhaps "a little Urdu". She presupposed that for verification they asked him in Urdu something like: "Do you want to go to Bulgaria?" "Because that is where he came from and he does not want to go back to, he heard Bulgaria, so he said no. But as soon as he began to listen to some legal text, he did not understand." The applicants' willingness to cooperate under time constraints led police officers to believe that the legal representative was unnecessarily prolonging the procedure. Yet she had only refused to ignore the limits of linguistic competence.

Imprecision in interpreting is higher where the interpreters claim that the differences in dialects, sociolects and regiolects are not substantial. Often it is the case with so called 'neighboring' languages. For example, Afghan translators normally speak Farsi and Pashtun. Since only one of those languages is their mother tongue and they are unaware of minute differences, some specific expressions are incorrectly translated. Words might sound the same, but vary (and are sometimes opposite) in meaning. Inaccurate interpreting in cases where the interpreter had insufficient command of the language in which the interview was conducted, was justified by the officials as an unintended side-effect of unavailability of court interpreters. For the applicant, the above-mentioned 'approximate' translation may produce a mass of inaccuracies in the final evaluation of his or her testimony. This deficiency has been observed in several cases where ad hoc interpreters were used, though rarely where certified court interpreters were employed (Tužinská 2020).

On the other hand, to ease the process of finding an interpreter, applicants themselves declare that they understand and speak English, Russian or French. In most cases, it was at a basic or intermediate level and/or a dialect. The language identification was itself an investigation and not only at the beginning of the asylum procedure. *Interpreting* is an ever-present and complex matter that changes the *interpretation* of the case in the course of procedure.

As Maryns (2006), Berk-Seligson (2002) and Eades (2008) have pointed out, there is a need to be aware of language registers as a linguistic mechanism for identity construction. Communication depends not just on which language is used per se but also on which kind of language register the participants use. Linguistic means are powerful tools which contribute to the shaping of asylum seekers' narratives. If both interpreters and officials unknowingly added words such as "probably, perhaps, some", it signified uncertainty. They might also have concealed the subject, which, in some languages more than in others, changed the claim from the first to the third person. What also changed the impression were prosodic features such as rhythm, intonation or emphasis. These linguistic means contributed to what was actually transcribed in the final report. Thus, for some it represents a subtlety, for others it might become a constitutive element of an asylum applicant's identity construction. We argue that in the process of language identification, the above-mentioned language features are usually considered to be subliminal.

As many scholars have already noted, those in charge decontextualize what the asylum applicant said and recontextualize it in their own words, within their own expert discourse (Berg-Seligson 2002; Maryns 2006; Eades 2008; Gibb and Good 2014; Gill and Good 2019 and others). In a similar vein, Spotti argues that there is a need to "shift the analysis here from differences between 'languages' to differences within languages, for example, 'ways of speaking', 'ways of narrating', and 'ways of naming things'." Register is connected with issues of belonging as well as expectations of how things should be narrated and named (Spotti 2019, 85). It is not only an "appropriate" register that is expected of asylum applicants. The use of 'legalese' on the side of the state also brings challenges for the interpreting process.

3.3 Communicating rights to asylum applicants

The asylum seeker enters an already established communication hegemony (Briggs 1984). In this sense, the language for institutions is constitutive, that is, the means by which the institution forms a coherent social reality (Vrábľová 2018). The institution justifies its interventions which obstruct narration and also obstruct qualified interpreting by rushed conduct of the interview, by posing closed questions and by frequently interrupting replies. The interpreter may not follow professional standards, and ignorance of professional terminology disadvantages the asylum seeker (Štefková 2013; Guldanová 2013, 2014; Lipovec Čebron-Pistotnik 2018; Petrovic 2018). Attitudes are diverse among all parties to the extent in which it is necessary to explain and understand the official procedure. This circumstance includes verifying whether both parties mean and understand the same thing when using "common" legal or cultural terms (more in Tužinská 2019).

The state conducts legal processes at the police station, at the migration office and in the courtroom with authoritative certainty. Yet, on the whole, asylum seekers view this lengthy process under time constraints as full of uncertainties. At the end of the minutes the sentenced person declares: "That's all I want to say to that matter, everything I have said is true, I have not silently concealed anything. During my testimony, no physical or psychological pressure was imposed on me by the police, I voluntarily denounced it. I do agree with the contents of the minutes, I do not wish to change or add anything."

Our ethnographic case studies confirmed rather the opposite: the interviewed asylum seekers did not say all they intended, they might have concealed some information out of fear or for other reasons, they reported being put under pressure, and the minutes might not be fully translated (Tužinská 2020).

Firstly, we inquired as to how the knowledge of the official procedures is constructed. When we asked a police officer to what extent she was concerned about verification of what asylum applicants understand from the procedure, she replied: "No one will ever explain even to an ordinary person the law exactly when we go into such details. I have always been taught that ignorance of the law does not justify (e.g., my mistake) and it did not justify me either."

Applicants themselves mentioned several areas of possible misinterpreting in the course of justification of their claims. In general, before anyone tells them in detail the procedural sequence and before they have a legal representative, they expect the officials to clarify their responsibilities. A legal representative spoke about a situation in which she observed a client being put under pressure to sign a declaration in a detention center (Tužinská 2020):

> They (asylum applicants) are told only that they just need to sign something. Many times we simply ask: why did you sign it? You did not understand it, and it's the most relevant thing, why did you sign it? Because they thought they had to. And I already understand it now when I saw one of the situations: imagine a relatively high-ranking cop, a strong young guy who's behind that computer… next to the poor boy sitting there with his head down, not understanding a single word from a poor interpreter.

In general, at the beginning of proceedings, asylum applicants are not informed of all their rights and responsibilities, or of the course of the interview, or of the possibilities for further official action. In most cases, the police report on the reasons for submitting an asylum application is abbreviated as the police do not inform applicants how detailed their report should be or what type of facts it should contain. When asked in the courts why asylum seekers did not state some facts earlier, they would say the instruction was: "Speak briefly!" Also, the interpreter personally encourages the applicant to condense his or her statements. However, further explanation of incompletely expressed opinions is often interpreted by officials as a deceitful or contradictory statement.

By not explaining the entire course of the proceedings to the applicant, the interviewer makes more interventions, which ultimately obstruct not only narration but also qualified interpreting. Despite these questions, interpreters are aware that their mere presence slows down the process, as in a judge's remark towards a lawyer: "Bear in mind, we have an interpreter!" The state representatives summarize decisions, in some cases with an interpreter; complete decisions are given to the applicants in written form, in the state language, Slovak.

Secondly, when it comes to legal terminology, actors in the migration field expressed a variety of restrictions. Ad hoc interpreters usually have limited command of legal vocabulary. For example, the interpreter sometimes translates inaccurately that applicants are going to be placed in a *reception* camp, when in fact they might be ultimately placed in a *detention* camp. Asylum applicants explicate this finding as a consequence of interpreters siding with the state as well as a means of protocolar swiftness. The migration office and courts rely on legal representatives as sufficient substitute for interpreters' incompetence in legal terminology. Some of the officials remarked that asylum applicants (a) would not actually understand the legal terminology and/or (b) leave the country as soon as possible anyway. More fundamental misunderstandings happen if the person who conducts the interview does not explain the term 'persecution' or poses the question regarding persecution verbatim. Applicants might not be conversant with the intentional meaning as stated in the Geneva Convention.

Fluency in the use of legal terminology in the field of migration is a matter of individual responsibility for each interpreter. However, with regard to their support, there are no publicly provided, specialized courses provided in this area. A policeman's stance towards precision of interpreting is succinctly described in his question to a legal representative (Tužinská 2020):

> Well, do you think it is necessary to interpret every page? When it is just a legal text? He will not understand anyway. Perhaps not even the interpreter would be able to do it, all those legal terms. Or do you think that everything needs to be interpreted? When he has a legal representative? You will explain it, so why shall we interpret it all?

At the same time, legal representatives may refrain from demanding a signature from an uninformed applicant on the spot. They usually consider interpreting of particular legal steps in plain language. However, police representatives are convinced that the selection of interpreters and the quality of their services are secured appropriately (Tužinská 2020):

> We do appoint those who do not have the stamp, but they are from that country. The people are fully integrated here. We already have such people basically in every language, so we appoint them and we see if the man nods and he confirms this with his signature in the minutes, he confirms each side of the minutes.

The accuracy of the decision is intertwined with the accuracy of the interpreting. If the applicant states that he or she did not say what is written in the report, there is no proof of any shift in meanings. Discrepancies may serve as proof of the asylum applicants' untrustworthiness in further proceedings. Unqualified interpreting can lead to misinterpreting in the official proceedings and subsequently impact the final decision.

At the court hearing, after the judge reads her statement, she usually asks a closed question: "Did you understand?" The asylum applicant nods and the judge puts into the record: "Reasoning understood." At the end of a hearing when the judge says: "It is cancelled", the interpreter either remains silent or turns his head towards the legal representative with a question "It's good?" and gets an answer after the hearing in the corridor of the court.

The interpreter's linguistic competence, including legal terminology, is verifiable on the spot only to a certain extent, and generally it is less probable that the asylum applicant will express discontent with the interpreting immediately during the proceedings, because the objection would have to be translated by the interpreter concerned. Applicants also hesitate to object to the state service, as it is the same entity they ask for protection. However, the quality of interpreting is conditioned by the interpreters' independence on or interdependence with the respective state institution. Balancing this power asymmetry requires awareness of its existence: "Although interpreters often lack institutional power, they may be equipped with power within the exchange as a result of their bilingual and bicultural expertise. They may exercise this power by adopting various verbal and non-verbal strategies to negotiate, coordinate, check and balance power relations" (Angelelli 2014, 5).

The stance of the state towards interpreting indicates how much symbolic space is given for communication with applicants. Similarly, in the following example, a legal representative reported on the police officer's stance towards her and the interpreters' presence in the interview (Tužinská 2020):

> "It would take a long time." Even now, when the cop has asked me, "Will you go on a lot? Let us not prolong it." You know, then it does not run so smoothly, according to them. I understand that they have a lot of work, they are under pressure with such a turnover, wishing to be finished as fast as possible. Especially when they know nothing will change their decision. "Whatever you say into the minutes, we will write it down, but it will not have any influence on our decision." She told me this straight in the beginning. (laughter) She also said they have a command from above not to let them go.

The restrictive attitudes of some political representatives in Slovakia and their presence in the media would require additional site-specific research.

4 Conclusion and recommendations

The description of the Slovak context shows that regulation in the field of institutional interpreting does not always follow current developments in migration and the diversified needs of the target groups. In many cases it is non-systematic, non-standardized, correlated with the political representation of specific minorities, stemming from the unwillingness of the political elites to provide the service in particular contexts and in sectors with no immediate profit. Based on the aforementioned observation, we pointed out some crucial aspects of institutional translation and interpreting in Slovakia that deserve further attention:

- Slovakia lacks **accredited, specialized institutional training for institutional translators and interpreters**, particularly in combinations of languages with limited diffusion; this is especially true for languages not sufficiently represented in our region. The existing courses for court interpreters and translators are focused on the knowledge of some partial areas of the legal system – the contents of the law regulating the translation and interpreting service for the state authorities. Interpreters and translators are relatively isolated in their work and are dependent on self-education.[18]
- Slovakia also lacks an **institutional framework** that would distinguish the performance of court interpreters and translators from the medical, social and educational domains. Specific attention should be paid to translation and interpreting services in asylum procedures. Such a framework could assure a standardized procedure of certification and evaluation of translators and interpreters in line with the aforementioned educational framework. This framework would offer an effective organizational structure to ensure the provision of translation and interpreting services where needed.[19]

---

[18] The first steps towards the education of institutional translators and interpreters in combinations of less common languages have been taken within the Erasmus+ project PACI (Professional, Accessible Community Interpreting). This project aims to create a generally applicable model of language-neutral intensive training of high-quality skills in the field of community interpreting and translation. (Project number: 2017-1-SK01-KA203-035412, https://www.kgns.info/paci.)

[19] Inspiration for the development of such a structure is provided by the Belgian model, see Štefková and Bossaert (2019) and Bossaert (2020).

- A **code of ethics for non-sworn interpreters** does not yet exist in Slovakia. Even though United Nations High Commissioner for Refugees has a specific code of ethics for translators and has organized training courses for interpreters in asylum proceedings, the interpreter sometimes does not know and does not adhere to the fundamental standards of interpreting. In practice, there is no established mechanism for inspecting and maintaining the level of interpreting and enabling disciplinary action in cases of breaches of the code of ethics, with criminal proceedings to be initiated in those cases where there is suspicion that a criminal offense has been committed.[20] "Interpreters are active participants in the often multilingual and intercultural exchanges that take place in asylum interviews and appeal hearings, although the mechanistic views of interpreting and ideas about the 'invisibility' of the interpreter that are sometimes found in these legal and administrative contexts can obscure this fact" (Gibb and Good 2014, 396). Dahlvik suggests a means to overcome the issues of remaining neutral yet professional: "Professionalism and professional ethics may require the right intervention at the right time: Sometimes it would simply be unprofessional or unethical for an interpreter not to intervene" (Dahlvik 2019, 150). Interpreters are active agents rather than passive transmitters of utterances from one language into another. Thus, it is crucial "to focus more on professionalism and ethics in community interpreting, especially in the context of international protection" (Dahlvik 2019, 134).
- We see another significant opportunity for **the development of professional standards** for translators and interpreters as well as defining their rights and position with respect to government agencies and other parties ordering translations or interpreting. The practice reveals the fact that ordering institutions often have no idea of the tasks of the translator and interpreter, do not know what they may require and are unable to assess the time needed to produce the translation, or the place of an interpreter in a specific setting. In line with Hertog (2010), we recommend that legal professionals should be trained in how communication operates across diverse languages and cultures. They should be offered training on working with interpreters in order to recognize when an interpreter is needed and to select a suitable interpreter from the approved register. Legal professionals also need to be aware of their requirement to brief

---

20 In the Slovak Republic according to § 347 of the Criminal Law "Untruthful expert opinion, interpreting and translation" or § 328 of the Criminal Law under such headings as "Corruption" and "Acceptance of bribes".

the interpreter, to recognize and respect their role and skills and their code of conduct and to facilitate relevant interpreting techniques, like consecutive or whispered simultaneous.
- Institutional translation and interpreting require **management of quality control** of the performance of the individual translator and interpreters active in the different domains and language combinations. Initiating specialized professional preparation is, in our view, the first step towards fixing these criteria and providing a system of quality evaluation, which can consequently be used in practice. We suggest standardizing methods and criteria for the evaluation of interpreters' performance at the national level in Slovakia or adopting a functioning model with appropriate modifications. The quality criteria must be documented with a material back-up, so as to make the interpreter's work recognizable as well as well-managed, systematic and purposeful.
- **A higher awareness of the context of communication,** starting before the interpreting itself, is needed. It entails the verification of the understanding between the participants of the communication, the knowledge of their institutional background and the overall setting of the interaction. Asylum applicants report the need to introduce all actors and their functions and to explain the purpose of the particularities in communication. Government representatives, on the other hand, expect either that applicants know the causes and circumstances of the communication already or that it will be explained by a legal representative. We need to develop criteria by which state administration might ascertain the asylum applicants' knowledge of languages and the interpreter's knowledge of languages. Additionally, people in charge need to pay sufficient attention to verifying that asylum applicants have understood their rights and are making an informed consent. Each right should be presented individually, with sufficient time for follow-up questions. Our research findings are in line with those of Maryns that there are "hidden asymmetries in the ability to decide what counts as reality. (…) The data have shown that what applicants say during their interviews is very often not made into a *sayable* because it does not match the institutionally inscribed codes, modes and views" (Maryns 2006, 342).
- In the case of translations which contain **expert terminology** (mainly of a legal or medical nature), there is a dual problem: (1) the interpreter must understand the expert and at the same time (2) adjust the information to the participant's language register. If interpreters communicate with applicants from a different educational background and detect possible misunderstanding, they may invite the participants to reformulate the

questions or provide additional explanation. In legal settings, there is a need to use standardized justifications in plain and clear language with frequently used words, short sentences with single clauses and in the active voice that clearly indicates the agent of the action. Such justifications should be drawn up in consultation with police officers, legal representatives and experts in linguistics. They must also be available in the state language as well as in the other most frequently used languages. We also recommend the adoption of the Guidelines established for the communication of rights to non-native speakers of European state languages (Guidelines 2015).[21]
- Issues of **cross-cultural communication** include generating and implementing respect among participants. The quest for more respectful communication is also widely reported by Slovak citizens themselves in communicating with representatives of state institutions. Both historical and new minorities in Slovakia experience the ethnicized interpreting of their accounts. Dialogic communication in power asymmetry is thus a professional challenge for both government officials and interpreters. To overcome the social and cultural bias "we recommend the adoption of an in-your-own words requirement" (Guidelines 2015). Where this fundamental focus is omitted "the denial of its inter-lingual as well as intra-lingual complexity is a source of rather fundamental, though often invisible, injustice" (Spotti 2019, 88).

Our report on the situation in Slovakia shows that the provision of language services to non-native speakers and the degree of institutionalization are closely linked to the position of the target groups of institutional translation and interpreting in society; these services are also connected to the tradition of certification and training of translators and interpreters, as well as the interest of public institutions in the quality of language services. A systematic approach at supranational level, cooperation with NGOs and educational institutions, sharing experience, knowledge and ethical principles, and practical approaches can make a major contribution to all countries concerned. It could even help to identify and implement measures to ensure effective models for providing institutional translation and interpreting with a view to quality, solidarity and safeguarding human rights.

---

21 https://www.aaal.org/guidelines-for-communication-rights.

Acknowledgement

This text is an output within the grant project *Moral narratives about religious and ethnic groups in teaching selected subjects at junior schools* 1/0194/20 and the Erasmus+ project PACI – *Professional and Accessible Community Interpreting – a Gateway to Migrant´s Integration*, project number: 2017-1-SK01-KA203-035412.

References

Angelelli, Claudia V. 2014. *The Sociological Turn in Translation and Interpreting Studies*. Amsterdam: John Benjamins.

Berg-Seligson, Susan. 2002. *The Bilingual Courtroom: Court Interpreters in Judicial Process*. Chicago: The University of Chicago Press.

Bossaert, Benjamin, 2020. "Institucionalizace a profesionalizace komunitního tlumočení ve Vlámsku." In *Komunitní tlumočení v České republice a v nizozemsky hovořících zemích*, edited by P. Knap-Dlouhá, B. Bossaert, D. Macáková and K. Pajerová, 130–132. Olomouc: UPOL.

Briggs, Charles. 1984. *Learning how to Ask: A Sociolinguistic Appraisal of the Role of the Interview in Social Science Research*. Cambridge: Cambridge University Press.

D'hulst, Lieven, Carol O'Sullivan, and Michael Schreiber. 2016. *Politics, Policy and Power in Translation History*. Berlin: Frank & Timme.

Eades, Diana. 2008. *Courtroom Talk and Neocolonial Control*. New York: Mouton de Gruyter.

Gibb, Robert, and Anthony Good. 2014. "Interpreting, Translation and Intercultural Communication in Refugee Status Determination Procedures in the UK and France." *Language and Intercultural Communication* 14: 385–399.

Gill, Nick, and Anthony Good, eds. 2019. *Asylum Determination in Europe: Ethnographic Perspectives*. Bristol: Palgrave Macmillan.

Good, Anthony. 2007. *Anthropology and Expertise in the Asylum Courts*. London: Routledge Cavendish.

Guldanová, Zuzana. 2013. "Problém preložiteľnosti/nepreložiteľnosti v kontexte súdneho tlmočenia/prekladu." In *Kontexty súdneho prekladu a tlmočenia II.*, edited by Zuzana Guldanová, 51–60. Bratislava: Univerzita Komenského.

———. 2014. "Niekoľko pohľadov na činnosť súdneho tlmočníka/prekladateľa zo súdnej praxe." In *Kontexty súdneho prekladu a tlmočenia III.*, edited by Zuzana Guldanová, 50–67. Bratislava: Univerzita Komenského.

Hale, Sandra. 2004. *The Discourse of Court Interpreting*. Amsterdam: John Benjamins.

———. 2007. *Community Interpreting*. Basingstoke: Palgrave Macmillan.

Hertog, Erik, and Bart van der Veer. 2006. "Taking Stock: Research and Methodology in Community Interpreting." *Linguistica Antverpiensia, New Series – Themes in Translation Studies* 5: 11-17.

Hertog, Erik. 2010. "Community Interpreting." In *Handbook of Translation Studies*, vol. 1, edited by Yves Gambier and Luc van Doorslaer, 49–54. Amsterdam: John Benjamins.

Kadrić, Mira. 2008. *Dolmetschen bei Gericht: Erwartungen – Anforderungen – Kompetenzen*. Viedeň: WUV.

Kainz, Claudia, Erich Prunč, and Rafael Schögler, eds. 2011. *Modelling the Field of Community Interpreting. Questions of Methodology in Research and Training*. Berlin: LIT Verlag.

Koskinen, Kaisa. 2014. "Institutional Translation: The Art of Government by Translation." *Perspectives* 22 (4): 479–492. https://doi.org/10.1080/0907676X.2014.948887.

Lipovec Čebron, Uršula, and Sandra Pistotnik. 2018. "(Im)mobile Populations and Health Rights: Accessing the Healthcare System in Slovenia." In *Healthcare in Motion: Immobilities in Health Service Delivery and Access*. Worlds in Motion, vol. 5., edited by Cecilia Vindrola-Padros, Ginger A. Johnson and Anne E. Pfister, 53–71. Oxford: Berghahn Books.

Maryns, Katrijn. 2006. *The Asylum Speaker: Language in the Belgian Asylum Procedure*. Manchester: St. Jerome.

Meylaerts, Reine. 2011. "Translation Policy." In *Handbook of Translation Studies*, vol. 2, edited by Yves Gambier and Luc van Doorslaer, 163–168. Amsterdam: John Benjamins.

Mikkelson, Holly. 2000. *Introduction to Court Interpreting*. Manchester: St. Jerome.

Pöllabauer, Sonja. 2004. "Interpreting in Asylum Hearings: Issues of Role, Responsibility and Power." *Interpreting* 6 (2): 143–180.

———. 2005. *"I Don´t Understand Your English, Miss." Dolmetschen bei Asylantenhörungen*. Tübingen: Günter Narr.

Rakšányiová, Jana, et al. 2017. *Quo Vadis Rechtsübersetzung?* Univerzita Komenského V Bratislave.

Spotti, Max. 2019. ""It´s All About Naming Things Right": the Paradox of Web Truths in the Belgian Asylum–Seeking Procedure." In *Asylum Determination in Europe: Ethnographic Perspectives*, edited by Nick Gill and Anthony Good, 69–90. London: Palgrave Macmillan.

Štefková, Marketa. 2013. *Právny text v preklade: Translatologické aspekty právnej komunikácie v kombináciách málo rozšírených jazykov*. Bratislava: Iura Edition.

———, and Benjamin Bossaert. 2019. "Equity, Quality and Vision Comparative Analysis of the Practices of Public Service Translation and Interpreting in Slovakia and Flanders." *FITISPOS* 6 (1): 168–182.

Tužinská, Helena. 2011. *Questions of Description and Translation: Using Data from Anthropology and Ethnology in the Conduct and Interpreting of Interviews with Immigrants*. Bratislava: Stimul.

——— et al. 2017. "Anthropology as Necessary Unlearning: Examples from Camps, Courts, Schools and Businesses." *Etnološka tribina* 40 (47): 3–42.

———. 2019. "Doing Things with Questions: Interpreting in Asylum Settings." *Lud* 103: 81–99.

———. 2020. *Medzi riadkami. Etnografia tlmočenia azylových súdnych pojednávaní*. Bratislava: Akamedia.

Vrábľová, Júlia. 2018. "Specifics of Institutional Management of the National Language in Slovakia." In *National Language Institutions and National Languages: Contributions to the EFNIL Conference 2017 in Mannheim*, 85–99. Budapest: Research Institute for Linguistics, Hungarian Academy of Sciences.

Wadensjö Cecilia. 1996. *Interpreting as Interaction*. London: Longman.

Flawless in translation?

Legal translations in the Flemish legal professional press (1889–1935)

Sebastiaan Vandenbogaerde

Abstract

At the end of the nineteenth century, lawyers took the lead within the Flemish Movement (*Vlaamse Beweging*) and relentlessly strove for the equal use of both French and Dutch as official legal languages in Belgium. However, Dutch – actually Flemish – was deemed incoherent and hence unsuitable as a legal jargon. Aware of this setback, *flamingant*[1] lawyers aspired to develop a legal 'Flemish' which would serve the needs of legal professionals. Through legal periodicals, these lawyers advocated a specific view on how French legal sources could and should be translated. In addition, they offered legal professionals the tools to adopt Flemish as a language in court. This contribution scrutinizes the actors of a handful of legal professional journals between 1889 and World War II, an era in which the so-called linguistic struggle soared. Even if the 1935 Act on Use of Languages in Court legally eased the linguistic tensions, editors and authors remained vigilant and kept offering translations for legal professionals. In this way, these lawyers positioned themselves at the front of Belgium's linguistic issue as gatekeepers for legal changes in administration, education and the judiciary.

1 Introduction

In 1899, the *Rechtskundig Tijdschrift voor Vlaamsch-België* (Legal Journal for Flemish Belgium) boldly opened with its infamous slogan "In Vlaanderen, Vlaamsch!" ("In Flanders, Flemish!"). Influential lawyers sympathized with the linguistic objectives of the review, even though it was not regarded as authoritative source for legal practice and scholarship (Vandenbogaerde 2018, 184). In 1909, the *Rechtskundig Tijdschrift* announced its new stance.

---

1 The word *flamingant* refers to all activists of the Flemish Movement. The term does not necessarily mean that they are Flemish-speaking or that they want to have an independent Flanders.

The editors desired no longer "een "vlaamsch" Tijdschrift te hebben, maar [...] betrachten vooral, een "degelijk" Rechtskundig Tijdschrift in België te verspreiden, dat kan opwegen tegen de beste Tijdschriften uit andere landen" ("to have a "Flemish" periodical, but [...] above all to circulate a solid legal journal able to compete with the best journals in other countries") (De Redactie 1909, 1–2). Although that year the 'Law of Equality' (*Gelijkheidswet*)[2] – having formally put French and Flemish on the same legal footing – had also celebrated its tenth anniversary, Flemish was still not common in Belgium's legal world. Judges and other members of the elite still considered it unsuitable as a legal language, as had been the case on the eve of that legislation (Y. 1897, 129–30; Vandenbogaerde 2018, 195).

In this debate, Flemish legal periodicals advocated otherwise and adopted a specific view on how French legal sources could and should be translated. In addition, they offered legal professionals the tools to adopt Flemish as a language in court. Until now, the visions and strategies these titles adopted on and for translating a mainly French world to Flemish have remained uninvestigated.

For decades, the social sciences have embraced the professional periodical press as a valuable object of study. Online access and computer technology have facilitated the analysis of titles all over the world and boosted the potential of periodical studies to unseen levels. The rise of periodical studies offers unique insights in the development of academic disciplines and the organization of different professional groups (Latham and Scholes 2006; Tesnière 2014a, 2014b; Velle 1985–1988; 1994; Vandenbogaerde 2018). The periodical press is a perfect means of communication between different actors (editors, authors, publishers and readership) in which they can share their views on societal issues. As a 'vector' or a carrier of information, journals are able influencers and inherently shape a (professional) group (Vandenbogaerde 2018, 413).

This contribution scrutinizes a handful of legal titles published in Flemish before World War II and spans the period from 1889, when the first reviews saw their publication, to 1935, when the adoption of the Act on Use of Languages in Court[3] at least legally eased the linguistic tensions. In this period of time, journals adopted their views on the translation of French legal texts and the development of a Flemish variant usable for lawyers. Hence, the editors offered translations for legal professionals to use in their practice. Lawyers positioned themselves at the forefront of Belgium's linguistic issue and demanded legal

---

2   *Wet betreffende het gebruik der Vlaamsche taal in de officiëele bekendmakingen* (Act concerning the use of the Flemish language in official announcements) of 18 April 1898, *Belgisch Staatsblad* 15 May 1898.
3   *Wet op het gebruik der talen in gerechtszaken* of 15 June 1935.

changes to secure Flemish language rights in administration, education and the judiciary. Among those lawyers, some harbored strong views on how a francophone professional group should revert to Flemish in courtrooms in Flanders. This chapter will focus on the translation actors of the periodicals: who were the editors, authors and publishers? How did they tackle the linguistic issue and more particularly the translation problems that came with it? What role did they assign to the periodicals? The answers will reveal the networks of authors and their views on the linguistic issue.

2 A cultural issue becomes a legal one

On the evening of 25 August 1830, riots erupted in the streets of Brussels against the Dutch King William I. The turmoil led to the secession of Belgium from the United Kingdom of the Netherlands, and the new country's Provisional Government (*Gouvernement provisoire/Voorlopig Bewind*), composed of a group of notables, promptly declared Belgium's independence.

Since Belgium united both francophone and Flemish-speaking people, the 1831 Constitution proclaimed in principle the free use of both languages.[4] However, the government adhered to the one-country-one-language principle that almost each nation-state throughout history had adopted. Moreover, it would show Belgium to be a true nation that merited its independence (Witte 2005, 196). French was a logical choice: it was the leading cultural language in the world, and the Belgian elite was educated in Molière's tongue. Therefore, it was selected as the sole official language in administration, higher education and the judiciary. To accommodate the Flemish population the government provided translations in Flemish of the legislative norms, but it was the French version that mattered in courtrooms (Gubin and Nandrin 2005, 408).

During the 1840s, the first petitions for the use of Flemish in public offices were filed, and the Flemish Movement (*Vlaamse Beweging*) took an active part in it. In this initially cultural movement, jurists took an early lead. One of them was Charles Louis Ledeganck (1805–1847), the justice of the peace (*juge de paix/vrederechter*) who translated the Napoleonic Civil Code from French in 1841 (Deprez 1998, 1810–1811; De Smedt 1997, 227–243). His initiative caused a stir in the francophone legal community, but he sold over

---

4 "L'emploi des langues usitées en Belgique est facultatif ; il ne peut être réglé que par la loi, et seulement pour les actes de l'autorité publique et pour les affaires judiciaires" ("The use of languages spoken in Belgium is optional: it can only by regulated by law, and only for acts of the public authorities and for judicial affairs"), Article 23, 1831 Belgian Constitution.

3,000 copies, a huge success at that time which illustrated the need for useful translations (Hoste 1859, v–vi).

Official legal documents such as laws and decrees were translated and published in official government journals and collections, but the overall quality of these translations was questionable. Together with the alleged impossibility to achieve a uniform Flemish legal terminology, the poor quality of State translations gave officials the ammunition to deem the language inferior to French. The lack of legal literature in Dutch and an abundance in French only compounded this problem (Dopp 1932). Some sensational court cases during the 1860s and 1870s resulted in great dissatisfaction among the pro-Flemish lawyers who urged for a legally imbedded linguistic equality (Victor 1935; Wils 1977; Van Goethem 1985, 1990; Gevers et al. 1998).[5] In the wake of this agitation, two legal monthlies were established in 1889: *Het Vlaamsch Bestuur* (The Flemish Administration) and the *Bestuurlijk Tijdschrift voor Vlaamsch-België* (Administrative Journal for Flemish Belgium).

3 Administrative law leads the way

The timing of these publications made perfect sense. At the end of 1888, Belgian members of Parliament had filed an amendment to the 1873 Act on the Use of Languages in Criminal Proceedings.[6] It followed the tenth anniversary of the 1878 Act on the Use of Languages Within the Administration.[7] Furthermore, secondary schools in Flanders had been legally obliged to educate students in Flemish since 1883.[8] These legislative operations generated law books written or translated in Flemish (see Martyn 2005), a

---

5   The most renowned case was the one of Coucke and Goethals. These two Flemish men were tried in French and sentenced to death for murder. They became the symbol of a people oppressed by an elite, since they allegedly did not understand a word of what was said in court.

6   From that moment on, incriminated Flemish civilians were supposed to be addressed in Dutch during their trial. The Act was fine-tuned on 3 May 1889 and 4 September 1891, when the Courts of Appeal in Brussels and Liège had to rule in Flemish if a Flemish was involved in any penal case concerning Flemish persons; *Loi étendant aux cours d'appel de Bruxelles et de Liège la loi du 3 mai 1889 sur l'usage de la langue flamande en matière répressive, et modifiant la loi d'organisation judiciaire et la loi sur les circonstances atténuantes*, Pasinomie 1891, 384–391.

7   *Loi sur l'emploi des langues en matières administratives* (Act on the Use of Languages in Administrative Matters) of 22 May 1878, Pasinomie 1878, 173–177.

8   *Loi réglant l'emploi de la langue flamande pour l'enseignement moyen dans la partie flamande du pays* (Act on the Use of Flemish in Secondary School in the Flemish Part of the Country) of 15 June 1883, Pasinomie 1883, 146–151. Since secondary education was conducted in Flemish, there was an urgent need for manuals written in Dutch. It prepared future generations of Dutch-speaking children for a career in administration.

revolution enhanced by the first (non-compulsory)[9] courses in Flemish of criminal law and criminal procedure at the universities of Louvain (1888) (Victor 1935, 45), Liège, Ghent (1890) and Brussels (1891) (De Pauw 1973, 345; Vandersteene 2009, 113).

In this time frame, the Catholic Limburg attorney-at-law and politician Adrien De Corswarem (1849–1909) (Roppe and Boudrez 1998, 804–805) initiated *Het Vlaamsch Bestuur,* while the Catholic civil servant Karel Brants (1856–1934) (*Rechtskundig Weekblad* 1933–1934, 548; De Redactie 1934, 219–220; *Tijdschrift der Gemeentebesturen* 1934, 89–90; Hardy and van Clemen 1998, 594–595) established the *Bestuurlijk Tijdschrift voor Vlaamsch-België.* Both periodicals focused on administrative law, which might have been the best developed legal branch at that time. After independence, Belgium's legislators hastened the institutional development of the country, in which the administration took a central position (*Het Vlaamsch Bestuur* 1889–1890, 222). Due to their office, most civil servants in Flanders were perfectly bilingual since they acted as intermediary between the Dutch-speaking population and the francophone central government (Dujardin et al. 2006, 396–397). The 1878 Act regulated languages in the national administration, and the editors-in-chief sensed a profound need for publications in support of civil servants in Flanders (Vandenbogaerde 2018, 170–172).[10]

Similarities put aside, both monthlies differed conceptually and ideologically from one another. *Het Vlaamsch Bestuur* dealt dispassionately with topics for all kinds of administrative institutions such as municipalities, churches and poor houses. It discussed legislation, decrees and the most noteworthy judgments in administrative law. Additionally, De Corswarem reviewed in a bibliographic section books regardless of the language they were written in. Furthermore, he answered practical questions about administrative law in a Q&A section (De Corswarem 1893). The politician regularly used the francophone *Revue de l'administration* (Administration Journal) as a source and translated its content. De Corswarem's efforts proved to be lucrative, since the number of subscriptions rose quite rapidly (*Het Vlaamsch Bestuur* 1889–1890b). Presumably, local civil servants in Flanders enthusiastically

---

9   Article 49, *Loi sur la collation des grades académiques et le programme des examens universitaires* (Act on Awarding Academic Grades and University Examination Program) of 10 April 1890 stipulated no one in Flanders could be appointed as a magistrate without knowledge of the Flemish language.

10 From then on, messages from civil servants to the public in Flanders had to be either in Dutch or bilingual. In their correspondence with local authorities or individuals, they had to use Dutch in principle, unless the addressee wished otherwise.

subscribed to this title published by one man who supported all Flemish initiatives (*Het Vlaamsch Bestuur* 1898, 32).

The *Bestuurlijk Tijdschrift voor Vlaamsch-België* took a more combative stand and opened with the line "In Vlaanderen, Vlaamsch!" The journal stated that it aimed to remain above all politics and to refrain from "valorizing the legislation and decrees mentioned". This title launched Karel Brants's career at the forefront of the Flemish Movement. He found a *compagnon de route* in his colleague, the secretary of the city of Lier, Aloïs Broëll (1831–1898)[11] and the Louvain attorney Hendrik Veltkamp (1857–1933) (Brants 1898, 285–286). As 'experience experts' they knew how civil servants in Flanders struggled with the use of both languages in Belgium and encouraged local representatives and civil servants to subscribe. The *Bestuurlijk Tijdschrift* did not explicitly ask for a complete 'flemification' of the government; rather, it intended to be a practical instrument for civil servants. The periodical embedded itself in administrative circles, and pretty soon it became the mouthpiece for the Flemish Association for Town Clerks. In this professional category, most executives had studied law. Hence, the *Bestuurlijk Tijdschrift* discussed administrative law in all its aspects, such as the military, elections, organization of schools and the like. In addition, it also translated and discussed legislation and relevant case law (see, for example, *Bestuurlijk Tijdschrift* 1889b, 207–210).

The very first article of this periodical sketched the history of how Belgium's municipalities were organized. The anonymous author, presumably Brants himself, seized the opportunity to heavily criticize the disproportionately large French influence on Belgian administrative law (*Bestuurlijk Tijdschrift* 1889a, 1–2). The author argued that despite genuine Belgian municipal law (1836) public civil servants and magistrates still looked to France when confronted with a legal problem. This situation was a vestige from when the Southern Netherlands were annexed as the *départements réunis* by France between 1795 and 1815. Brants reinforced his point by referring to the time before the French dominated 'ancient Flanders' with its *châtellenies* and decentralized administration.[12] To his way of thinking, Belgium's administrative organization imposed by Brussels was uncharacteristic for the Flemish *Volksgeist*, as well as the use of French.

---

11 Not much is known about Aloïs Hendrik Roëll, except that he was the municipal secretary at Lier and a board member for the local chapter of the Catholic Flemish association called the *Davidsfonds*.

12 During the *Ancien Régime*, the regions that would become later Belgium stood rather independent from the Habsburg ruler.

Like many other Romantic thinkers, Brants ascribed a common language to such *Volksgeist*. He blamed the French annexation for the fact that "onze geest [...] zoo diep van die uitheemsche vakwoorden en uitdrukkingen doordrongen [is], dat onze taal, in bestuurszaken, ons eene vreemdelinge is geworden" ("our spirit [is] permeated by foreign words and expressions in such way that our language has become a stranger to us in the context of the administration") (*Bestuurlijk Tijdschrift* 1889c). Consequently, public civil servants had no experience whatsoever in using Flemish correctly, which was also caused by a lack of decent works in that language (*Bestuurlijk Tijdschrift* 1889c; Het Volksbelang 1889, 6).[13] Aware of 'gallicisms', or *bastaardwoorden* as they called them, the editors strove to a pure and united administrative legal language (*Bestuurlijk Tijdschrift* 1889c). To that end, the editors introduced a section *Rechtstaal* (Legal Language) in 1890.

The section responded directly to a failed competition organized by the Royal Flemish Academy of Belgium for Science and the Arts. In 1889, this cultural organization called for a project to draft a "Nederlandsch-Fransche en Fransch-Nederlandsche woordenlijst van rechtstermen en –uitdrukkingen" ("Dutch-French and French-Dutch glossary of legal terms and expressions"). A three-member jury of the prominent *flamingants* Theophiel Coopman (1852–1915) (Vervliet 1998, 791–792),[14] Jan Van Droogenbroeck (1835–1902) (Sieben 1998, 990)[15] and Julius Obrie (1849–1929) assessed the lists handed in by two anonymous contenders (Coopman et al. 1890). The first one was named "Eigen recht in eigen taal" ("Justice in own language"), whereas the second adopted the title "Rust roest" ("To rest is to rust"). The members of the jury heavily criticized both submissions as incomplete inventories of terms and expressions, lacking any sense of methodology. The section "Rechtstaal" had the ambition to do better.

As a concept, this section's strength was its simplicity: it brought legal terms and proverbs in French or Latin together in a list and translated them into Flemish. Felix Rodenbach (1827–1915) – political propagandist, tax specialist and secretary of the city of Elsene – drafted those vocabulary lists and justified each specific translation (Rodenbach 1890, 175–177; 1891, 11–13,

---

13 This clearly shows the opinion of Karel Brants.
14 Initially, Coopman was an accountant. As a civil servant he helmed the translation section of the Railway Department. He was very active in the Flemish Movement and wrote poems and songs devoted to Flanders.
15 Van Droogenbroeck started his career as a teacher, but he became a civil servant at the *Bureau des Affaires flamandes* of the *Algemeen Bestuur van Letteren, Wetenschappen en Kunsten,* which was a subdivision of the Ministry of Internal Affairs. He became an active member of several associations to promote Flemish in theater and poetry.

176–177, 240–243, 305–308; 1892, 17–19, 45–49; 1893, 106–109, 172–176, 235–238, 262–267). Apart from the fact that Rodenbach authored several other legal works in both languages, little is known about him (Victor 1935, 37). However, as will become clear further on in this text, he and Brants eventually took a leading role in the translation of legal terminology.

During its ten-year existence, the *Bestuurlijk Tijdschrift* faced a high turnover in the editorial staff. Eventually, it all came down to Karel Brants, who had to take full responsibility for the journal. The final issue appeared in September 1899. Publication was halted as it likely suffered from the strongly francophone-oriented legal world. However, the main reason for its disappearance is probably the dedication of Brants as founder and editorial secretary to another, new and more broadly circulated general legal journal: the *Rechtskundig Tijdschrift voor Vlaamsch-België*.

4   *Rechtskundig Tijdschrift*: Old wine in new bottles

Even if it was published eight years after the *Bestuurlijk Tijdschrift*, historians designate the *Rechtskundig Tijdschrift voor Vlaamsch-België* as Belgium's first legal periodical in Flemish (Victor 1935, 46; Van Overwalle 1988, 16).[16] It is, however, more correct to consider it the first journal addressing 'actual legal professionals' – that is, attorneys, magistrates, notaries – making it the first 'judicial' journal.

Its structure was conventional. Each copy opened with a contribution on doctrinal matters, followed by (sometimes commented) case law and a bibliographic section. It ended mostly with "novelties" about the legal world. Its major achievement was its long-term publication until it ingloriously perished in 1964, due to financial issues. Throughout its history, the *Rechtskundig Tijdschrift* never succeeded in shaking off its label as "eternal promise" (*Rechtskundig Tijdschrift* 1963, 1), but it merits every acclaim since it paved the road to important successes such as the *Rechtskundig Weekblad* (Legal Weekly) and the *Tijdschrift voor Notarissen* (Journal for Notaries) (Van Goethem 1985b, 13–99; 1990; 1998c, 2566).

The *Rechtskundig Tijdschrift* found its roots in the *Vlaamsche Conferenties* (Flemish Conferences) and the *Bond der Vlaamsche Rechtsgeleerden* (Union

---

16   Van Overwalle considered the *Rechtskundig Tijdschrift* as the oldest she could lay hands on; Victor mentioned *Het Vlaamsch Bestuur* in his oeuvre *Een eeuw Vlaamsch rechtsleven*. However, *Het Vlaamsch Bestuur* and the *Bestuurlijk Tijdschrift voor Vlaamsch-België* are mentioned in the bibliographic section of the first issue of the *Rechtskundig Tijdschrift voor Vlaamsch-België*.

of Flemish Legal Scholars). These associations united attorneys around one goal: improving the position of Flemish as a legal language (about the Flemish Conference in Ghent (1873): Baert 1974; about the Flemish Conference in Antwerp: Meerts 2012, 193–223; Quintelier 2013, 90–92; Van Goethem 1985a; 1998a, 538-540; Matheeussen 1992). Protagonists in the Brussels legal scene – such as Edmond Picard (1836–1924) (Coppein 2011; Aron and Vanderpelen-Diagre 2013; Van Eeckhoutte and Maes 2014), Victor Jacobs (1848–1924) (*Rechtskundig Tijdschrift* 1924, 234–235) and Jules Lejeune (Christiaensen 2004; Matheeussen 1992, 37–40) – supported those associations and the Flemish demands. The announcement of the 1898 Law of Equality, which stated that French and Dutch had equal standing in legislation, directly lies at the root of the *Rechtskundig Tijdschrift* (De Opstellers 1897–1898, 1).

The new journal modeled itself on its predecessor, the *Bestuurlijk Tijdschrift*. After all, the day-to-day management was in the hands of the inescapable Karel Brants who, again, was editorial secretary and took full responsibility for the journal's smooth running. The first editorial staff was helmed by Juliaan Van der Linden and was firmly rooted in the Brussels legal world, yet could also rely on cooperation from outside Belgium's capital (Vandenbogaerde 2018, 171).

The presence of Brants explains the similarities between the titles in terms of both form and content. Like *Het Bestuurlijk Tijdschrift voor Vlaams België* the opening statement "In Vlaanderen, Vlaamsch!" had two objectives. First of all, it propagated the use of Flemish in Flanders' court rooms. In the editor's opinion, the Law of Equality was a mere first step in the creation of a Flemish legal culture. Therefore, the correct use of Dutch-language legal language was highly necessary (De Opstellers 1897–1898, 2), and the journal adopted a specific method for it:

> Het ligt in het plan van het Rechtskundig Tijdschrift, op rechtsgebied het zijne bij te dragen tot het bevorderen en het verspreiden der Nederlandsche rechtstaal in België door het leveren van taalkundige studiën en het verklaren van vakwoorden. Naar onze meening, bestaat daartoe geen doelmatiger middel dan het volgende: bij iedere aflevering de voornaamste rechtstermen en rechtsuitdrukkingen, die in deze of gene bijdrage dier aflevering voorkomen, aanteekenen met aanwijzing van de artikels onzer Wetboeken en mededeeling van andere termen en uitdrukkingen die tot hetzelfde vak behooren.

> (The *Rechtskundig Tijdschrift* aims to contribute to the promotion and dissemination of Dutch as a legal language in Belgium by providing linguistic studies and explaining professional words. In our opinion, there is no more effective means of achieving this than to take notice of important

legal terms and expressions that appear in this or that issue and indicate the articles of our codes as well as convey other terms and expressions that belong to the same discipline.) (Brants 1897–1898a, 26)

Karel Brants and Felix Rodenbach, in particular, provided linguistic contributions and glossaries (Brants 1897–1998a, 26). Sometimes they entered into discussions with each other (Rodenbach 1897, 47–51; 1897-1898, 115–118; De Opstelraad 1897–1898, 51–52; Brants 1897–1898, 118–120). However, at that time most *flamingants* felt no need to invent a new legal language since an appropriate and well-developed legal language did already exist in the Netherlands. Some strongly defended the opinion that Flanders should adopt the legal language from the Netherlands "as far as possible" (Van Goethem 1998b, 1465–1466). On the occasion of Paul Bellefroid's (1869–1959) *Dictionnaire français-néerlandais des termes de droitI,* Hendrik de Hoon (1850–1932) wrote in the *Rechtskundig Tijdschrift*: "Ons standpunt is gekend: de Nederlandsche rechtstaal behoeft niet in het leven geroepen te worden, zij bestaat; wij hebben slechts te putten in den woordenschat, dien onze Noordelijke taalgenooten bezitten en die het gemeenschappelijk goed is van allen die de Nederlandsche taal spreken." ("Our point of view is known: the Flemish legal language does not need to be created, it exists; we only have to use the vocabulary that our fellow Northerners possess, and which is the common good of all who speak Dutch.") (De Hoon 1898–1899, 37).

Nevertheless, the attention to the Dutch language did not last long and the linguistic section disappeared.[17] The *Rechtskundig Tijdschrift* published translated judgments from French and the editors corrected in footnotes any mistakes to purify the texts from 'gallicisms' (van Gerwen 2017, 14). The new secretary, Albéric De Swarte, labelled the journal as "the best way to study Dutch legal language". However, he also recommended Dutch journals, including the *Rechtsgeleerd Magazijn* (Legal Magazine), *Tijdschrift voor Strafrecht* (Journal of Criminal Law), *Paleis van Justitie* (Palace of Justice), *Weekblad van het Recht* (Weekly Journal of the Law), *Rechtsgeleerde Bijdragen* (Legal Contributions) and *Themis* (Deswarte 1900–1901, 89).

Over time, the editors became aware that the magazine did not benefit from an exclusive focus on the development of the Dutch legal language.[18]

---

17 In 1903, the section was called "Taal- en Rechtskundige Aantekeningen" ("Linguistic and Legal Notes").
18 That is why the tenth volume was announced as following: "Wij betrachten niet alleen een "vlaamsch" Tijdschrift te hebben, maar we betrachten vooral, een "degelijk" Rechtskundig Tijdschrift in België te verspreiden, dat kan opwegen tegen de beste Tijdschriften uit andere landen, zooals bijvoorbeeld, het Rechtsgeleerd Magazijn uit Holland" ("Not only are we trying to have a

In addition to its linguistic purpose, the journal had to pursue a practical and scientific goal and reshuffled its objectives in 1909. A call for more professionalism was made (De Redactie 1909, 2).[19]

Viewed from a distance, all the ingredients seemed present to make the *Rechtskundig Tijdschrift* a success story. The editors were involved in all kinds of Flemish legal associations, promoted the use of Dutch within legal practice and provided the necessary tools. Nevertheless, the formula never worked out, and the *Rechtskundig Tijdschrift* faded away, due to its irregular publication frequency. In fact, it just came about too soon, since the legal world was simply too frenchified for legal professionals to justify an expensive subscription to "a linguistic magazine".

The most important merit of the *Rechtskundig Tijdschrift* is perhaps that it encouraged other Flemish lawyers to start publishing a Dutch-language legal journal as well. In that sense, it succeeded in its mission: the development of a Flemish legal culture. In the wake of the *Rechtskundig Tijdschrift*, new Dutch-language initiatives arose that were supported by the former, such as the *Vlaamsch Museum* (Flemish Museum), a now forgotten monthly magazine devoted to "Staathuishoudkunde, bestuurlijke aangelegenheden, onderwijs, wetenschappen, letteren en schoone kunsten" ("State Economics, Administrative Affairs, Education, Science, Literature and Fine Arts"). On 1 October 1900, the first issue of the *Tijdschrift voor Belgische Notarissen* (Journal for Belgian Notaries) appeared, the first journal completely published in the Dutch language for the notaries. Its first year was unilingual in Flemish, but the next year it appeared as a bilingual journal, which attests to the fact that Belgium's legal world was too francophone. However, this journal merged with the francophone *Annales du notariat et de l'enregistrement* (Annals of Notaries and Registration) as a supplement in Dutch in 1908. It became a direct precursor to the *Tijdschrift voor Notarissen* (Vandenbogaerde 2013, 7–30).

The last major pre-war achievement was the *Tijdschrift der Gemeentebesturen* (Journal of Local Governments) which was founded in 1902, by, once again, Karel Brants. Seven years later, this title took over *Het Vlaamsch Bestuur* when

---

"Flemish" journal, but above all we are trying to distribute a "solid" *Rechtskundig Tijdschrift* which can compete with the best journals from other countries, such as, for example, the *Rechtsgeleerd Magazijn* from Holland." (De Redactie 1909, 1–2).

19 "Bij het samenstellen van ieder nummer beoogen wij een drievoudig doel: 1. het leveren van grondige rechtsstudiën; 2. het verzamelen van al wat nieuws en meldenswaardig is op rechtsgebied in binnen- en buitenland; 3. het mededeelen van al wat ons beroepsleven aangaat" ("In compiling each issue, our aim is threefold: 1. to provide thorough legal studies; 2. to collect all that is new and noteworthy in the field of law at home and abroad; 3. to share all that concerns our professional life.")

de Corswarem died. More initiatives were to come, but the August 1914 German invasion halted all publications during the course of the war.

Before World War I, the attempts for legal periodicals to familiarize legal practitioners with Flemish terminology seemed to have little effect. The very few contributions were limited to an even fewer number of pages. One thing was clear: in the genre of legal periodical, Felix Rodenbach and Karel Brants took the lead. Nevertheless, little is known about their approach to the task. A glimpse can be found in an article Karel Brants published in 1921.

5 Insights in translation: The method of Karel Brants

After World War I, the godfather of Flemish legal titles kept actively translating legal terminology from French. In 1921, the Catholic monthly *Dietsche Warande en Belfort* published Brants's article on *Nederlandsche rechts- en bestuurstaal* (Dutch [i.e., Flemish] legal and administrative language), in which he emphasized the formal equality of legal texts both in Flemish and French. However, he added, the Flemish translation in most of those texts were poorly drafted and showed no uniformity. The application of a decent legal Flemish required a linguistically impeccable translation (Brants 1921b, 298).[20]

In two contributions – more were foreseen, but never published – Brants discussed two terms, namely *témoin/getuige* (witness) (Brants 1921b, 299–303). and *impôts/belastingen* (taxes) (Brants 1921c, 608–613). He did not explain the rationale behind these choices. As before, he argued for preferred translations and, for the first time, he disclosed his sources and method. Brants seemed to have taken a very prosaic and pragmatic approach, for he took popular Dutch dictionaries, such as Van Dale, Kramers and Koenen, as a starting point. In addition, he relied on less-known, general dictionaries that translated French to Dutch (Heremans 1867; Herckenrath 1906). From that point on, he looked into Dutch legal texts in depth, such as the 1838 Dutch Civil Code – which in a sense can be considered a translation of the Napoleonic Code – and the Dutch Procedural Code. Other sources were the aforementioned French-Dutch legal dictionary, published by Paul

---

20 "*Welk de oorzaken van een zoo betreurenswaardigen toestand zijn, willen wij thans niet nagaan: het volstaat dien toestand vast te stellen en er op te wijzen dat, waar, krachtens de taalwet van 1898, de Vlaamsche stukken in de meeste gevallen even officieel, even wettelijk zijn als de Fransche, die stukken behoeven onberispelijk te zijn in taalopzicht.*" ("We do not want to examine at this moment the causes of such a deplorable situation: it suffices to establish the situation and to point out that, where, by virtue of the linguistic law of 1898, the Flemish documents in most cases are as official, as legal, as the French ones, those documents need to be flawless from a linguistic point of view.")

Bellefroid, or Dutch handbooks (e.g., De Boer 1900). When a translation was not satisfactory for Brants, he consulted all other texts and specialist handbooks, regardless of the language they were published in (e.g., de Brouckère and Tielemans 1834–1856). Brants assembled all dictionaries, legal texts and handbooks that could help to explain the term correctly, from which a satisfactory translation could be distilled.

Almost simultaneously, Brants published his *magnum opus* on Belgium's municipal law (Brants 1921a; Vandenbogaerde 2020, 169–172). Moreover, after the war he had obtained the position of *bestuurder der Vlaamsche Diensten aan de Kamer der Volksvertegenwoordigers* (Director of the Flemish Services at the House of Representatives).[21] His never-ending commitment to the Flemish cause must have enabled him to acquire access to Belgium's highest political circles. It resulted in a seat in the 1923 *Centrale Commissie voor de Nederlandse Rechtstaal en Bestuurstaal in België* (Central Commission for Flemish Legal and Administrative Language in Belgium), headed by Hendrik de Hoon and later by Emiel Van Dievoet (1886–1967).[22] This commission was set up at the request of the *Bond der Vlaamsche Rechtsgeleerden* (Flemish Lawyers Assocation) and could count on the support of the *Rechtskundig Tijdschrift* (Vandenbogaerde 2018, 205).The commission based its translations heavily on the 1838 Dutch Civil Code and saw its work before the start of World War II rewarded with the adoption of a translated Constitution (1925), Penal Code (1926) and Municipal Law (1927). It took until 1939, before the Belgian government had approved a translated Civil Code (Van Dievoet 2003, 109).

At that moment, the Flemish Movement had witnessed important breakthroughs, such as the 1935 Act on the Use of Languages in Court. This law appeased, at least formally, the discussion between Flemish and francophone lawyers. A crucial victory in the road to that appeasement was the complete 'flemificiation' of Ghent University in 1930. From that moment onward, students could study law in their mother tongue, which opened the doors for a new influential legal weekly, which would then take up the issue of translational policies (Vandenbogaerde 2018, 237).

---

21 Unfortunately, we do not know – yet – what kind of position it was.
22 Koninklijk besluit over de oprichting van een *Commissie voor de vertaling in het Vlaamsch van de bepalingen der Grondwet, der wetboeken, der voornaamste geldende wetten en besluiten waarvan geen officieele Vlaamsche tekst werd bekendgemaakt* (Royal Decree of 18 September 1923 on the installation of Commission for the Translation in Flemish of the Constitution, Codes, most Important Acts and Decrees in force of which no official Flemish text was promulgated) of 18 september 1923, *Moniteur belge* 28 September 1923.

6 *Rechtskundig Weekblad* (1931–today)

On Sunday, 11 October 1931, the *Rechtskundig Weekblad* published its first issue with the goal of providing Belgian lawyers reports on legal life in Dutch on a weekly basis. It was an immediate success, and to this day it is considered to be one of the most important Flemish legal journals in existence (Victor 1935–1936, 1735–1740; *Rechtskundig Weekblad* 1961–1962a, 2507–2518; 1961–1962b, 2521–2544; Van Oevelen 2011–2012, 1–6). It could count on a new generation of students – first those at Ghent University; a few years later Louvain and Brussels followed suit – trained in law only in Flemish. In addition, shortly after the launch of this journal, the Act on the Use of Languages in Court was adopted.[23]

The aims of the *Rechtskundig Weekblad* can be found in the opening statement, written by editor-in-chief René Victor (1897–1984) (Verstraete 2018) and endorsed by all the members of the Board (De Voorloopige Redactie 1931–1932, 1–4; Ooms 1961–1962, 2073). First and foremost, the new publication stood at the service of the Flemish legal practitioner, especially through the publication of the most important judgments ruled in Dutch (not Flemish, as there were very little). In doing so, the editorial board took a great risk, as it refused to translate any cases from any other language (De Redactie 1968–1969).[24] Hence, it faced the same problems as its illustrious predecessor the *Rechtskundig Tijdschrift*, since, in practice, for the time being, there were no Flemish-language judgments from the Court of Cassation, and Courts of Appeal rarely allowed Flemish in civil proceedings (De Redactie 1931–1932, 19).

The *Rechtskundig Weekblad* served a scholarly purpose. Almost every issue opened with a contribution on doctrinal matters, which was not always as thorough as it could have been (De Redactie 1931–1932, 18), but at least

---

23 In the Flemish districts, the entire administration of justice is conducted in Dutch. In the Walloon arrondissements, it is done in French, except for the courts in the district of Eupen, where German is the language of administration of justice. For the judicial district of Brussels, there is a complicated arrangement. This judicial district contains unilingual Dutch municipalities and bilingual municipalities (Dutch-French).The parties can unanimously request that the proceedings be continued in another language. The case is then referred to a court of the other language area.
24 It was only in 1968 that the *Rechtskundig Weekblad* published its first 'translated' case. The so-called Belgian Linguistic Case (Belgium v. Belgium, ECHR (1968), Appl. No. 1474/62; 1677/62; 1691/62; 1769/63; 1994/63; 2126/64.) was a ruling by the European Court for Human Rights and had a high symbolic value for René Victor and the *Rechtskundig Weekblad*. By fully translating the judgment in Dutch, the journal fought against its own program statement that only Dutch language case law would be published. René Victor saw the ruling as a confirmation of his ideals in the field of language policy in Belgium. .

it discussed topical issues at that time (e.g., Vander Planken 1932–1933, 545–550; Fredericq 1932–1933, 513–518; Ooms 1932–1933, 497–506). The editors wanted to contrast this approach of theirs with those who regarded the law as a mere technique: "Het blijkt voor de meeste leden van onze rechtskundige congressen, die zich hoofdzakelijk bezighouden met de praktijk van het recht, uitsluitend een techniek. [...] Aan een zuiver wetenschappelijke verhandeling wordt door de meeste onzer juristen al te dikwijls weinig belang gehecht" ("For most of the members of our legal conferences, who are mainly concerned with the practice of law, this appears to be exclusively a technique. [...] Too often, most of our lawyers attach little importance to a purely academic treatise") (*Rechtskundig Weekblad* 1931–1932, 467). The editors copied their *modus operandi* from the *Nederlandse Juristenvereniging* (Dutch Lawyers Association) (De Nederlandse Juristenvereniging 1970), which presented thoroughly elaborated papers at professional conferences (Vandeputte 1932–1933, 553). René Victor admired Dutch law and its legal scholars (Vandeputte 1984–1985, 2872). Together with other members of the editorial board, he believed there was no cultural boundary between Flanders and the Netherlands. Moreover, his opinion was that in law there should be more solidarity and co-operation between Flemish and Dutch lawyers (Victor, 1961–1962, 2527). Even if the Dutch turned out to be not very ardent fans of Flemish legal life at that time (C.R.C. Wijkerheld Bisdom 1961–1962, 2528), the seeds were planted for a more intense Flemish-Dutch co-operation.

The scholarly goal did not stand on its own, yet was seen as a necessary element to emancipate and to elevate the Flemish people (*Rechtskundig Weekblad* 1931–1932, 466).[25] After all, law was a cultural product and played a prominent role in society (De Voorloopige Redactie 1931–1932, 2). Hence, according to the editors, the *Rechtskundig Weekblad* would contribute to the general culture and intended to mobilize the masses with influential lawyers as perfect guides (Roost 1961–1962, 2529). The gap between the courthouses and the Flemish people had to be reduced in order to develop a full-fledged Flemish legal culture. In this respect, the program differed little from that of *La Belgique Judiciaire* (Judiciary Belgium) and the *Journal des Tribunaux* (Tribunals' journal), both of which also aimed at the popularization of the law (Vandenbogaerde 2018, 237).

---

25 "Stellig niemand zal betwisten dat vooral in ons land volksverlichting het hoogste doel dient te zijn van de wetenschap." ("Certainly no one will dispute that, especially in our country, popular enlightenment should be the highest goal of science.")

This could only happen once Flemish lawyers had embraced and mastered Flemish as a legal language. The editors wanted to familiarize all legal actors with Flemish, all the more so because

> in vele vonnissen en arresten [...] fouten voor[komen] die niet slechts aan onachtzaamheid te wijten zijn maar die het vermoeden wekken dat de stellers de Nederlandsche taal niet behoorlijk kennen. Dit gebrek zal dan eerst afdoende kunnen bestreden worden wanneer de afgestudeerden der Nederlandsche hoogescholen van Gent en Leuven een overwegende plaats zullen innemen in de magistratuur, in de balie en in het notariaat

> (many judgments and rulings contain errors that are not only due to negligence, but which give rise to the suspicion that the composers do not know the Dutch language properly. This shortcoming can only be adequately combated when the graduates of the Dutch colleges of Ghent and Leuven will occupy a dominant position in the judiciary, in the bar and in the civil-law notary's office.) (*Rechtskundig Tijdschrift* 1933, 619)

A thorough knowledge of their mother tongue would also give the Flemish lawyers greater self-confidence:

> Wij voelen elken dag vóór onze Rechtbanken hoe aarzelend en onzeker velen onzer magistraten en confraters, zelfs wanneer ze van Vlaamsche afkomst zijn, de Nederlandsche rechtstaal gebruiken. [...] Voor de Vlaamsche juristen ligt hier een geweldig arbeidsveld en ons blad wil een praktisch werktuig zijn om hen in hun taak te helpen. De taal onzer rechtspraktijk dient geschaafd en geslepen te worden. De onvolmaaktheden die zullen voorkomen in de uitgegeven beslissingen zullen aanleiding geven tot kritiek en tot studie en de vruchten hiervan zullen gemeengoed worden van de heele Vlaamsche rechtswereld.

> (Every day before our Courts we feel how hesitantly and insecurely many of our magistrates and co-counsels, even if they are of Flemish origin, use Dutch. [...] For Flemish lawyers, lots of work remains to be done, and our journal wants to be a practical tool to aid them in their task. The language of our legal practice needs to be brushed and polished. Imperfections in published case law will give cause for criticism and investigation, the fruits of which will become commonplace in the entire Flemish legal world.) (De Redactie 1931–32, 19)

In order to remedy these shortcomings (Van Dievoet 1932–1933, 601–604; Bellefroid 1933–1934, 137–150; Le Paige 1933–1934, 661–668) judgments of Dutch courts were regularly included in the journal, and a section with professional terminology in Flemish was published (De Redactie 1931–1932, 19). The comments were drafted by lawyer and Germanic philologist Guido Spanoghe (1910–1994). At that time, the later professor was a young man who enthusiastically read the *Rechtskundig Weekblad*. However, he was annoyed by the multitude of errors published in the weekly and wanted to prevent that such frequent mistakes would be adopted as correct legal language. He contacted the editorial board and was allowed to point out all faulty terminology. At the same time, he proposed solutions (Spanoghe 1932–1933a, 347–350). He opposed the use of words in Latin – which is common in the legal world – since it did not contribute to a clear and uniform legal language. In later contributions, he replied to translation questions from readers (Spanoghe 1932–1933b, 425–28). Contrarily to his predecessor Brants, we cannot distinct the sources Spanoghe uses to found his argument. However, he refers several times to the Dutch legal language, which was a continuation of Brants's philosophy. In addition, one cannot deny that Spanoghe was educated as a philologist who understood the importance of correct application of language rules.

Although these glossaries drew inspiration from Dutch legal terms, the editors did not consider it desirable to simply copy the legal terminology from the Netherlands (De Redactie 1931–1932, 19). This position contrasted with the former generation of Flemish lawyers and opened the door for a more 'Belgian Dutch'. Paul Bellefroid – after World War I, a professor at Nijmegen University – published a plea for proper Flemish legal terminology independent of the Dutch vocabulary. Through examples he described the shortcomings of a mere adoption of Dutch legal terminology. According to him, a unified legal language between Flanders and the Netherlands is impossible and not desirable, since both countries had developed a different legal system. He invigorated his argument by referring to the terminological differences in Austria and Germany. Bellefroid questioned the Belgian government that had imposed in law education and administration the translations made by the 1923 Commission. In his opinion, a government cannot regulate a language, which is a lively aspect of human interaction which alters over time. Bellefroid could not support a lawyer who promoted himself as a "taalverbeteraar" ("improver of language"), one who felt superior to the people, because such a person could only cause confusion. The professor advocated for a close connection to the language the population uses on a daily basis and called out for patience. A Flemish legal language would flourish once the first generation law students, who were trained in their mother tongue, would fill the chambers of attorneys, public notaries and the judiciary (Bellefroid 1933–1934, 150). In hindsight, Bellefroid might have assessed the situation correctly.

7 Conclusion

Legal periodicals are nodes in networks bringing together like-minded actors. The case of titles published in Flemish illustrates the importance of such networks and how they adopted a vision of the official language and translation policy. One general observation was that official translations were of poor quality and would not help the Flemish people to emancipate themselves in the Belgian nation. Therefore, the editors used their medium to give the tools needed to legal practitioners.

Aware of their role as an elite to guide the people, lawyers used the means of periodical publications in an attempt to construct a uniform legal language. Therefore, they adopted one particular method: drafting vocabulary lists and inventories of translations with a justification for the choices made. Authors did not systematically mention the sources they relied on, but it is perhaps clear that, based on an article by Karel Brants, Flemish lawyers took a very pragmatic approach. They referred to a wide variety of (translating) dictionaries and handbooks to distill a uniform legal language and used their journals to disseminate – and maybe impose – 'their' legal language.

At the turn of the nineteenth and twentieth centuries, Flemish lawyers increasingly consulted Dutch vocabulary and explained their approach because of the language shared between Dutch and Flemings. It did not work out. Firstly, Belgium's legal world remained heavily embedded in the French tradition and its professionals remained francophone – roughly until World War II – and secondly, there seemed to have been little support by legal practitioners to simply adopt a 'foreign' legal language. When Ghent University became monolingually Flemish, a generation of lawyers, educated with one legal terminology, could stand up and introduce their mother tongue in legal practice. From then on, it was only a matter of time before a proper Flemish legal terminology had developed.

It is remarkable that pre-World War II legal periodicals published in Flemish were sustained by a very small group of civil servants and lawyers who expressed the desire to adopt a Dutch-inspired legal language. Particularly Karel Brants proved essential to this evolution. Even if he did not fully succeed in establishing a clear and uniform legal language in Flemish, his influence in the professional press makes clear that he can deservedly be considered the 'godfather' of all Flemish legal journals.

Acknowledgement

This contribution is written with the support of the FWO-Vlaanderen Scientific Research Fund. The first draft was corrected by Dr. Matthias Van Der Haegen. Remaining mistakes are all mine.

References

Aron, Paul, and Cécile Vanderpelen-Diagre. 2013. *Edmond Picard: Un bourgeois socialiste belge à la fin du dixneuvième siècle*. Brussels: Musées royaux des Beaux-Arts de Belgique.

Baert, Geert. 1974. *De Vlaamse Conferentie der Balie van Gent. 1873–1973*. Ghent: Vlaamse Conferentie der Balie van Gent.

Bellefroid, Paul. 1933–1934. "Beschouwingen over de Nederlandsche Rechtstaal in Vlaanderen." *Rechtskundig Weekblad* 3 (9): 137–150.

Bestuurlijk Tijdschrift. 1889a. "De Belgische Gemeenteïnrichting." *Bestuurlijk Tijdschrift* 1 (1): 1–2.

———. 1889b. "Kieswetten. Beknopt overzicht der arresten van het Verbrekingshof." *Bestuurlijk Tijdschrift* 1 (3): 207–210.

———. 1889c. "Prospectus." *Bestuurlijk Tijdschrift*.

Brants, Karel. 1897–1898a. "Bijdrage tot het samenstellen eener Nederlandsch-Fransche en Fransch-Nederlandsche woordenlijst van rechtstermen en rechtsuitdrukkingen." *Rechtskundig Tijdschrift* 1 (1): 26.

———. 1897–1898b. "Wederantwoord." *Rechtskundig Tijdschrift* 1 (4): 118–120.

———. 1898. "A.H. Roëll." *Bestuurlijk Tijdschrift* 10 (9): 285–286.

———. 1921a. *Het Belgisch gemeenterecht: samenstelling, inrichting en bevoegdheid der gemeentebesturen*. Lier: Van In.

———. 1921b. "Nederlandsche rechts- en bestuurstaal." *Dietsche Warande en Belfort* 21 (3): 299–303.

———. 1921c. "Nederlandsche rechts- en bestuurstaal." *Dietsche Warande en Belfort* 21 (5): 608–613.

Christiaensen, Stef. 2004. *Tussen klassieke en moderne criminele politiek: Leven en beleid van Jules Lejeune*. Leuven: Universitaire Pers.

Coopman, Theophiel, Julius Obrie, and Jan Van Droogenbroeck. 1890. "Vierde prijsvraag: Eene Nederlandsch-Fransche en Fransch-Nederlandsche woordenlijst van rechtstermen en –uitdrukkingen." *Verslagen en mededelingen van de Koninklijke Vlaamse Academie voor Taal- en Letterkunde*: 289–325.

Coppein, Bart. 2011. *Dromen van een nieuwe samenleving: Intellectuele biografie van Edmond Picard*. Brussels: Larcier.

De Boer, W.C. 1900. *Handleiding voor het Notarisambt*. Medemblik: K.H. Idema.

De Brouckère, Charles, and F. Tielemans. 1834–1856. *Répertoire de l'administration et du droit administratif de la Belgique*. Brussels: Weissenbruch.

De Corswarem, Adrien. 1893. "Vragen en antwoorden." *Het Vlaamsch Bestuur* 4 (6): 184–185.

De Hoon, Hendrik. 1898–1899 "De Nederlandsche Rechtstaal." *Rechtskundig Tijdschrift*: 37.

De Nederlandse Juristenvereniging. 1970. *Honderd jaar rechtsleven: (1870–1970)*. Zwolle: Tjeenk Willink.

De Opstellers. 1897–1898. "Tot inleiding." *Rechtskundig Tijdschrift* 1 (1): 1.

De Opstelraad. 1897–1898. "Aanmerkingen." *Rechtskundig Tijdschrift* 1 (2): 51–52.

De Pauw, Frans. 1973. "Het ontstaan van de Nederlandstalige faculteit der rechtsgeleerdheid aan de Vrije Universiteit te Brussel." In *Recht in beweging, opstellen aangeboden aan prof. Mr. Ridder R. Victor*, 345. Antwerp: Kluwer.

Deprez, Ada. 1998. "Ledeganck, Karel L." In *Nieuwe Encyclopedie van de Vlaamse Beweging*, edited by Ludo Simons, 1810–1811. Tielt: Lannoo.

De Redactie. 1909. "Een woordje vooraf bij den aanvang van den 10en jaargang." *Rechtskundig Tijdschrift voor Vlaamsch-België* 10 (1–2): 1–2.

De Redactie. 1934. "In Memoriam Karel Brants." *Rechtskundig Tijdschrift* 29 (3): 219–220.

De Redactie. 1931–32. "Ons doel." *Rechtskundig Weekblad* 1 (2): 19.

———. 1968–1969. "Het arrest van Straatsburg." *Rechtskundig Weekblad*: 1.

De Smedt, Marcel. 1997. "Karel Lodewijk Ledeganck (1805–1847)." *Wetenschappelijke Tijdingen* 56 (4): 227–243.

Deswarte, Albéric. 1900–1901."Over de studie der Nederlandsche rechtstaal." *Rechtskundig Tijdschrift* 3 (3): 89.

De Voorloopige Redactie. 1931–1932. "Aan onze lezers." *Rechtskundig Weekblad* 1 (1): 1–4.

Dopp, Herman. 1932. *La contrefaçon des livres français en Belgique (1815–1852)*. Leuven: Librairie universitaire.

Dujardin, Vincent, Emmanuel Gerard, Michel Dumoulin, and Mark van den Wijngaert. 2006. *Nieuwe geschiedenis van Belgïe II 1905–1950*. Tielt: Lannoo.

Fredericq, Louis. 1932–1933. "Het privaat recht der Soviëts." *Rechtskundig Weekblad* 2 (29): 513–518.

Gevers, Lieve, Arie W. Willemsen, and Els Witte. 1998. "Geschiedenis van de Vlaamse beweging." In *Nieuwe Encyclopedie van de Vlaamse Beweging*, edited by Ludo Simons, 35–86. Tielt: Lannoo.

Gubin, Eliane, and Jean-Pierre Nandrin. 2005. "Het liberale en burgerlijke België, 1846–1878." In *Nieuwe Geschiedenis van België 1830–1905*, edited by Els Witte, Jean-Pierre Nandrin, Eliane Gubin and Gita Deneckere, 239–440. Tielt: Lannoo.

Hardy, J., and S. van Clemen. 1998. "Brants, Karel, G." In *Nieuwe Encyclopedie van de Vlaamse Beweging,* edited by Ludo Simons, 594–595. Tielt: Lannoo.

Herckenrath, C.R.C. 1906. *Fransch Woordenboek.* Groningen: J.B. Wolters.

Heremans, Jacob. 1867. *Dictionnaire français-néerlandais.* Antwerp: Imprimerie J.P. Van Dieren.

Het Vlaamsch Bestuur. 1889–1890a. "Nieuwe boeken." *Het Vlaamsche Bestuur* 1 (6): 222.

———. 1889–1890b. Announcement in annex. *Het Vlaamsch Bestuur* 1 (7,8).

———. 1898. "Nieuwe boeken." *Het Vlaamsch Bestuur* 9 (1): 32.

Het Volksbelang. 1889. "Bestuurlijk Tijdschrift voor Vlaamsch België." *Het Volksbelang*: 6.

Hoste. 1859. "Berigt des uitgevers." In *Het Burgerlyk Wetboek uit het Fransch Vertaeld en Beknoptelyk uitgelegd door C. Ledeganck. Vierde uitgave,* edited by Louis De Hondt. Ghent: H. Hoste.

Latham, Sean, and Robert Scholes. 2006. "The Rise of Periodical Studies." *PMLA* 121 (2): 517-531.

Le Paige, A. 1933–1934. "Enkele opmerkingen over taal en wetgeving." *Rechtskundig Weekblad* 3 (35): 661–668.

Martyn, Georges. 2005. "Het Burgerlijk Wetboek en de evolutie van de 'Vlaamse' rechtstaal in België." In *Napoleons nalatenschap. Tweehonderd jaar Burgerlijk Wetboek in België/Un héritage Napoléonien. Bicentenaire du Code civil en Belgique,* edited by Dirk Heirbaut and Georges Martyn, 271–300. Mechelen: Kluwer.

Matheeussen, Constant. 1992. *Honderd jaar Vlaams Pleitgenootschap bij de Balie te Brussel 1891–1991.* Tielt: Lannoo.

Meerts, Jan. 2012. "Geschiedenis van de Vlaamse Conferentie bij de balie te Antwerpen." In *1812–2012. 200 Jaar orde van advocaten te Antwerpen,* edited by Jan Verstraete, Stefanie Verstraete, Pierre Bogaerts, Frederic Dupon, Bart Lange, Cathy Lannoy, Jan Meerts, Frank Roosendaal and Guy Van Doosselaere, 193–223. Bruges: Die Keure.

Ooms, Emiel. 1961–1962. "Dertig jaar geleden." *Rechtskundig Weekblad* 30: 2073.

Ooms, R. 1932–1933. "Goethe. Stud. iuris en advokaat (1765 tot 1774)." *Rechtskundig Weekblad* 2(28): 497–506.

Quintelier, Bart. 2013. *Een (rechts)geschiedenis van de Belgische advocatuur (1795–2006), met nadruk op het tuchtrecht, toegelicht aan de hand van de Antwerpse casus.* Unpublished PhD diss., UGent, Faculty of Law.

Rechtskundig Tijdschrift. 1924. "In Memoriam. Mr. Victor Jacobs." *Rechtskundig Tijdschrift* 15–16: 234–235.

———. 1933. "Beschouwingen over de Nederlandsche rechtstaal in Vlaanderen." *Rechtskundig Tijdschrift*: 619.

———. 1963. *Rechtskundig Tijdschrift* 53 (1): 1.

Rechtskundig Weekblad. 1931–1932. "Beschouwingen over het Rechtskundig Congres." *Rechtskundig Weekblad* 1 (1): 466–467.

———. 1933–1934. "Karel Brants." *Rechtskundig Weekblad* 3 (28): 548.

———. 1961–62a. "Feestnummer ter gelegenheid van het vijfentwintigste jubileum van het "Rechtskundig Weekblad"."*Rechtskundig Weekblad* 25 (40): 2507–2518.

———. 1961–1962b. "Viering van het vijfentwintigjarig jubileum van het Rechtskundig Weekblad." *Rechtskundig Weekblad* 25 (41): 2521–2544.

Rodenbach, Felix. 1890. "Rechtstaal." *Bestuurlijk Tijdschrift* 2: 175–177.

———. 1891. "Rechtstaal." *Bestuurlijk Tijdschrift* 3: 11–13; 176–177; 240–243; 305–308.

———. 1892. "Rechtstaal."*Bestuurlijk Tijdschrift* 4: 17–19; 45–49.

———. 1893. "Rechtstaal."*Bestuurlijk Tijdschrift* 5: 106–109; 172–176, 235–238; 262–267.

———. 1897. "Eigen muur met vensters of openingen-verkrijging der mitoyenniteitgevolgen." *Rechtskundig Tijdschrift*: 47–51.

———.1897–1898. "Antwoord op de aanmerkingen van den opstelraad." *Rechtskundig Tijdschrift* 1 (4): 115–118.

Roost, Marcel. 1961–1962. "Viering van het vijfentwintigjarig jubileum van het Rechtskundig Weekblad." *Rechtskundig Weekblad* 25 (41): 2529.

Roppe, Louis, and Filip Boudrez. 1998. "Corswarem, ridder Adriaan J.L. de." In *Nieuwe Encyclopedie van de Vlaamse Beweging*, edited by Ludo Simons, 804–805. Tielt: Lannoo.

Sieben, Luc. 1998. "Droogenbroeck, Jan A." In *Nieuwe Encyclopedie van de Vlaamse Beweging*, edited by Ludo Simons, 990. Tielt: Lannoo.

Spanoghe, Guido. 1932–1933a. "Taalonkruid in het Rechtskundig Weekblad." *Rechtskundig Weekblad* 2 (19): 347–350.

———. 1932–1933b. "Beschouwingen over onze rechtstaal." *Rechtskundig Weekblad* 2 (24): 425–428.

Tesnière, Valérie. 2014a. "Les revues médicales depuis 1800." *Revue de Synthèse* 135 (2–3): 202–219.

———. 2014b. "Une morphologie de la circulation des savoirs la revue depuis 1800." *Revue de Synthèse* 135 (2–3): 175–202.

Tijdschrift der Gemeentebesturen. 1934. "In Memoriam Karel Brants." *Tijdschrift der Gemeentebesturen*: 89–90.

Vandenbogaerde, Sebastiaan. 2013. "Geschiedenis van het Tijdschrift voor Notarissen (1937–2012)." In *Gestaan en gelegen: Taal en Notariaat, 75 jaar Tijdschrift voor Notarissen*, edited by Karl Hendrickx, Marc Demaeght and Sebastiaan Vandenbogaerde, 7–30. Bruges: Die Keure.

———. 2018. *Vectoren van het recht: Geschiedenis van de Belgische juridische tijdschriften*. Bruges: Die Keure.

———. 2020. "Het Belgisch Gemeenterecht: samenstelling, inrichting en bevoegdheid der gemeentebesturen – 1921 – Karel Brants (1856–1934)." In *Juristen die schreven en bleven,* edited by Georges Martyn, Louis Berkvens and Paul Brood, 169–172. Hilversum: Uitgeverij Verloren.

Vandeputte, Robert. 1932–1933. "Op den uitkijk naar het Noorden." *Rechtskundig Weekblad* 2 (32): 553.

———. 1984–1985. "Leven en werk van R. Victor." *Rechtskundig Weekblad* 48 (42): 2872.

Vander Planken, C. 1932–1933. "De burgerlijke partij voor het Assisenhof. Wijzigingen aangebracht door de wet van 21 december 1930." *Rechtskundig Weekblad* 2(31): 545–550.

Vandersteene, Liesbeth. 2009. *De geschiedenis van de Rechtsfaculteit van de Universiteit Gent: van haar ontstaan tot aan de Tweede Wereldoorlog.* Ghent: Maatschappij voor Geschiedenis en Oudheidkunde.

Van Dievoet, Guido. 2003. "Het Nederlands als wetstaal in België in de negentiende en de twintigste eeuw." *Pro Memorie* 5 (1): 96–118.

Van Dievoet, Emile. 1932–1933. "Voor de practische vervlaamsching van onze burgerlijke rechtsvordering." *Rechtskundig Weekblad*: 601–604.

Van Eeckhoutte, Willy, and Bruno Maes, eds. 2014. *Genius, grandeur & gêne: Het Fin de Siècle rond het Justitiepaleis te Brussel en de controversiële figuur van Edmond Picard/La Fin de Siècle autour du Palais de Justice de Bruxelles et le personnage d'Edmond Picard.* Ghent: Knops.

Van Goethem, Herman, ed. 1985a. *Honderd jaar Vlaams rechtsleven 1885–1985: Bij het eeuwfeest van de "Vlaamse Juristenvereniging" en de vijftigste verjaardag van de vernederlandsing van het gerecht.* Ghent: Story-Scientia.

———. 1985b. "De Bond der Vlaamse Rechtsgeleerden (1885–1964)." In *Honderd jaar Vlaams rechtsleven,* edited by Herman Van Goethem, 13–99. Ghent: Story-Scientia.

———. 1990. *De taaltoestanden in het Vlaams-Belgisch gerecht, 1795–1935.* Brussels: Koninklijke academie voor wetenschappen, letteren en kunst.

———. 1998a. "Bond der Vlaamsche Rechtsgeleerden." In *Nieuwe Encyclopedie van de Vlaamse Beweging,* edited by Ludo Simons, 538–540. Tielt: Lannoo.

———. 1998b. "Hoon, Hendrik de." In *Nieuwe Encyclopedie van de Vlaamse Beweging,* edited by Ludo Simons, 1465–1466. Tielt: Lannoo.

———. 1998c. "Rechtskundig Tijdschrift (voor Vlaamsch-België)." In *Nieuwe Encyclopedie van de Vlaamse Beweging,* edited by Ludo Simons, 2566. Tielt: Lannoo.

van Gerwen, Heleen. 2017. "'In Vlaanderen Vlaamsch!' Translation practices in Flemish legal journals: the case of *Rechtskundig Tijdschrift voor Vlaamsch-België* (1897–1898)." *Journal of European Periodical Studies* 2 (1): 3–20.

Van Oevelen, Aloïs. 2011–2012. "75 Jaar Rechtskundig Weekblad." *Rechtskundig Weekblad* 75 (1): 1–6.

Van Overwalle, Geertrui. 1988. "Het Nederlandstalig juridisch tijdschrift in België." *VJV*: 16.

Velle, Karel. 1985–1988. "Bronnen voor de medische geschiedenis: de Belgische medische pers (begin 19e eeuw–1940)." *Annalen van de Belgische Vereniging voor de Geschiedenis van de Hospitalen en de Volksgezondheid*: 67–120.

———. 1994. "Les revues juridiques et administratives des XIXe et XXe siècles: une source sous-estimée pour l'historien des institutions." In *4ᵉ Congrès de l'association des cercles francophone d'histoire et d'archéologie de Belgique*, 255–269.

Verstraete, Jan. 2018. *René Victor (1897–1984): Strijder voor het Vlaams rechtsleven*. Antwerp: Het Laatste Woord.

Vervliet, Raymond. 1998. "Coopman, Theophiel." In *Nieuwe Encyclopedie van de Vlaamse Beweging*, edited by Ludo Simons, 791–792. Tielt: Lannoo.

Victor, René. 1935. *Een eeuw Vlaamsch rechtsleven*. Antwerp: De Sikkel.

———. 1935–36. "Na ons eerste lustrum." *Rechtskundig Weekblad* 5 (43): 1735–1740.

———. 1961–1962. "Viering van het vijfentwintigjarig jubileum van het Rechtskundig Weekblad." *Rechtskundig Weekblad* 25 (41): 2527.

Wijkerheld Bisdom, C.R.C. 1961–1962. "Viering van het vijfentwintigjarig jubileum van het Rechtskundig Weekblad." *Rechtskundig Weekblad*: 2528.

Wils, Ludo. 1977. *Honderd jaar Vlaamse beweging*. Leuven: Davidsfonds.

Witte, Els. 2005. "De constructie van België, 1828–1847." In *Nieuwe Geschiedenis van België 1830–1905*, edited by Els Witte, Jean-Pierre Nandrin, Eliane Gubin and Gita Deneckere, 196, Tielt: Lannoo.

Y. 1897. "Législation bilingue." *La Belgique Judiciaire*, 129–130.

Translating the Belgian Civil Code

Developments after 1961

Willem Possemiers

Abstract
Since the 30 December 1961 Act, the Belgian Civil Code has had an official Dutch text, superseding the previous non-authentic translation. This achievement of the Van Dievoet Commission, which oversaw the translation, is impressive. The commission worked from 1954 to 1961 on the revision of the translation of a previous commission, also presided by Emiel Van Dievoet, which worked on the Civil Code from 1923 to 1939. The final result is a Dutch text of very high quality, based on an in-depth study of legal history and comparative law, in which the terminology is almost always consistent, with the legal language in the Netherlands used as the prime example. Unfortunately, even though the commission existed until 2008, it was rarely asked to give advice on amendments of the Civil Code after 1961. It cannot come as a surprise that the quality of the Dutch text of new acts of Parliament rarely came up to the 1961 standard. Over the years, this has led to an eclectic Civil Code: the pre-1961 articles being of excellent quality as far as the Dutch text is concerned, the post-1961 articles sometimes, though certainly not always, being marked by poor grammar, spelling mistakes, and the re-introduction of obsolete terminology. In this chapter, examples are given of some of the novelties used by the legislators in post-1961 articles and of how these have been problematic for the consistent 1961 terminology used throughout the Civil Code. The current practice of hasty translations shows a lack of interest by the government in a well-drafted Dutch (and French) text of the law. However, poorly written law diminishes its prestige and leads to a great loss of time for students, academics, lawyers and judges alike, all of whom need to understand the meaning of the law texts.

1 Introduction

This chapter starts with a short overview of the development of the Dutch translation of the Belgian Civil Code. A brief discussion of the 1961 Dutch text follows. An analysis of some of the developments regarding the quality of the Dutch text after 1961 concludes this chapter. The main argument is that, while the linguistic quality of the 1961 Dutch text was excellent, most of the amendments to the Civil Code are not of the same quality, as the legislators did not consult the commission that prepared the 1961 Dutch text when amending the Civil Code. This shortcoming tends to result in an eclectic Civil Code, where the articles predating 1961 form an excellent text, with a uniform terminology and without language mistakes, whereas the succeeding amendments are often mediocre at best.

2   Translating the Civil Code into Dutch

Following the annexation by France in 1795, the Southern Netherlands and the Prince-Bishopric of Liège were reorganized into nine departments which formed the northern corner within the so-called "natural borders of France" (Sahlins 1990, 1443–1446). New French laws applied within this new 'Greater France', and the Civil Code was no exception.

The French text of the Civil Code was the only authentic one, and after having been promulgated in the form of thirty-six different laws, the entire French Civil Code was published on 30 ventôse year XII (21 March 1804) (Heirbaut and Baeteman 2004). This *Code civil des Français* was republished by the law of 3 September 1807 under a new name, the *Code Napoléon*, and the terminology was updated, seeing as France had been an empire since the new Constitution of 28 floréal year XII (18 May 1804) (Van Dievoet 2004). From the viewpoint of Belgian law, this was the last time the entire Civil Code had been promulgated[1] and this version, though heavily amended in the past two hundred years, is still applicable in Belgium, being the French text of the Civil Code (Heirbaut and Baeteman 2004, lii). In 1814–1815, the Southern Netherlands reunited with the Northern Netherlands. For the Civil Code, however, the Dutch period is irrelevant as it was not amended in these years (Van Dievoet 2004, XIV).

---

1   The original thirty-six laws were promulgated in the then-occupied Southern Netherlands, but the Civil Code of 21 March 1804 was not. Most likely, this was simply an oversight by the occupying French government. In France, the Civil Code was promulgated again in later years, but at that time the Southern Netherlands did not belong to France anymore. Neither the Dutch nor the Belgian government has ever promulgated the Civil Code in full again (Van Dievoet 2004). However, the French Civil Code was replaced by a Dutch Civil Code in 1838 and has been replaced in Belgium by a Belgian Civil Code since 2020.

Belgium declared independence on 4 October 1830,[2] and French was swiftly declared the official language of legislation. The decree of 16 November 1830[3] established French as the sole authentic language of the decrees of the National Congress, the constitutional assembly. This choice was confirmed by the law of 19 September 1831 concerning the sanctioning and promulgation of laws.[4] At this time, the Civil Code had not changed at all since 1807; even the references to France and the French Empire remained in the Civil Code (they would only be corrected in 1949; Van Dievoet 1949–1950).[5]

A definitive and authentic 'Dutch' text of the Civil Code, however, took much more time to materialize (Heirbaut 2004a). In 1804, alongside the thirty-six different laws, a Dutch or, to be more precise, a "Flemish"[6] translation was published in the bilingual edition of the official journal, the *Bulletin des lois*;[7] the quality of the translation was nevertheless very poor. Commercial translations of a somewhat higher quality were prepared and published. In the Northern Netherlands, an excellent translation of the Civil Code by Joannes van der Linden saw the light of day. This translation was commonly used in the Southern Netherlands as well, when they were part of the Netherlands. After the creation of the independent Belgian state, a translation was prepared by Karel Lodewijk Ledeganck, which became the standard translation in Belgium for the decades to follow. Ledeganck's translation, however, was also flawed in several ways, especially its lack of consistent terminology and its use of uncommon words. Most importantly, it had never been granted government approval, as this was a purely private initiative.[8]

2   *Indépendance de la Belgique* (Independence of Belgium), 4 October 1830, *Bulletin officiel* 8 October 1830.
3   *Arrêté du Gouvernement provisoire: Le Bulletin officiel des lois restera publié en français: les gouverneurs des provinces où le flamand et l'allemand sont plus en usage que le français, sont autorisés à faire traduire* (Decree of the Provisional Government: The Official Bulletin of Laws will remain published in French: the governors of the provinces where Flemish and German are more in use than French, are authorized to have it translated) of 16 November 1830, *Bulletin officiel* 20 November 1830.
4   Loi concernant la sanction et la promulgation des lois (Act concerning the sanction and promulgation of laws) of 19 September 1831, *Bulletin officiel* 1831 No. XCIII.
5   Wet tot verbetering van de verouderde termen van de Franse tekst van het Burgerlijk Wetboek en tot vaststelling, in die tekst, van sommige stilzwijgende opheffingen (Act to correct the obsolete terms of the French text of the Civil Code and to determine, in that text, certain tacit repeals) of 15 December 1949, *Belgisch Staatsblad* 1–3 January 1950.
6   It was common to refer to the Dutch language spoken in the South as "Flemish" and in the North as "Hollandic", a usage which disappeared in the twentieth century, at least in formal speech.
7   Not to be confused with the *Bulletin hollandais* that existed in the Netherlands after its annexation by France (D'hulst 2015).
8   See the commission's report, which can be found in the parliamentary proceedings. *Wetsontwerp tot invoering van de Nederlandse tekst van het Burgerlijk Wetboek*, Parl.St. Chamber of Representatives 1959–1960, No. 507/1, 5–9.

The real turning point was the Law of Equality of 18 April 1898.[9] From then on, the entire legislative process would be completely bilingual, from the work in Parliament until publication in the official journal.[10] This meant that the new laws that changed the old Civil Code would be authentic in both languages, implying that those changed articles would be authentic in both languages, but that the other articles, predating 1898, remained authentic in French only. In other words, the 1898 law changed nothing for the Civil Code, except for the articles that were changed after 1898. This situation was unsustainable in the long term, and demands grew for an official Dutch translation of the laws predating 1898.

The issue was first tackled by a short-lived commission, set up by the German occupier during World War I. A more serious attempt was made by the Belgian government by royal decree of 18 September 1923, which instated a commission first chaired by Hendrik De Hoon and, from 1932 on, by Emiel Van Dievoet; their task was to translate the Constitution, the codes and the laws predating the 1898 Law of Equality. The commission prepared a translation of the Civil Code, promulgated part by part, which was to be the only one to be used for the purpose of education and the drafting of future legislation. As the translations made by the commission were published by royal decree and not voted in Parliament, they were not authentic.[11] The commission did not survive World War II, but a new commission was set up to replace it in 1954 (Van Haver 1990, 601–620).[12] Unlike the 1923 commission, this commission, again presided by Emiel Van Dievoet, was authorized to

---

9   *Wet betreffende het gebruik der Vlaamsche taal in de officiëele bekendmakingen* (Act concerning the use of the Flemish language in official publications) of 18 April 1898, *Belgisch Staatsblad* 15 May 1898.

10 At least in theory. In practice, almost all parliamentary work was done in French for decades to come (Doms 1965).

11 The government preferred not to vote on these texts in parliament, as, at that time, it was assumed that Article 41 of the Constitution required such texts to be voted on article by article, which would take too much time (Victor 1935, 96–7). Interestingly, the translations prepared by the commission at the Ministry of Colonies, which translated the decrees dating from the time of the Congo Free State, were authentic in both languages. This means that those parts of the Civil Code for which an official translation had been published already had an authentic text in both languages in Belgian Congo long before this was the case in Belgium. However, court proceedings in Belgian Congo remained in French only until the decree of 15 February 1957 regulating the use of the French and the Dutch language in judicial cases, which, according to Article 3 of the Colonial Charter, would already have been promulgated by 1913 (Meeuwis 2015, 59).

12 For the royal decree, see *Koninklijk Besluit houdende oprichting van de Commissie belast met de voorbereiding van de Nederlandse tekst van de Grondwet en de voornaamste wetten en besluiten* (Royal Decree establishing the Commission charged with the preparation of the Dutch text of the Constitution and the most important laws and decrees) of 5 April 1954, *Belgisch Staatsblad* 5 April 1954.

prepare an 'authentic' Dutch text of laws predating 1898, which had to be passed in Parliament before taking effect.[13]

This difference is of utmost importance. Until then, for texts predating 1898, only the French version was authentic; the Dutch translation was not. This distinction meant that, in case of any uncertainty about the meaning of the text, only the French version would be taken into account.[14] The new commission, however, would not prepare a Dutch translation but instead a Dutch 'authentic' text of the laws it was working on. Now, the French and the Dutch text would be of equal status.[15] The commission first finished its work on the Constitution,[16] immediately followed by the Dutch text of the Civil Code. In 1961, the text approved by the commission was passed in Parliament and published in the official journal on 18 May 1962.[17]

3 The Dutch text of the Belgian Civil Code of 1961

The Dutch text of the Civil Code is generally praised as a masterpiece.[18] The 1954 Van Dievoet Commission was composed of some of the finest experts in both the legal field and the linguistic field (Van Haver 1990). The commission was chaired by former minister Emiel Van Dievoet, a renowned law professor with an excellent knowledge of legal history[19] as well as a great interest in

---

13   In rare cases, there were exceptions to these rules. This was the case when post-1898 laws were closely linked with pre-1898 laws, or if it was necessary to change the terminology of old laws to the new terminology established in, for example, the new Dutch text of the Civil Code.

14   This situation still exists in Belgium with regard to the German translation, which is still not authentic, with the exception of the German text of the Constitution (Muylle and Stangherlin 2006).

15   For the importance of the difference, see Herbots (1973).

16   The Dutch text of the Constitution was written in a relatively short period of time, yet was only enacted in 1967. From 1954 until 1958, the Christian People's Party blocked any amendment to the Constitution to protest the government's education policy; in 1959, the text was approved by the Chamber of Representatives but rejected by the Senate, and no agreement could be reached until the government fell over the Unitary Law in 1961. From 1961 until 1965, the Chambers lacked the competence to amend the Constitution (see Article 131 of the Constitution). It was only after the 1965 elections that an agreement on the Dutch text could be reached.

17   *Wet tot invoering van de Nederlandse tekst van het burgerlijk wetboek* (Act 30 December 1961 to introduce the Dutch text of the Civil Code) of 30 December 1961, *Belgisch Staatsblad* 18 May 1962.

18   In general, all the translations prepared by the Van Dievoet Commission have been extremely well received. Only very rarely did some of the texts it produced give rise to some mild criticism, such as the text of the Criminal Code (Leliard 2007–2008).

19   He was the author of the standard work of comparative Belgian-Dutch legal history (Van Dievoet 1943).

legal language. He was a man with excellent political connections[20] and an important proponent of Belgian-Dutch cooperation.[21]

Among the members were other important jurists and high-ranking civil servants, as well as Emiel Van Dievoet's son, Guido Van Dievoet, who would become chairman of the commission in 1967 until his death in 2008, when the commission was disbanded.[22] The commission did not lack well-known linguists, either, like Edgard Blancquaert, Jan Lodewijk Pauwels and Willem Pée. Not only did the commission ensure a balance between jurists and linguists: it also harmonized the four different universities in Belgium at the time.

In preparing the Dutch text of the Civil Code, the commission consulted previous translations, including the translation made by Joannes van der Linden and, most importantly, the translation by the 1923 commission, which had been published by royal decree in various phases between 1932 and 1939. The commission also took into account the 1838 Dutch Civil Code, as well as the draft of the new Dutch Civil Code by Eduard Maurits Meijers. It consulted doctrine from the North and, occasionally, the commission had a look at the terminology used in Germany or in the legal history of the Northern and the Southern Netherlands themselves, which had a rich tradition of customary law. For more specific topics, the commission was expanded with a temporary member, always an expert in the field, usually a university professor (Victor 1960–1961).[23] Of course, dictionaries were also consulted, including general dictionaries (Van Dale), legal dictionaries (Fockema Andreae, Verdeyen/Moors) and the *Woordenboek der Nederlandsche Taal* (Dictionary of the Dutch Language, the world's largest dictionary). Last but not least, the remarks of a short-lived mixed Belgian-Dutch commission, which had existed from 1938 to 1941, were also taken into account (Van Dievoet 1997).

One of the major points of contention was the influence of the legal language of the Netherlands. Though some had proposed a more "Flemish" translation (e.g., Paul Bellefroid), it was generally agreed that the

---

20   From 1919 until 1936, Emiel Van Dievoet was a member of the Chamber of Representatives for the Catholic Party. He was the Belgian agriculture minister in 1931–1932 and justice minister in 1939.

21   Emiel Van Dievoet and Eduard Maurits Meijers were the driving forces behind the Association for the Comparative Study of the Law of Belgium and the Netherlands (Victor 1947–1948).

22   For the composition of the commission at the time of the Dutch text of the Civil Code, see *Wetsontwerp tot invoering van de Nederlandse tekst van het Burgerlijk Wetboek, Parl. St.* Chamber of Representatives 1959–1960, No. 507/1, 3.

23   This practice is also explained in the commission's report in the parliamentary proceedings. *Wetsontwerp tot invoering van de Nederlandse tekst van het Burgerlijk Wetboek, Parl.St.* Chamber of Representatives 1959–1960, No. 507/1, 10–11.

Netherlands were the model to follow.[24] This conviction was already shared by Herbert De Hoon[25] and Emiel Vliebergh in the 1930s, and also by Emiel Van Dievoet, who explained the commission's methodology in the following way:

> Dat de Nederlandse rechtstaal in België en in Nederland één dient te zijn vloeit reeds voort uit de taaleenheid van het Nederlands sprekende volk in Noord en Zuid. Voor de rechtstaal gezien als technische taal, is zulks des te meer noodzakelijk omdat het gebruik van twee uitdrukkingen voor een zelfde begrip misverstand en verwarring kan teweegbrengen.
>
> (The Dutch people in North and South speak the same language and the legal language, as a technical language, requires uniformity, as the use of two different expressions for one term would produce misunderstandings and confusion.) (Van Dievoet 1964, 13).

This was not easy, however, as the language of the Dutch Civil Code at the time, which dated from 1838, was already considered archaic by the 1950s,[26] and, of course, Dutch law and Belgian law had developed differently since North and South separated in 1830.)

The commission worked on the translation for several years, convening six hours per week; a quick calculation demonstrates that this equals just a few articles per session. Discussions in the commission were extremely lengthy, and the research produced before cutting the knot on a particular topic is

---

24 The insistence on following the Dutch model did sometimes lead to remarkable situations. For example, Lodewijk De Hondt, who translated the Criminal Code and was a staunch proponent for the unity of Dutch legal language, translated the French *prévenu* with the Dutch *beklaagde* (English: "the accused"), a word borrowed from the 1838 Dutch Criminal Code but completely unknown in Belgium at the time. In 1921 however, a new Criminal Code was promulgated in the Netherlands, which replaced *beklaagde* by *verdachte*. Since then, the term *beklaagde* only continues to exist in the Dutch legal language as used in Belgium (Bellefroid 1933–1934, 140). This is also explained in the commission's report. *Ontwerp van wet 1° tot verbetering van de verouderde termen in de Franse tekst van het Wetboek van Strafvordering en tot opheffing van een aantal daarin nodeloos geworden bepalingen; 2° tot invoering van de Nederlandse tekst van hetzelfde Wetboek en van de wet van 20 april 1874 op de voorlopige hechtenis, Parl.St.* Senate 1966–1967, 37, 9–10.

25 De Hoon famously said in this regard: "De Nederlandsche rechtstaal bestaat in Holland; niet noodig veel te zoeken, er valt maar over te neemen wat ze daar hebben." ("There is no need to draw up a Dutch legal language as it already exists in Holland.") (Bellefroid 1933–1934, 138)

26 See the commission's report in the parliamentary proceedings. *Wetsontwerp tot invoering van de Nederlandse tekst van het Burgerlijk Wetboek, Parl.St.* Chamber of Representatives 1959–1960, No. 507/1, 11–12.

remarkable.[27] The result was an excellent translation of the French original, or, more precisely, a new Dutch text of the Civil Code, with a consistent terminology throughout the text. The translation was universally praised, both by contemporary sources and by more recent doctrine (Victor 1961–1962; Hendrickx 2003, 25–28).

4 Developments after 1961

The tragedy of Dutch legislative language in Belgium is that the almost fanatic work by the Van Dievoet Commission has never been followed up by the legislators. Amendments to the Civil Code after 1961 were rarely, if ever, sent to the Van Dievoet Commission for further review.[28] The Belgian Council of State thus became the only official body to examine the linguistic quality of new laws, but due to its increasing workload and the lack of time granted to the Council to advise on new legislation – often as little as a few days– this aspect of its work has become less and less important (Hendrickx 2003). This lack of interest in the quality of legal language is part of a broader phenomenon, which includes the partial recognition of separate Dutch language standards in Belgium and the Netherlands, especially in spoken language, and the decline of linguistic purism in Flanders.[29]

Nevertheless, the general structure of the 1961 Civil Code text has been preserved, and the terminology used in the Civil Code is now widely used by the Dutch-speaking legal world in Belgium. However, occasionally, the legislators has decided not to stick with the terminology. A striking example is the

---

27 The report made by the commission concerning the translation of the Civil Code, which is seventy-three pages long, provides excellent testimony of this attitude. *Wetsontwerp tot invoering van de Nederlandse tekst van het Burgerlijk Wetboek, Parl.St.* Chamber of Representatives 1959–1960, No. 507/1, 3–75.

28 This did happen in the early years of the commission (e.g., the Motor Vehicles Compulsory Insurance Act).

29 The main commercial dictionary of the Dutch language, the *Van Dale Groot woordenboek van de Nederlandse taal*, famously introduced the terms 'Dutch Dutch' (*Nederlands-Nederlands*) alongside the already existing 'Belgian Dutch' (*Belgisch-Nederlands*) in its 2015 edition. In fact, the term 'Belgian Dutch' itself was unthinkable up until only a few decades ago, when all Belgian Dutch words and expressions were simply classified as 'regional' (*gewestelijk*) in all major dictionaries. Furthermore, for example, in the 1950s Standard Dutch was widely used throughout the Dutch language area in film and popular music, radio and television. Now, the usage of more informal speeches such as *tussentaal* (language register between Standard Dutch and Belgian Dutch dialects) or *Polder Dutch* (informal language register used in the Netherlands, especially in the western part of the country) are more accepted, the opposition to the use of loan words has diminished, etc.

translation of the French word *adoption*. When the 1923 commission had to translate this word, there was no legal term available in the Netherlands, as the North had no adoption law until 1956. Two Dutch alternatives were proposed: *adoptie*, or *aanneming van kinderen* ("taking up children").[30] (Interestingly, the Civil Code of Belgian Congo translated *adoption* with *aanneming van een kind*.) The latter was more similar to the German terminology *Annahme an Kindesstatt*.[31] The commission opted for the latter one, probably for reasons of linguistic purism. The exact reason will never be known, as the commission did not keep minutes. However, as noted, the commission's translation was not authentic. Interestingly, on 22 March 1940 a new Belgian Adoption Law was adopted, altering the Civil Code but keeping the term *aanneming van kinderen*. As its text was authentic in both languages, this became the official legal term. Unfortunately, in 1956, when the Netherlands introduced its own adoption law, the choice was to opt for the Latin-derived term *adoptie*.[32] When preparing the authentic text of the Dutch Civil Code, the Van Dievoet Commission decided to keep the old Belgian terminology – a rare instance where it did not follow the Dutch model. As such a decision was inevitably going to be controversial, it was justified in a seven-page note attached to the report made by the commission.[33] In this note, the commission explained the two different possible terminologies; then, it examined the terms used in Dutch during the *Ancien Régime* – for example, an edict by Albert and Isabella of 14 December 1616; the *costumen* (customs) of the town of Oudenaarde of 27 March 1615; a decision by the States of Guelders of 27 September 1653, and so on – all of which used the term *adoptie* or *adoptatie*. The first use of the term *aanneming van kinderen* seemed to stem from Hugo Grotius, well-known for his habit of 'inventing' Dutch legal terms. After consulting different dictionaries, including the *Middelnederlandsch Woordenboek* (Dictionary of Middle Dutch) and the aforementioned *Woordenboek der Nederlandsche Taal*, the commission decided to choose *aanneming van kinderen* for pragmatic reasons: it had been the official Dutch term in Belgium since 1940.

---

30 The word *aanneming* also has a completely different meaning in the Civil Code, being the translation of *entreprise* in *entreprise d'un ouvrage* (Article 1794) or *marché* (Articles 1711, 1779 and 1787) (Moors and Theissen 2015, v° aanneming).
31 § 1741 BGB. Now *Annahme als Kind*.
32 A draft law prepared by the Belgian government in the same year retained the 'Belgian' terminology. Wetsontwerp tot wijziging van Hoofdstuk I van Titel VIII van Boek I van het Burgerlijk Wetboek betreffende de aanneming van een kind, *Parl.St.* Senate 1956–1957, 27.
33 The report can be found in the parliamentary proceedings. Wetsontwerp tot invoering van de Nederlandse tekst van het Burgerlijk Wetboek, *Parl.St.* Chamber of Representatives 1959–1960, No. 507/1, 15–21.

Adoption law, however, was a field of law which was quickly evolving at the time, and the 1940 law was already seen as outdated by the time the Dutch text of the Belgian Civil Code was enacted. In 1962, a new adoption law was proposed,[34] again altering the provisions of the Civil Code. In the original proposal, the 1961 terminology would be retained.[35] However, the Justice Committee of the Chamber of Representatives decided to switch the terminology from *aanneming van kinderen* to *adoptie* when it convened in 1965,[36] without giving any reasoning behind it.[37] After the adoption of the new law, *adoptie* became the legal term in Belgium.

The new Adoption Law was closely connected with the law of 8 April 1965 on the protection of youth. Both laws were criticized for their lack of consistency with the 1961 authentic text. Baert[38] gave a few examples of this inconsistency in an article in the *Rechtskundig Weekblad* (Baert 1967–1968, 1636): the translation of *quinze ans* as *vijftien jaar* ("fifteen year", singular, whereas the 1961 text always translates as plural *vijftien jaren*, "fifteen years"), *en tout cas* as *alleszins* ("fully", instead of *in alle gevallen* ,"in all cases"), and the translation of *spécial* as *speciaal* ("special") instead of the preferred translation *bijzonder*. Baert notes: "Wanneer de wetgever op die manier verder gaat zal binnen korte tijd zeker een nieuwe taalcommissie aan het werk moeten gezet worden." ("If the legislature will continue this way, it will only take a short time before a new language commission will have to be set up").

In one case, the legislators, when drafting amendments to the Civil Code, even reverted to a translation predating the 1961 translation. In 1970, the 1951 Commercial Lease Act, which is incorporated in the Civil Code and thus received an authentic Dutch text in 1961 as well, was amended, and its Article 13 was rewritten on the basis of the Dutch text of the original 1951 Act, even though it was completely rewritten by the Van Dievoet Commission in the 1961 text (Heirbaut 2004b, lvi–lvii).

Another example is the translation of the French terms *défunt* ("deceased") and *testateur* ("testator") in Belgian inheritance law. In 1961, the Van Dievoet

---

34 The proposal was made by three Flemings and three Walloons, one from each of the three important political parties. *Wetsvoorstel tot wijziging van het eerste hoofdstuk van Titel VIII, eerste Boek, van het Burgerlijk Wetboek*, Parl.St. Chamber of Representatives 1961–1962, 436/1.

35 The same is true for a different adoption-related proposal in 1963. *Voorstel van wet tot wijziging van artikel 344 van het Burgerlijk Wetboek*, Parl.St. Senate 1963–1964, 22.

36 *Verslag over het wetsvoorstel tot wijziging van het eerste hoofdstuk van Titel VIII, eerste Boek, van het Burgerlijk Wetboek*, Parl.St. Chamber of Representatives 1961–1962, 436/2.

37 The change was not discussed in the plenary meeting either. *Hand*. Chamber of Representatives 1964–1965, 11 February 1965, 23–38.

38 Geert Baert would join the commission in 1978 and remain a member until the end of the commission in 2008.

Commission was very clear: *défunt* is translated as *overledene*, *testateur* as *erflater*. However, already in the 1970s the legislators did not seem to pursue this logic anymore: the 19 September 1977 Act[39] amended Article 720, writing *défunt* in the French text and *erflater* in the Dutch text. The Act, however, was implementing the Benelux Agreement on Commorientes and stuck with its terminology (Puelinckx-Coene and Perrick, 1978). Article 1 of the annex to this agreement used the word *de cujus* in French, which is not used in the Belgian Civil Code. Apparently, the legislators replaced this term in the French text with the correct term *défunt*, yet did not take the Dutch text into account when making this change, which still used the word *erflater*. Had the legislators taken a look at the Dutch text, they would have noted that the correct Dutch translation of *défunt* would have been *overledene*.

Another peculiar case was the 1987 law[40] that also reformed the rules on paternal power, from then on to be known as "parental authority". Interestingly, this change in the French text of title IX of book I of the Civil Code, from *De la puissance paternelle* ("paternal authority") to *De l'autorité parentale*, was already partially foreshadowed by the 1961 Dutch text of the Civil Code, which used the term *ouderlijke macht* instead of *vaderlijke macht*, thus translating it as "parental power". As a matter of fact, in the authentic Dutch text of the Congolese Civil Code before the colony's independence in 1960, *de l'autorité paternelle* (paternal authority, not paternal power) was already translated as *ouderlijk gezag* (parental authority).[41] Apparently, the translators at both the Ministry of Justice and the Ministry of Colonies were not that fond of the idea of paternal power or authority.

Even though the general terminology of the Van Dievoet Commission has been largely preserved up to the present day – partially because key parts of the Civil Code, such as the law of obligations, have hardly been amended at all in subsequent decades – the Civil Code reform currently proposed in Belgium will cause further deviation from the original. For example, if the reform for the law of obligations is implemented, the terms *convention* (*overeenkomst*, "agreement") and *contrat* (contract) would be unified into the single term of *contrat* (contract). This move is somewhat unfortunate, as the

---

39 *Wet houdende goedkeuring van de Beneluxovereenkomst inzake commorientes, en van de bijlage, ondertekend te Brussel op 29 december 1972* (Act approving the Benelux agreement on commorientes and its annex, signed in Brussels on 29 December 1972) of 19 September 1977, *Belgisch Staatsblad* 10 January 1978.

40 *Wet tot wijziging van een aantal bepalingen betreffende de afstamming* (Act amending a number of provisions on filiation) of 31 March 1987, *Belgisch Staatsblad* 27 May 1987.

41 Decree of 25 March 1953 *"Nederlandse tekst van het boek: "Personen" van het Congolees Burgerlijk Wetboek"*, *Ambtelijk Blad van Belgisch-Congo* 15 April 1953.

Dutch term *overeenkomst* is the one normally used in Dutch law, as well as in European Union law, which always has only one Dutch text for both Belgium and the Netherlands. Furthermore, in other fields of Belgian law, the term *overeenkomst* is preserved, as in *arbeidsovereenkomst* ("labor agreement", but in French *contrat de travail*). Interestingly, the 2018 reform of matrimonial property law retained the term *huwelijksovereenkomst* (*convention matrimoniale*, "marriage contract"), except in the new Article 1469/2, § 4, where it uses the term *huwelijkscontract* (*contrat de mariage*). Why a different term is used here is not clear. The fact that another article, Article 299, uses *contrat de mariage* in the French text, but *huwelijksovereenkomst* in the Dutch text, seems to prove that the legislators did not really pay attention when drafting this law.[42]

Another interesting term is the French term *faute*. The Van Dievoet Commission almost never translated this word by the most obvious translation *fout* ("error" or "mistake"), as, in most cases, this translation is considered incorrect (or 'Belgian Dutch'); the correct translation in those cases is *schuld* ("fault" or "guilt"). The commission did seem overly sensitive toward this issue, as in some cases the translation *schuld* proposed by the commission is not the most appropriate. However, the proposed reform of the Civil Code tends to go to the other extreme, simply translating *faute* with *fout* and replacing *schuld* by *fout* everywhere, no matter what is meant exactly. Apparently, the rationale is that the mistake is so common in Belgium nowadays that it makes no sense to oppose it anymore. Though most Flemings would effectively suggest that *faute* can always be translated by *fout*, even in the meaning of *schuld*, it is certainly strange that the legislators would impose a linguistic error throughout the Civil Code.

The Dutch text of the new Civil Code can be criticized, because, even though all of the members of the commissions which prepared the texts were among the best jurists of the country, they did not have the time nor the responsibility to draft a text at the level of the one prepared by the Van Dievoet Commission; not only do the new commissions lack linguists, but they also had less time to write a new Civil Code than the Van Dievoet Commission had to translate the old one.

---

42   *Wet tot wijziging van het Burgerlijk Wetboek en diverse andere bepalingen wat het huwelijksvermogensrecht betreft en tot wijziging van de wet van 31 juli 2017 tot wijziging van het Burgerlijk Wetboek wat de erfenissen en de giften betreft en tot wijziging van diverse bepalingen ter zake* (Act amending the Civil Code and various other provisions as regards matrimonial property law and amending the Act of 31 July 2017 amending the Civil Code as regards inheritances and gifts and amending various provisions in this regard) of 22 July 2018, *Belgisch Staatsblad* 27 July 2018.

In fact, other recent law texts are even more problematic. An excellent example is the 2017 reform for inheritance law.[43] Before the reform, most of the provisions of Belgian inheritance law had not been changed since 1804 (Heirbaut and Baeteman 2004, 2254). In particular, the insistence on differentiating movable and immovable property was considered outdated. Though the reform retained the general framework of the Civil Code, the sheer number of amendments to the Code is impressive.

However, from a language point of view, the reform is rather disappointing: the consistent translation by the Van Dievoet Commission in 1961 has basically been nullified. This can come as no surprise; even for new legislation of this importance, the Council of State was only given thirty days to provide its recommendations. Despite the poor Dutch (and French) text of the act, the Council of State only gave two remarks related to the quality of the texts.[44]

For example, the legislators still mix up *défunt (overledene)* and *testateur (erflater)*. Where the new Article 843 correctly translates *défunt* as *overledene*, the new Article 205bis translates the same word as *erflater*. Even stranger is the use of new terminology in the new Articles 922 and 922/1, where *testateur* is not translated as *erflater*, but as *testator*. Notable, too, is the heavy use of the word *verzaken* as a translation of the French *renoncer* ("to renounce"); two times in the matrimonial property law reform, and no less than thirty-three times in the inheritance law reform. *Renoncer* was normally only translated as *verwerpen*. However, in this meaning, *verzaken* is Belgian Dutch, which is why it was never used in this sense by the Van Dievoet Commission.[45] This is not a surprise, as, with very few exceptions, the commission always used terms the same way as they are used in the Netherlands.

A typical example is the new Article 205bis of the Civil Code, which speaks of *bloedverwanten in opgaande lijn* ("relatives in ascending line") as a translation of *ascendants*. In the Civil Code of 1961, however, *ascendants* is always translated as *bloedverwanten in 'de' opgaande lijn*, as it is in the Netherlands, for example, in the Articles 747, 750, 907 and 935 of the Civil Code. The same mistake is made several times with the translation of the term *descendants*, for

---

43 *Wet tot wijziging van het Burgerlijk Wetboek wat de erfenissen en de giften betreft en tot wijziging van diverse andere bepalingen ter zake* (Act amending the Civil Code as regards inheritances and gifts and amending various other provisions in this regard) of 31 July 2017, *Belgisch Staatsblad* 1 September 2017.

44 Adv.Rvs nr. 60.998/2 bij het wetsvoorstel tot wijziging van het Burgerlijk Wetboek wat de erfenissen en de giften betreft en tot wijziging van diverse andere bepalingen ter zake, Parl.St. Kamer 2016–2017, n.d.

45 Moors and Theissen 2015, v° *verzaken*. See also the *Woordenboek voor correct taalgebruik* and the *Van Dale Groot woordenboek van de Nederlandse taal*.

example, in the new Articles 843 and 1100/7. The new law is very consistent in this mistake; however, the old articles in the Civil Code remain unchanged, so both translations will now inevitably have to co-exist.

Article 10, 1° of the 2017 law, amending only the Dutch text of Article 745quater, is also interesting, replacing *vorderen* with *vragen* (both meaning "to demand"). This seems logical, as the French text uses the word *demander*, which is closer in meaning to *vragen*. However, even though the French word *demander* is usually translated as *vragen* (see Articles 878, 881, 921, 1143 and 1184), it is also sometimes translated as *vorderen* (for example, in Articles 826, 1004, 1006 and 1011). In this way, the purpose of this amendment is not very clear. Another typical detail is the translation of the French *alinéas 4 à 6* in the same article, which is translated as *vierde tot en met zesde lid*, whereas elsewhere in the Civil Code, *vierde tot zesde lid* is consistently used (for example, in Article 353–4bis). Moreover, in Article 745sexies, in the French text we read *il en va de même* (normally: *il en est de même*), translated as *zo ook* (normally: *hetzelfde geldt*[46]) meaning "the same applies to". In Article 817, the French text is correct (*il en est de même*), but the Dutch translation is here *zo ook* instead of *hetzelfde geldt*.

Article 816 translates *mede-erfgenamen* as *héritiers* ("heirs") instead of *cohéritiers* ("co-heirs"); perhaps a typographical error, but in that case it should have been corrected before the vote in Parliament (even if the Council of State did not notice it either). Another peculiarity is Article 820: *avant de* is translated as *vooraleer* ("before") instead of *alvorens*. In Article 835, it is translated as *vóór*. *Vooraleer* is a common word in Belgium, but not in the Netherlands; in the North, it is seen as very formal and not used in the Civil Code.

Another potential typographical error can be found in the new Article 820. In the old text, the French *le numéraire, les comptes en banque et les valeurs de portefeuille* were translated as *het gereed geld, de bankrekeningen en de beleggingswaarden aan toonder*. In the new article, the Dutch text is *het gereed geld en de bankrekeningen*, the French text *les comptes en banque et les valeurs de portefeuille*. Clearly, different words were deleted in both texts; in this case, the Dutch text is correct, as it clearly reflects the will of the legislators.

On a different note, we encounter strange expressions in a legal context, such as in Article 822 *in principe* instead of *en principe* ("in principle") and *er wordt naar gestreefd* ("it is being pursued"). A common spelling mistake can be found in Article 855, writing *teniet gedaan* ("negated") as two words instead of one. In Article 823, *une disposition conventionnelle* is translated as

---

46 Except for Article 1042, where the Van Dievoet Commission wrote *"Hetzelfde heeft plaats"*, probably because the 1923 commission wrote it that way.

een conventionele bepaling ("contract clause"). *Conventioneel*, however, was not used in this sense in the Civil Code; *conventionnel* was translated as *uit overeenkomst* or as *bedongen*. And in Article 858 and 1100/7, we find a mistake against the classic *hen/hun*-rule (two forms for 'them'): in Dutch, *hen* should be used as an accusative or in connection with a preposition, *hun* should be used as a dative. The text uses *hen* as a dative in both cases, which is incorrect.

It must be said that the legislators did implement two small points of criticism from a language point of view made by the Council of State, which, unfortunately, only had thirty days to give its recommendations. The Justice Committee of the Chamber of Representatives also did correct a few mistakes, though mostly when the Dutch and the French text clearly did not have the same meaning. A striking example can be found in the same report, which summarizes the problem of the current translation practice in Belgium. In the Dutch text of Article 823, the wording *ten bezwarende titel* ("for valuable consideration") was present, whereas the French equivalent *à titre onéreux* was not. Therefore, the Judiciary Committee decided to add these words to the French text.[47] Unfortunately, nobody noticed that the Dutch *ten bezwarende titel* is in fact incorrect; it should have been *onder bezwarende titel*.[48] The Judiciary Committee only had to look at Article 1106 of the Civil Code, which defines a contract *onder bezwarende titel*, to know the correct terminology.

The 2018 matrimonial property law reform, which is closely related to the inheritance law reform, both being in force since 1 September 2018, is equally inconsistent. For example, the new Article 299 translates *sauf convention contraire* ("notwithstanding any clause to the contrary") as *behoudens overeenkomst in tegenovergestelde zin*, whereas Article 301 still translates it as *tenzij de partijen anders overeenkomen* and Article 1449 as *tenzij anders is bedongen*. In short, the linguistic quality of the text has some serious defects, especially in the Dutch text.

Some expressed hope that these two acts of parliament would be an exception, as the government was preparing a new Civil Code which would replace the old code entirely anyway. So far, two books of the new Civil Code have been published in the official journal. However, the text of the new Civil Code is not unproblematic either. For example, in many articles of the old

---

47 Wetsvoorstel tot wijziging van het Burgerlijk Wetboek wat de erfenissen en de giften betreft en tot wijziging van diverse andere bepalingen ter zake. Wetvoorstel tot wijziging van het Burgerlijk Wetboek met betrekking tot het erfrecht. Wetvoorstel tot wijziging van het Burgerlijk Wetboek wat de globale erfovereenkomst over een niet-opengevallen nalatenschap betreft. Verslag van de tweede lezing namens de Commissie voor de Justitie, uitgebracht door de heer Gautier Calomne, Parl. St. Chamber of Representatives 2016–2017, 54-2282/9.
48 Article 1106 Civil Code. Moors and Theissen 2015, *v° titel*.

Civil Code (e.g., Article. 3 CC, 838 CC, 966 CC, 1244 CC, 1595, 2° CC), the structure *même + adjective* is used (*même* meaning "even"); since it is not possible to translate such a construction literally into Dutch, the Van Dievoet Commission translated the sentences in which this construction is used in a way that is appropriate for the Dutch language. However, in Art. 8.3 of the new Civil Code, we can read *Le droit, même étranger, ne doit pas être prouvé* translated as *Het recht, zelfs buitenlands, moet niet bewezen worden*. Literally this means "the law, even foreign, does not have to be proven"; a very unnatural-sounding wording in Dutch. In fact, even the French text of the law has some issues. For example, the word *entrainer* (to entail) is spelled without an *accent circonflexe* on the i (otherwise, it would be *entraîner*); this alternative spelling has been allowed since the French spelling reform of 1990. Interestingly, however, Book 7 of the Civil Code is titled *Les sûretés* (Securities) instead of *Les suretés*, which would be the recommended spelling when implementing the 1990 reform.

5   Conclusion

While it is impossible to summarize the entire development of the Dutch text of the Belgian Civil Code in this chapter, the examples mentioned above do give us a good general overview. None of the Dutch translations of the Civil Code predating 1961 were authentic, and especially the nineteenth-century translations had major flaws. However, the quality of the 1961 text was excellent, prepared by extremely skilled scholars in both the legal and the linguistic field. Unfortunately, after the enactment of this text, amendments to the Civil Code were generally no longer reviewed by the Van Dievoet Commission.[49] The linguistic quality of amendments was already criticized in the 1960s, but the most recent reforms of the Civil Code are of particular concern. As the Van Dievoet Commission does not exist anymore, only the Council of State still offers some healthy criticism on the legislature's proposals; however, throughout the years, the Council has been offering less and less linguistic advice due to time constraints (Hendrickx 2003; Van Damme and De Sutter 2013, 184–186).[50] At present, neither the quality of the Dutch and the French

---

49   In fact, during its later years, even the translations prepared by the Van Dievoet Commission of laws predating 1898 were completely ignored by the government and by the legislature. As such, 128 translations were made, but never implemented (Leliard 2008–2009).

50   According to Article 84 of the Council of State Act and to the Council of State's own *Vademecum adviesprocedure voor de afdeling wetgeving 2018*, the Council often only reviews the language used by the proposal if it does not have a limit to give its advice, which rarely happens.

text nor the equivalence of both texts is thoroughly checked by any official government body. Still, at a time when more and more scholars advocate a new Law of Equality for the German text of the law, addressing this issue should be the first priority.

References

Baert, Geert. 1967–1968. "Beschouwingen over de burgerrechtelijke bepalingen van de wet van 8 april 1965 betreffende de jeugdbescherming." *Rechtskundig Weekblad*, 1609–1636.

Bellefroid, Paul. 1933–1934. "Beschouwingen over de Nederlandsche rechtstaal in Vlaanderen." *Rechtskundig Weekblad*, 137–150.

D'hulst, Lieven. 2015. "« Localiser » des traductions nationales: Le Bulletin des lois en version flamande et hollandaise sous la période française (1797–1813)." In *Nationenbildung und Übersetzung*, edited by Dilek Dizdar, Andreas Gipper and Michael Schreiber, 93–108. Ost-West-Express 23. Berlin: Frank & Timme.

Doms, Philippe. 1965. "L'emploi des langues dans les chambres législatives en Belgique." *Res Publica*, 126–140.

Heirbaut, Dirk. 2004a. "Editing and Translating the Code Civil in Belgium, 1804–2004." *The Legal History Review* 2004, 215–229.

———. 2004b. "Inleiding tot de Cumulatieve editie van het Burgerlijk Wetboek in België: gebruikte bronnen en methodologische problemen." In *Cumulatieve editie van het Burgerlijk Wetboek*, edited by Dirk Heirbaut and Gustaaf Baeteman, xlv–lxxxii. Ghent: Kluwer.

Heirbaut, Dirk, and Gustaaf Baeteman. 2004. *Cumulatieve editie van het Burgerlijk Wetboek: de huidige en de originele tekst met alle wijzigingen in België van 1804 tot 2004*. Ghent: Kluwer.

Hendrickx, Karl. 2003. *Taal- en formuleringsproblemen in de regelgeving: de taalopmerkingen in de adviezen van de Raad van State*. Bruges: die Keure.

Herbots, Jacques. 1973. *Meertalig rechtswoord, rijkere rechtsvinding*. Ghent: Story-Scientia.

Leliard, Jos. 2007–2008. "De weergave van de begrippen wil, wetenschap, doel, bedoeling en voornemen in de tweetalige tekst van het Strafwetboek." *Rechtskundig Weekblad*, 922–927.

———. 2008–2009. "De receptie van de ontwerpen van de commissie belast met de voorbereiding van de Nederlandse tekst van de Grondwet, de wetboeken en de voornaamste wetten en besluiten." *Rechtskundig Weekblad*, 1074–1082.

Meeuwis, Michael. 2015. "Language Legislation in the Belgian Colonial Charter of 1908: A Textual-Historical Analysis." *Language Policy* 14 (1): 49–65.

Moors, Joseph, and Siegfried Theissen. 2015. *Juridisch Woordenboek*. Bruges: die Keure.

Muylle, Koen, and Katrin Stangherlin. 2006. "Federale wetteksten in het Duits: over de niet-naleving van een arrest van het arbitragehof en de nood aan een nieuwe gelijkheidswet." *Tijdschrift voor Wetgeving*, 3–25.

Puelinckx-Coene, Mieken, and Steven Perrick. 1978. "De Benelux-Overeenkomst van 29 december 1972 of de nieuwe commoriëntenregel." *Tijdschrift voor Privaatrecht*, 43–65.

Sahlins, Peter. 1990. "Natural Frontiers Revisited: France's Boundaries since the Seventeenth Century." *The American Historical Review*, 1423–1451.

Van Damme, Marnix, and Benny De Sutter. 2013. *Raad van State: Afdeling Wetgeving*. Bruges: die Keure.

Van Dievoet, Emiel. 1943. *Het burgerlijk recht in België en in Nederland van 1800 tot 1940: de rechtsbronnen. Bijdragen tot de vergelijkende rechtsgeschiedenis*. Antwerp: De Sikkel.

———. 1964. "De Nederlandse tekst van de Belgische wetboeken." *Klasse der Letteren* XXVI (5): 3–20.

Van Dievoet, Guido. 1949–1950. "De wet van 15 december 1949 tot verbetering van de verouderde termen van de Franse tekst van Het Burgerlijk Wetboek en tot vaststelling, in die tekst, van sommige stilzwijgende opheffingen (Belgisch Staatsblad, 1, 2 en 3 Januari 1950)." *Rechtskundig Weekblad*, 817–820.

———. 1997. "E.M. Meijers en de herziening van de vertaling van het Belgisch Burgerlijk Wetboek door een Nederlands-Belgische commissie (1938–1941)." *The Legal History Review* 2004, 497–504.

———. 2004. "Het Burgerlijk Wetboek van 1804 tot heden." In *Cumulatieve editie van het Burgerlijk Wetboek*, edited by Dirk Heirbaut and Gustaaf Baeteman, xiii–xxviii. Ghent: Kluwer.

Van Haver, Jozef. 1990. "De wetboekencommissie en het taalbeleid van de overheid." In *Houd voet bij stuk. Xenia Iuris Historiae G. Van Dievoet Oblata*, edited by Fred Stevens and Dirk Van den Auweele, 601–620.

Victor, René. 1935. *Een eeuw Vlaamsch rechtsleven*. Antwerp: De Sikkel.

———. 1947–1948. "Commissie Voor de vergelijkende studie van het recht van België en Nederland. Eerste vergadering te Brussel (19 en 20 september 1947)." *Rechtskundig Weekblad*, 49–64.

———. 1960–1961. "De Nederlandse vertaling van ons Burgerlijk Wetboek." *Rechtskundig Weekblad*, 1755–1762.

———. 1961–1962. "De Nederlandse tekst van ons Burgerlijk Wetboek." *Rechtskundig Weekblad*, 1929–1932.

Translation in administrative interactions

Policies and practices at the local level in the Dutch language area of Belgium

Jonathan Bernaerts

Abstract

Linguistic diversity is leading to a number of legal and practical challenges in multilingual societies. The communication between administrative authorities and resident non-majoritarian language speakers is just one of the areas where these challenges arise. This contribution focuses on translation policies and practices at the regional and local level with regard to municipalities without language facilities in the Dutch language area in Belgium. It considers both formal and informal translations and interpretations provided by various actors. This contribution first addresses the relevant legal provisions on the use of translators and interpreters in interactions between administrative authorities and resident non-majoritarian language speakers. It considers the Belgian language model based on the general principle 'the language of the area is the administrative language', as well as specific norms at the Flemish level on translation and interpretation. Moreover, it discusses the relevant advisory practice of the Belgian Standing Committee for Linguistic Supervision and the Flemish government's approach to this issue. Second, this contribution presents fieldwork results on translation policies and practices in municipalities without language facilities in the Dutch language area. The findings are drawn from semi-structured interviews with the involved parties, observations and an analysis of local language and translation policies. It provides empirical accounts of the use of translators and interpreters in interactions between administrative authorities and resident non-majoritarian language speakers. The presented empirical findings are lastly analyzed in light of the current legal framework.

1   Introduction

A complex set of rules applies to language use in administrative interactions in Belgium and its four language areas, namely, the monolingual Dutch, French and German language areas and the bilingual area Brussels-Capital (Clement 2003; De Pelsmaeker et al. 2004; Gosselin 2017). Yet if one considers the relevant provisions regarding language use in administrative interactions in the Dutch language area, the legal framework appears rather straightforward for municipalities without language facilities.[1] It holds that only Dutch may be used by civil servants and residents in their administrative interactions. Translation policies, next to the clear-cut provisions on language use (Meylaerts 2011, 744–745), add nuance to this straightforward notion. These provisions and policies on language use and translation raise the question of how interactions unfold between allophone residents and administrations at the local level.

This contribution aims at providing insights into these interactions. It is based on qualitative empirical data that were collected during fieldwork in several municipalities in the Dutch language area and, more specifically, in municipalities "without" language facilities. The data gathered include 150 semi-structured individual interviews with civil servants and non-Dutch speakers, observations in administrative offices and written documents.[2] The fieldwork took place at eleven field sites in the Dutch language area from autumn 2015 to summer 2018. The qualitative data do not allow for statistical claims regarding the overall situation in the Dutch language area, but they cover several types of services and municipalities (two in the periphery of Flemish municipalities around Brussels (*Vlaamse Rand*); two in the province of Flemish Brabant outside this Flemish periphery; two at the language border outside of Flemish Brabant; two larger cities (*centrumsteden*); one touristic center; and two municipalities with a considerable number of persons with a migration background).[3]

---

1   There are twenty-seven municipalities with language facilities located in monolingual language areas in Belgium. In these municipalities, a special regime applies to the interactions between the administration and its residents, as the administration is under the obligation to use another language in certain cases.
2   The broader research examines the direct use of other languages by civil servants, as well as the use of translators and interpreters in local administrations.
3   The names of the municipalities are consistently not mentioned in publications related to this research in order to avoid identification of individual civil servants. Short descriptions of their profiles give nonetheless some background information.

Throughout this fieldwork, a broad variety of actors who offer translation and interpretation services was present, including formal translators and interpreters, multilingual colleagues and informal translators and interpreters (e.g., children, friends or mediators within a community). Formal translators and interpreters include those actors who are subject to some sort of certification, including sworn translators and interpreters (*beëdigde vertalers en tolken*), as well as community translators and interpreters (*sociaal vertalers en tolken*) provided by the Flemish Agency for Integration or by municipalities.[4] These actors differ from informal translators and interpreters who are not certified for these tasks. This paper focuses on formal and informal translation and interpreting.

The analysis opens with a brief discussion of the legal framework, including the position of supervisory bodies on the use of translators and interpreters (2). This overview sketches the legal complexity of the use of translators and interpreters by administrations and provides background information to policies and practices at the local level. Thereafter, empirical findings on local policies and practices are presented, followed by an analysis of some legal challenges (3).

2 The legal framework on language use in administrative settings

Language use in administrative interactions in Belgium is governed by a legal framework that recognizes four language areas and differentiates between several types of services and administrative operations. This framework builds on a number of constitutional provisions as well as the Coordinated Laws of 18 July 1966 with regard to language use in administrative affairs (henceforth the Administrative Language Law).[5] The principle holding that 'the language of the area is the administrative language' applies to interactions between local authorities and residents in the monolingual Dutch language area. The introduction of this so-called principle of territoriality in the Belgian legal framework was the result of several factors, including the idea of protecting the linguistic character of the different language areas in Belgium (Clement

---

4   The concept 'community translators and interpreters' (*sociaal vertalers en tolken*) refers to the Flemish Integration Decree, as discussed in Section 2.2.
5   *De bij koninklijk besluit gecoördineerde wetten op het gebruik van de talen in bestuurszaken* (the coordinated Laws of 18 July 1966 with regard to language use in administrative affairs), *Moniteur belge* 2 August 1966.

2003, 805–814). This historical protection of the Dutch-speaking character of Flanders is currently reinforced by a context of (renewed) monolingual ideologies leading, for example, to language courses and tests for immigrants (Blommaert 2011, 241; Meylaerts 2018, 462–463).

In the following overview, we will see that the Administrative Language Law has remained largely unmodified since its adoption and that it results in rather strict provisions on language use in administrative interactions on the local level. This strict impression is, however, softened by the Flemish Integration Decree and by supervisory bodies.

2.1 Relevant constitutional and legislative provisions

Three Articles of the Belgian Constitution are most relevant for language use in administrative settings, namely, Articles 4, 30 and 129. Article 4 constitutionally entrenches the division of Belgium into four language areas: the French language area, the Dutch language area, the German language area and the bilingual area Brussels-Capital. This provision further guarantees the constitutional protection of the priority of the designated language in the monolingual areas.[6]

The principle of language freedom is secured by Article 30 (the former Article 23) of the Belgian Constitution. According to this provision, language freedom may only be regulated[7] by the law for judicial affairs and for acts of public authorities (Velaers 2001, 52; Clement 2003, 772–787; Vande Lanotte et al. 2015, 621).[8] Article 129 (the former Article 59*bis*, § 3) of the Belgian Constitution explicitly mentions *bestuurzaken* (administrative affairs) as a domain for which language use may be regulated, and it attributes the legislative competence, in principle, to Parliaments of the Communities.[9]

---

6   *Grondwettelijk Hof* (Constitutional Court) No. 17, 26 March 1986.
7   The Belgian Constitutional Court stated in a 1986 judgment that "regulate" refers to "imposing the use of a specific language, as well as the prohibition on the use of a specific language, as well as the prohibition on prohibiting the use of a specific language." See *Grondwettelijk Hof* (Constitutional Court) No. 17, 26 March 1986.
8   *Raad van State* (Council of State) No. 140.635, 15 February 2005.
9   'Communities' are entities at the sub-state level in Belgium that exercise competence in cultural matters, education, person-related matters and for the use of languages in several spheres. There are three Communities in Belgium, namely the Flemish, the French and the German Communities, which are, in principle, competent in their respective language areas. Article 129 § 2 of the Belgian Constitution holds that the federal level has the competence to regulate language use for the so-called municipalities with facilities, "services whose activities extend beyond the language

Several laws were adopted throughout Belgian history to regulate language use in administrative affairs (Clement 2003). Articles 11 and 12 of the Administrative Language Law of 1966 are the most relevant for language use in interactions between local administrations and their residents in monolingual municipalities without language facilities. Article 11 § 1 of the Administrative Language Law obliges local services located in the Dutch or French language area, to publish messages, announcements and forms addressed to the public exclusively in the language of the area. According to its Article 12, "[i]edere plaatselijke dienst, die in het Nederlandse, het Franse of het Duitse taalgebied is gevestigd, gebruikt uitsluitend de taal van zijn gebied voor zijn betrekkingen met de particulieren" ("Every local service, located in the Dutch, French or German language area, uses exclusively the language of its language area in its interactions with individuals").[10] Although the Administrative Language Law does contain some provisions on translators and interpreters for other types of interactions,[11] it is silent on the use of translators and interpreters in these specific interactions in the monolingual areas.

The Administrative Language Law of 1966 is supplemented by a 1981 Flemish decree stipulating that individuals who are based in a municipality without a special language regime in the Dutch language area must exclusively use Dutch in their interactions with the local and regional administrative services.[12] The report on the parliamentary discussions of this decree shows that it was the explicit choice of the Flemish legislature not to opt for a system with translators and interpreters.[13] Article 12 of the Administrative Language Law and this Flemish decree result in the obligation for both local civil servants and residents in the monolingual Dutch language area to use Dutch in their interactions. A strict application of these provisions would

---

area within which they are located", and "federal and international institutions designated by the law whose activities are common to more than one Community."

10   Article 12 of the Administrative Language Law determines the language use for individualized interactions, whereas Article 11 covers texts that are disseminated without distinction on the basis of the recipient (De Pelsmaeker et al. 2004, 42–43, 6).

11   Article 17 § 1, Article 13, § 1 and Article 14, § 1 of the Administrative Language Law.

12   *Decreet van het Vlaams Parlement van 30 juni 1981 houdende aanvulling van de artikelen 12 en 33 van de bij Koninklijk Besluit van 18 juli 1966 gecoördineerde wetten op het gebruik van de talen in bestuurszaken wat betreft het gebruik van de talen in de betrekkingen tussen de bestuursdiensten van het Nederlands Taalgebied en de Particulieren* (Decree of the Flemish Council of 30 June 1981 concerning complementing Articles 12 and 33 of the Administrative Language Law with regard to language use in relations between the administrative services and private persons), *Moniteur belge* 10 November 1981.

13   Proposition of Decree, Report of the commission of language decrees and language protection (M. Bourry), *Parl. Doc.* Flemish Council 1980–1981, No. 127/2, 5 and 7.

entail that civil servants and non-Dutch speaking residents, without any further assistance, are legally trapped in a dialogue of the deaf during their administrative interactions (see Velaers and Adams 1993, 178).

Article 50 of the Administrative Language Law adds that the appointment of private collaborators or experts, such as contractors for road works and publishers of municipal magazines, does not exempt the administrative services from their language obligations, despite the fact that these private parties are not subject to a specific language regime.[14] Consequently, monolingual administrative services located in the Dutch language area are obliged to monitor that their private collaborators respect the obligations under the Administrative Language Law. Otherwise, these services expose themselves to the obligation of translating into Dutch the documents drafted by these private partners.[15]

2.2 Flemish Integration Decree

The Flemish Integration Decree of 2013 seemingly adds nuance to this stringent picture represented by the Administrative Language Law and the 1981 Flemish decree. The Flemish Integration Decree sets out the framework for community interpreting and translating (*sociaal tolken en vertalen*). These concepts are understood in this decree as instruments that support spoken and written communication with non-Dutch-speaking clients.[16] These tools may be used by services, organizations and public administrations active in the Dutch language area or in the bilingual area Brussels-Capital (Article 42, § 1 and § 3, 2 of the Flemish Integration Decree). The Explanatory Memorandum of the Flemish Integration Decree states that these instruments can be utilized in emergency situations, to impart complex messages, as well as in cases where language learning takes time.[17]

---

14 Report of the draft law on the use of languages in administrative affairs (H. De Stexhe), *Parl. Doc*. Senate 1962–1963, No. 304, 30. See, also SCLS, No. 51.223, 5 July 2019.
15 Draft law on the use of languages in administrative affairs, Report of the commission for internal affairs (Saint-Remy), *Parl. Doc*. Chamber of Rep. 1961–1962, No. 331/27, 39.
16 Articles 41 and 42 of *Decreet betreffende het Vlaamse integratie- en inburgeringsbeleid* (decree on the Flemish integration and civic integration policy) of 7 June 2013, *Moniteur belge* 26 July 2013 (henceforth referred to as the Flemish Integration Decree).
17 *Ontwerp van decreet betreffende het Vlaamse integratie- en inburgeringsbeleid* (draft decree on the Flemish integration policy), Explanatory Memorandum, *Parl. Doc*. Flemish Parl. 2012–2013, 1867, No. 1, 83.

According to the Memorandum, the administration may engage community interpreters or translators (ibid.). The legislative materials do not contain an explicit procedure as to how an institution is to proceed with the decision as to whether a community interpreter or translator has to be provided (Roels et al. 2015, 151). The Explanatory Memorandum recommends that this decision should be part of a language policy and takes into account the specific context and the service's tasks in order to be effective and efficient (ibid.).

Another insufficiently settled element is the financing of these interpreting and translating services. The Flemish policy towards community interpreting organized by the Flemish Agency for Integration[18] underwent a significant change, as the responsibility for the costs was transferred from Flemish ministries to the local level.[19] Parliamentary debates show that the financing of these translation and interpretation services has remained a thorny issue, as the Flemish government appeared to cut back its funding and to transfer the costs to the allophone speakers using the service.[20]

2.3 Supervisory bodies

A further nuance in the picture that emerges from the Administrative Language Law comes from the Standing Committee for Language Supervision (henceforth referred to as SCLS)[21] and the Flemish government. The SCLS oversees the implementation of the Administrative Language Law and issues opinions on the matter that are merely advisory, albeit with a high degree

---

18 The Flemish government used the option listed in Article 25 § 1 of the Integration Decree to assign tasks to local administrations. As such, the cities of Antwerp and Ghent are responsible for community interpreting and community translating (Article 17, 2, 2° of the Flemish Integration Decree).
19 Articles 4 and 5 of the *Besluit van de Vlaamse Regering van 15 juni 2012 houdende de erkenning en subsidiëring van een Vlaamse centrale dienst voor sociaal telefoontolken en sociaal vertalen, vermeld in de artikelen 45/1 en 45/3 van het decreet van 28 april 1998 betreffende het Vlaamse integratiebeleid en houdende de vaststelling van de regels voor de betaling van de te presteren tolkprestaties, vermeld in artikel 45/3, vierde lid, en artikel 45/4, § 1, van het voormelde decreet* (Decision of the Flemish Government of 15 June 2012 concerning the recognition and subsidization of a Flemish central service for social telephone interpreting and social translation, as referred to in Articles 45/1 and 45/3 of the Decree of 28 April 1998 on the Flemish integration policy and establishing the rules for payment of the interpreting services to be provided, as referred to in Article 45/3(4) and Article 45/4(1) of the aforementioned Decree), *Moniteur belge* 16 July 2012.
20 Plenary meeting of the Flemish Parliament of 20 March 2019, Debate on the waiting lists for integration courses, *Parl. Doc.* Flemish Parl. 2018–2019.
21 *Vaste Commissie voor Taaltoezicht; Commission permanente de contrôle linguistique.*

of moral authority (De Pelsmaeker et al. 2004, 247). The Flemish government is charged with the regular supervision of municipalities in the Dutch language area[22] and has the power to annul documents that are at odds with the Administrative Language Law.[23] These annulment decisions appear to be rather limited, but some indications of the approach of competent Flemish ministers can be found in a ministerial circular and in their responses to parliamentary questions.

Besides these supervisory bodies, jurisdictional appeals to the Council of State and to courts and tribunals are possible, in accordance with the competence of these bodies, against acts that violate the Administrative Language Law. As the case law on the use of translators and interpreters by local services in monolingual municipalities is rather limited,[24] we focus on the SCLS's advisory practice and the responses by competent Flemish ministers.

2.3.1 Standing Committee for Language Supervision

In its advisory practice, the SCLS has allowed certain exceptions to the use of other languages by local administrations (De Pelsmaeker et al. 2004, 83–84; Bernaerts 2019, 307–328). Four criteria can be distilled from the SCLS's standing advisory practice on the use of other languages in written messages and announcements to the public, namely, (i) the use of other languages should be exceptional rather than systematic; (ii) it should be for a specific goal; (iii) it should be in addition to the prescribed administrative language; and (iv) it should be targeted at a specific audience. The SCLS's advisory opinions on individual interactions are fewer.[25]

---

[22] The system of administrative supervision, which differs from the hierarchical and the jurisdictional supervision, consists of the *regular* and the *specific* supervision. The former refers to the supervision within the framework of *Decreet Lokaal Bestuur* (Local Authorities Decree) of 22 December 2017, *Moniteur belge* 15 February 2018. The latter relates to tasks regarding specific regulations, for which the Federal authorities, the Regions and the Communities may organize specific administrative supervision for matters within their competences (Article 7, § 1, first and second sub-clause of *Bijzondere wet tot hervorming der instellingen* (the Specific Institutional Reform Act) of 8 August 1980, *Moniteur belge* 15 August 1980). See *Raad van State* (Council of State) No. 22.453, 30 July 1982.

[23] Articles 327 and 332 *Decreet Lokaal Bestuur* (Local Authorities Decree) of 22 December 2017, *Moniteur belge* 15 February 2018.

[24] In fact, we did not come across a single judicial decision on the use of a (community) interpreter or translator within an interaction between a local administration and an allophone resident in a monolingual Dutch municipality.

[25] For the distinction between messages and announcements to the public, on the one hand, and interactions with individuals, on the other hand, see Section 2.1.

In addition, and more relevant for this contribution, the SCLS has issued some advisory opinions on translation and interpretating. Within the limited advisory practice on the matter, a distinction can be made between the 'organization' and the 'use' of these services. We did not come across any SCLS advice under the new current Flemish Integration Decree; as such, the SCLS's position on the current organization remains to be seen. At the time of the predecessor of the Integration Decree, the Decree on the Flemish policy regarding ethnic-cultural minorities of 1998,[26] the SCLS examined the functioning of interpreters who were working on the basis of cooperation agreements (and not as civil servants) and who received a lump sum for their services.[27] The SCLS was of the opinion that these persons did not fall within the scope of the Administrative Language Law, and even if they did, the SCLS held that nothing in the Administrative Language Law would prohibit the drafting of these cooperation agreements by a local service.[28]

In a second category of advisory opinions, the SCLS considered the *use* of translators and interpreters by administrations under the Administrative Language Law. The SCLS stated that interpreting during a meeting with residents was acceptable, as they were exceptional, the goal was specific, and the use of the other language was limited.[29] In another advisory opinion on an information meeting, short interventions by an interpreter were also considered to be in conformity with the Administrative Language Law "*in het licht van een betere integratie van de allochtone bevolking*" ("in light of better integration of the non-native population").[30] The limited number of cases renders it difficult to derive general principles on the matter solely from the SCLS's advisory practice.

2.3.2 Regular oversight

The Flemish government monitors the Administrative Language Law in the Dutch language area as part of its regular administrative oversight. Several Flemish ministers exercising the regular administrative oversight have exhibited a certain flexibility with regard to newcomers in the monolingual Dutch

---

26 *Decreet van het Vlaams Parlement van 28 april 1998 inzake het Vlaamse beleid ten aanzien van etnisch-culturele minderheden* (Flemish Decree of 28 April 1998 on the Flemish policy regarding ethnic-cultural minorities), *Moniteur belge* 19 June 1998.
27 SCLS, 21 October 2004, No. 36.014; SCLS, 5 December 2008, No. 40.156.
28 SCLS, 21 October 2004, No. 36.014; SCLS, 21 October 2004, No. 35.252; SCLS, 5 December 2008, No. 40.156.
29 SCLS, 19 October 1998, No. 30.130.
30 SCLS, 24 May 2007, No. 38.160 and No. 38.161 (my translation).

language area in their interpretation of the Administrative Language Law and the supplementary 1981 Flemish decree.[31] The responsible ministers' answers to parliamentary questions show that they see the use of other languages as temporary exceptions to facilitate communication with administrative authorities during the integration process.[32]

With regard to the organization and use of translators and interpreters, these parliamentary interventions by the responsible Flemish ministers also contain some indications of their approach. Minister Van Grembergen stated in 2004 that local administrations may decide on the modalities and situations in which they organize such services.[33] The subsequent responsible minister, Keulen, endorsed this view and confirmed it in a 2005 ministerial circular.[34] In this ministerial circular, he did not consider the use of translation and interpretation services to be a violation of the relevant legislation.[35] Certain elements come to the fore in the approach of these ministers: (i) the use of translators and interpreters has to be part of an integration policy; (ii) it has to be temporary; and (iii) it does not lead to any rights.

---

31 Commission for Administrative Affairs, Internal Administration, Decree evaluation, Integration and Tourism, 8 October 2013, Question No. 2208 Van Hauthem, *Parl. Doc.* Flemish Parl. 2012–2013.

32 Question of Van Nieuwenhuysen for Marino Keulen on allophone desks or counters for non-autochthonous persons in town halls, *Acts* Flemish Parl. 2006–2007, 17 April 2007, No. C159-BIN13, 2; Question of Van Hauthem for Geert Bourgeois on the use of French by municipal services in De Panne, *Acts* Flemish Parl. 2010–2011, 1 March 2011, No. C157-BIN11, 9; Commission for Administrative Affairs, Internal Administration, Decree evaluation, Integration and Tourism, 8 October 2013, Question No. 2208 Van Hauthem, *Parl. Doc.* Flemish Parl. 2012–2013; *Questions and Answers* Flemish Parl. 2014, 17 September 2014 (Question No. 31 T. Van Grieken; Answer Homans). See question of Stefaan Sintobin for Liesbeth Homans on the organization of Arabic language courses by a PSCA, *Acts* Flemish Parl., 2017–2018, No. 1269, 7.

33 Question of Van Nieuwenhuysen for Van Grembergen, *Acts* Flemish Parl. 2003–2004, 20 January 2004, No. C100-BIN11, 7.

34 Question of Van Nieuwenhuysen for Keulen on the compliance with the language legislation by local authorities during the reception of Francophones and allophones, *Acts* Flemish Parl. 2004–2005, 26 October 2004, No. C29 – BIN3, 21; *Questions and Answers* Flemish Parl. 2004–2005, 29 October 2004 (Question No. 31 Van Goethem; Answer Keulen); *Circulaire, BA-2005/3 betreffende het taalgebruik in de gemeente- en O.C.M.W.-besturen en in de intergemeentelijke samenwerkingsverbanden (interpretatie en gevolgen van de arresten van de Raad van State van 23 december 2004)* (Circulaire, BA-2005/3 with regard to the language use in municipal and PSAC's administrations and the intra-municipal partnerships (interpretation and effects of the judgments of the Council of State of 23 December 2004, 8 July 2005), 5–6 (henceforth referred to as Circulaire Keulen); Question of Van Nieuwenhuysen for Marino Keulen on allophone desks or counters for non-autochthonous persons in town halls, *Act* Flemish Parl. 2006–2007, 17 April 2007, No. C159-BIN13, 2.

35 Circulaire Keulen, 5–6.

Thereafter, the following minister, Bourgeois, distinguished the use of another language by civil servants from the use of community interpreters and translators. He envisaged the use of community interpreters in the context of "asielzoekers, mensen die in een noodsituatie zitten, [...], bij de arts bijvoorbeeld" ("asylum seekers, people in an emergency situation, [...] for example, at the doctor's").[36] The Explanatory Memorandum of the 2013 Flemish Integration Decree appears to build on these positions. As mentioned in Section 2.2, the Memorandum to this decree holds that community interpreting can be used when the learning of Dutch takes time, in emergencies or to communicate complex messages.[37]

2.4 Conclusion on the legal framework

We started our overview of the legal framework with the strict provisions on language use in administrative interactions which are contained in the Administrative Language Law and the 1981 Flemish decree. This strict impression was nuanced by the Flemish Integration Decree and the position of supervisory bodies. These sources mention a limited or exceptional use within an integration framework as recurring characteristics justifying the use of (community) translators and interpreters. As such, these tools are, in their view, not intended for persons who have already been in Belgium for a long time or for persons belonging to 'old', historical minorities (whatever these minorities might be in Belgium or the Dutch language area).[38]

The relation between the Flemish Integration Decree and the Administrative Language Law is not entirely clear. In light of Articles 30 and 129 of the Belgian Constitution, the question arises whether the reference to translators and interpreters in the Integration Decree installs a language regulation that deviates from the obligations in the Administrative Language Law. Without going into detail, it appears that the Integration Decree does not establish another language regulation (Bernaerts 2019, 322–323). Consequently, the Administrative Language Law forms the relevant framework for the organization and use of translators and interpreters in these interactions. In this understanding, the main problem is whether translators and interpreters provided for or employed

---

36 *Questions and Answers* Flemish Parl. 2011–2012, 7 December 2011 (Question No. 116 Segers; Answer Bourgeois).
37 Explanatory Memorandum, *Parl. Doc.* Flemish Parl. 2012–2013, No. 1867/1, 83.
38 For the discussion on which groups are to be considered the historical minorities in Belgium and in the Dutch language area, see Velaers (2009, 103–158).

by authorities fall within the scope of the Administrative Language Law or whether they are exempted from it by the Flemish Integration Decree.

Furthermore, the organization and the use of translators and interpreters in these administrative interactions have to respect Article 4 of the Belgian Constitution, in particular the priority of Dutch in the Dutch language area. As such, fully bilingual services or interactions entirely in another language are possibly at odds with Article 4 of the Belgian Constitution (Vande Lanotte et al. 2015, 1157).

3 Policy and practice at the local level

Following the foregoing analysis of the legal framework, we now turn to the empirical findings on local language policies and practices. First, we list three types of local language policies and their diverse approaches to translation and interpretation (3.1). Thereafter, we present data on the use of translators and interpreters by civil servants and residents (3.2), followed by some empirical and legal observations (3.3).

3.1 Three types of local language policies

While space does not allow us to discuss 'language policy' or 'translation policy' in detail (Meylaerts and González Núñez 2017, 2–3), our approach nevertheless requires some clarifications of these concepts. The empirical material on local language policies was not determined by legal criteria. This means that not only were statutory rules considered, but also local norms, guidelines and recommendations for civil servants, even if they do not necessarily conform to the Constitution or represent an obligation for civil servants or a right for residents (Patten and Kymlicka 2003, 26). Furthermore, we focus on policies at the 'local' level instead of on 'national' or 'regional' language policies (Backhaus 2012, 226–242). More specifically, we examine the parts of these policies that relate to the interactions between administrative services and their residents, being only one aspect of local language policies. Within the empirical data, a translation policy is often part of a local language policy.

Taking into account these conceptual clarifications, three ideal types of language policies were identified at the field sites, namely a 'strict Dutch-only policy', an 'in-between policy', and a 'flexible language policy'. These types have in common that they allow allophones to speak a language other than Dutch if this language is understood by the personnel in the administration.

As such, these policies do not insist on the obligation for residents to use Dutch in the Dutch language area, as embedded in the 1981 Flemish Decree. The differences between the three policies are mainly apparent with regard to 'when' the use of languages other than Dutch is allowed for the administration. This use of another language is permitted under 'strict Dutch-only policies' only in very limited situations; under 'in-between policies' in some situations, but generally only as a last resort to enable communication; and under 'flexible policies' in numerous situations and earlier on in the interaction between a civil servant and a resident.

If we consider the translation policies embedded in these types, we see that the use of translators and interpreters is often restricted to informal translators and interpreters[39] in 'strict Dutch-only policies'. Under this type of policy, providing informal interpreters is often required of residents if they do not understand Dutch. Several 'strict Dutch-only policies' do not specify requirements for these informal interpreters, while other services that follow this type of policy mention that interpreters either should be or must be adults.

The use of community translators and interpreters is rarely addressed in 'strict Dutch-only policies'; consequently, this type of translator and interpreter is generally not used by civil servants working under this policy. In some municipalities, however, these policies are combined with pragmatic initiatives, such as interpreting interventions by integration officers or welcome sessions by non-profit organizations. These initiatives enable administrations to bypass strict language policies by, for example, distributing information on municipal services in another language, while administrative services in general are allowed only to use Dutch.

'In-between policies' leave more room for the use of translators and interpreters. Concrete guidelines on which types of translators and interpreters can or should be used, when, and with whom are also rather rare with 'in-between policies'. They often remain limited to including the use of community interpreters, as well as the request that residents bring an informal interpreter, on a flowchart detailing the steps involved in establishing communication between the administration and allophone residents.

'In-between policies' thus also request the assistance of informal interpreters, who are to be arranged by the private individual. In contrast to the 'strict Dutch-only policies', an informal interpreter often only stands as one of the last options in a flowchart outlining how to enable communication. Sometimes these 'in-between policies' mention that an adult interpreter is preferable or

---

39   For our understanding of 'informal interpreters' and the difference with 'community interpreters', see Section 1.

should be requested. Pragmatic initiatives, often in cooperation with partner non-profit organizations, are also present with 'in-between policies'.

'Flexible language policies' share a lack of guidelines in general and as such the use of translators and interpreters is also not addressed extensively in this category. This non-regulation at the municipal level leads to divergent approaches in local administrations under flexible language policies. Some administrations require that residents bring an informal interpreter only if no common language can be found and after verifying the availability of a community interpreter. One supervisor operating under a 'flexible language policy' stated that, as a rule, they first try to solve the situation themselves before searching for or requesting an external (informal) interpreter.[40] Some 'flexible language policies' also revert the suggested steps to establish communication in comparison with 'in-between policies', for example, by stating that for "*gevoelige/emotioneel belastende, psycho-sociale, juridische/complexe onderwerpen*" ("sensitive/emotional, psycho-social, legal/complex issues"),[41] a community interpreter should be used instead of an informal interpreter available on site. Lastly, some 'flexible language policies' also require adult interpreters or explicitly forbid the use of children, while other policies of this type allow child interpreters only in emergencies.

3.2 Two groups of translators and interpreters in practice

As mentioned in the introduction, a broad variety of actors offer translation and interpreting in administrative interactions. We examine two groups, namely formal and informal translators and interpreters, which we introduce with short examples. The presented material includes quotes from civil servants which are accompanied by footnotes providing some additional context regarding the location, the service, the applicable local language policy and the civil servant's position.

3.2.1 Formal translations and interpretations

> Ze [anderstaligen bij het Openbaar Centrum voor Maatschappelijk Welzijn (OCMW)] hebben altijd recht op een tolk [...] om een gelijkheid aan kwalitatieve dienstverlening te bieden, denk ik. Als onze sociaal werkers bijvoorbeeld in Pashto moeten proberen iets uitleggen met handgebaren

---

40 Larger Flemish city 2, municipal office, flexible language policy, supervisor.
41 Language policy in a touristic center.

ofzo dan gaat er heel veel informatie verloren. En we vinden dat wel
belangrijk voor de klanten dat ze voldoende geïnformeerd zijn.

(They [non-Dutch speakers in the Public Social Assistance Centre (PSAC)]
always have the right to an interpreter [...] to ensure equality in the high-
quality provision of services, I assume. If our social workers, for example,
in Pashto [a language that they do not speak] have to explain something
with hand gestures or something then a lot of information gets lost. And
we find it important for the clients that they are sufficiently informed.)[42]

The supervisor in this example discusses the use of formal translators and
interpreters. Some PSACs have their own service with certified translators
and interpreters, while other local administrations use community translators
and interpreters provided by the Flemish Agency for Integration or by their
municipality.

Community translators and interpreters can be distinguished from 'guides
in diversity' (*toeleiders in diversiteit*), who are present in several Flemish
municipalities, albeit in different setups. These guides in diversity are defined
by their organizations as 'experts by experience' who help to familiarize
newcomers with the local society or provide assistance in bridging the gap
between newcomers and the administration. Their tasks do not necessarily
include, in theory at least, translating or interpreting.

An initial issue with regard to the use of formal translators and interpreters
in practice is closely related to the local language policy. It deals with the
structural question of who (the administration or the private individual)
provides the formal translator or interpreter. Some municipalities or administrations take upon themselves the responsibility to provide interpreters. In
some PSACs, interpreters on-site or at the PSAC's council can be arranged
by social workers; this service is paid for by the administration, especially in
administrations under 'in-between' and 'flexible language policies'. In some
PSACs, formal interpreters for several languages are always at hand at council
meetings, while at other services interpreters for certain languages are present
on a fixed day of the week. In this regard, the supervisor in the example above
considered it the state's obligation to provide translators and interpreters in
all interactions between a social worker and the PSAC's clients.[43]

In other administrations, community interpreting is not used, as there is a
belief that it would raise the same issues as the direct use of other languages

---

42 Larger Flemish city 1, PSAC, 'flexible language policy', supervisor.
43 Larger Flemish city 1, PSAC, 'in-between language policy', supervisor.

by civil servants, such as criticism from private individuals or from local politicians. Furthermore, several civil servants were unaware of this kind of service. As such, these administrations shift the responsibility for facilitating communication onto private individuals by, for example, requesting that they bring their own informal interpreters.

Apart from the structural provision of translators and interpreters, there are criteria regarding for whom, for which languages and when to provide or to request the presence of a translator or interpreter. This is often left to the civil servant's discretion, as only a limited number of local language policies have guidelines on when to use these services.

In practice, some administrations only provide for formal translations when no common language is available between the civil servant and the private individual. As such, formal interpreters for French or English are not used in these services, as the supervisors or the civil servants believe that they can handle these languages themselves. A supervisor leading the municipal office in a larger Flemish city explained that interpreters are also not used for the Turkish language, as there are enough Turkish-speaking colleagues in the office.[44]

Some services under a 'flexible language policy' usually use community interpreters for non-Dutch speaking clients, even as early as the initial scheduling of appointments by telephone. For several civil servants, the use of interpreters depends on the complexity of the issue. In this regard, some civil servants indicated that they prefer formal interpreters for complex situations, while others, on the contrary, preferred not to have interpreters present during these interactions.

Other civil servants referred to the interpreting services' characteristics to explain their use or non-use of interpreters. Some find telephone interpreting quick, the easiest tool, or just useful. A social worker based in a PSAC located at the language border indicated that her clients say more when a formal interpreter is used.[45] Other civil servants found it cumbersome, said that awkward interactions are generated by telephone interpreting, or complained about the waiting time or the need for an appointment and thus the inconvenience of having to plan the session in advance. In addition, some civil servants doubted the quality or the professional attitude of community interpreters (despite their certification). As such, several civil servants indicated that it is faster to switch to another language (if indeed they have mastery of that language) than to use a formal interpreter.

44   Larger Flemish city 2, municipal office, 'flexible language policy', supervisor.
45   Flemish municipality at the language border 1, PSAC, 'in-between policy', social worker.

3.2.2 Informal translations and interpretations

A civil servant under a 'strict Dutch-only language policy' switched the conversation to persons who have lived in the municipality for five to six years. She stated:

> Ze moeten toch een minimum aan Nederlands begrijpen. Vooral als ze dan kinderen hebben die hier naar het Nederlands onderwijs gaan. [zucht] Het komt ook vaak voor dat mensen komen met hun kinderen. Dat is dan ook [sic], ik vind dat ook lastig. Je moet dan soms een bevel gaan betekenen en daar zit een kind bij, want die ouder begrijpt niet wat hij krijgt en dan moet je aan dat kind gaan zeggen "het is geweigerd."

> (They should understand a minimum of Dutch. Especially as they have children who go to Dutch-speaking schools. [sighs] It also frequently occurs that people come with their children. That is also [sic], I think it's also troublesome. Sometimes you have to give notice of an order and then there is a child present, because the parent does not understand it, and then you have to say to the child, "It has been refused.")

The civil servant concluded her reflection by clarifying that there are no guidelines in this regard: "We zijn al blij dat ze meekomen. Ik bedoel als die vertrekken, zeg ik 'dank u om te vertalen'."("We are just happy that they come along. I mean, when they leave, I say, 'Thank you for translating'.")[46] A supervisor leading a municipal office under a strict language policy located in another municipality explained:

> [Informal interpreters are] fantastisch, dat is fantastisch, dat is integratie binnen de integratie. Mensen gaan mensen helpen, buren gaan vragen "spreekt gij Nederlands", "alleh, komt gij ne keer mee naar het stadhuis." We zien nu soms mensen die drie of vier keer per dag, die er een soort sport of hobby van maken. De nauwe contacten van de burgers worden op die manier beter. Ja, we zien dat het een soort groepsgesprek aan het worden is.

> ([Informal interpreters are] fantastic, that is fantastic, that is integration within the integration. People are helping people, neighbors go to ask, "Do you speak Dutch?" "c'mon then, come with me to the city hall." We now see

---

46 Flemish municipality in province of Flemish Brabant outside the Flemish periphery around Brussels, municipal office, 'Dutch-only/in-between language policy', civil servant.

some people [interpreters] three or four times a day – they make it a sort of sport or hobby. In this way close contacts between citizens get better. Yes, we see that it is becoming a sort of group conversation.)[47]

These examples highlight two sorts of informal interpreters, namely children and mediators within a community. Other actors, such as family members and random persons in the waiting room, also perform these informal translations and interpretations. They are neither certified translators nor are they working within the administration, although in some cases they are arranged or solicited by the administration.

Certain authorities under 'in-between' and especially under 'strict Dutch-only language policies' specifically demand that non-Dutch speakers bring an interpreter. This requirement is conveyed to the general public or private individuals via, for example, a verbal request, a multilingual leaflet that requires that persons "who do not speak (sufficient) Dutch" bring an interpreter, or in the invitation letters for appointments with social workers or for hearings at the PSAC council. These requirements are not always followed in practice. One civil servant who works in an administration under a 'strict Dutch-only policy' where such a written demand is formulated in leaflets, indicated that she hardly ever uses this document, as rarely does a person not speak French, English or German, in other words, the languages that she knows.[48] Other civil servants, however, almost automatically point to this paper in their conversations with non-Dutch speakers to justify their refusal to switch to a contact language.

In some administrations operating under a 'flexible language policy', informal interpreters are only requested of private individuals if there is no community interpreter (in that language) or no other communication channel available. In other administrations under a 'flexible language policy', there are no specific guidelines, and the principle of effective provision of aid to clients prevails.

Despite their informal character, some administrations arrange this informal translation and interpreting by actively using known networks and third parties to spread the message. Civil servants working in municipal emergency services, for example, indicated that they know who or which organizations to contact in case of an emergency in a certain area or when they need an

---

47 Flemish municipality at the language border 1, municipal office, 'strict Dutch-only policy', supervisor.
48 Flemish municipality at the language border 2, municipal office, 'strict Dutch-only policy', civil servant.

informal interpreter for a certain language.[49] Besides these more organized initiatives by administrations, amounting in certain places to an institutional policy, there are *ad hoc* searches by civil servants to find an interpreter. A city warden (*stadswacht*) operating in a municipality in the Flemish periphery around Brussels indicated that she herself searches for informal interpreters, as that is the fastest way to find one, and she knows whom to trust.[50]

More often, such informal interpreting is arranged by non-Dutch speaking residents. The examples already mentioned two types of actors. Among the recurring actors are mediators in a certain community. They are known persons within a community who are also familiar with the administration, for example, because of their (recognized) role within an organization for persons from a certain country of origin. In some municipalities, these informal translation services have coalesced into a whole system in certain communities, whereby some interpreters give the impression that they can "work out" something with the administration.

Other frequently recurring actors are children. As mentioned above, a number of local language policies state that children are not allowed to be interpreters. Accordingly, some administrations actively inform their users that they do not accept children as interpreters by, for example, posting a sign to this effect in the waiting area. Other services adopt a more pragmatic approach, as is illustrated by one service that only allows child interpreters outside of school hours.

Civil servants expressed divergent feelings about children acting as interpreters. Several civil servants stated that they are not happy if a child performs this role, but still allow it, even if it goes against a local language policy. Others find that they have no other choice than to work with child interpreters. Some civil servants found child interpreters bothersome or felt that it puts the children in a difficult position. Another group of civil servants indicated that they had not reflected on the potential difficulties but, rather, were more concerned with the immediate efficacy of child interpreters – some found it useful, while others held that it is an inadequate solution because children do not understand administrative jargon.

Apart from their differing degrees of appreciation for the interventions by children, civil servants also reflected on other informal interpreters (such as friends or neighbors) and expressed a range of feelings in this regard. On

---

49 Larger Flemish city 1, municipal office, 'flexible language policy', supervisor; Larger Flemish city 2, municipal office, 'flexible language policy', supervisor.
50 Flemish municipality in the Flemish periphery around Brussels 1, municipal office, 'in-between policy', civil servant.

the one hand, some civil servants experienced these informal translations as very useful. On the other hand, several civil servants highlighted problematic aspects with informal translations. First, they indicated a lack of control over the informal translation and raised concerns regarding the quality of the interpreting. As such, civil servants would do the interpreting themselves to be sure that the information was conveyed correctly. Multilingual civil servants, even those who are not allowed to or who refuse to use another language, still do have some control over the interventions of informal interpreters. If they hear that something is not being conveyed correctly, they can either correct the interpreter in Dutch or use the other language. Situations where there is no contact whatsoever with the user generate a related difficulty. Civil servants indicated that they feel tempted to request a formal interpreter in these situations, but they do not want to raise extra costs for the private individual.

Civil servants noted a final recurring challenge posed by the use of interpreters, that is, the change from a one-on-one conversation with their client to an unbalanced conversation, as the situation with an informal interpreter creates a majority situation with the private individual and the interpreter on one side and the civil servant on the other.

3.3 Analysis

The empirical data generated more insights with regard to local language policies and practices. From a legal perspective, a mixed response is evident regarding the conformity of local language policies with the legal framework. On the one hand, the competence of administrative authorities to adopt a local language policy on language use in administrative settings is limited, as the Belgian Constitution holds that language use in this domain may only be regulated by the law. As such, the adoption and the content of local languages policies are in a tense relationship with the constitutional framework. On the other hand, the Flemish Integration Decree mentions *taalbeleid* (language policy) as one of the tools for the Flemish Agency for Integration to be applied by local authorities.[51] In 2014, in addition to this provision, the Flemish minister responsible for Interior Administration and Integration did not oppose a local language policy that included guidelines

---

51 Article 17, 2, 2°, b) of the Flemish Integration Decree. See also Explanatory Memorandum to Flemish Integration Decree, 15 January 2013, No. 1867, 33.

on the use of translators and interpreters.[52] However, the wording of the Flemish Integration Decree and its Explanatory Memorandum indicate that language policy is not necessarily understood as including the regulation of language use in administrative affairs. Although it appears that some guidelines within these local language policies comply with the approach of supervisory bodies, other elements clearly go beyond the rare and exceptional use of other languages, as is stressed by these bodies (see Section 2.3). As such, several constitutional and legal obstacles to the adoption and content of these local language policies remain.

With regard to the practice, the empirical data show that several administrations do not provide formal interpreting services, which confirms the limited attention this form of interpreting receives in general in local language policies. This finding should not be overemphasized, however. It does not mean that all administrative interactions occur in Dutch, nor that no translator or interpreter plays a role in these administrations. Moreover, in other administrations, either in other municipalities or other types of administrations, interventions by community interpreters occur frequently.

Previous research suggesting arbitrary use of community interpreting (Roels et al. 2015, 149–156) is confirmed by the empirical data. Cascade reasoning is often present for spoken interactions in administrations where community interpreting is used (ibid., 155–175). The cascade reasoning is generally accompanied by an implicit understanding that community interpreting is regularly restricted to cases where no common language (such as French or English), no multilingual colleague, and no informal interpreter is available.

We have already pointed out that the use of translators and interpreters has received little attention in case law and jurisprudence. However, several aspects of the empirical data generate legal questions, for example, with regard to the Administrative Language Law and the non-discrimination and equality principle. Conformity of the current organization and use of interpretation services with the Administrative Language Law is a technical issue and depends on the specific circumstances of the case (Bernaerts 2019, 318–326). On the one hand, employees of administrative services remain bound by the Administrative Language Law, although they might refer to the SCLS's advisory practice on the use of other languages. On the other hand, Article 50 of the Administrative Language Law applies to the situation in which private collaborators are hired by services covered by this law.

---

52 *Questions and Answers* Flemish Parliament, 17 September 2014 (Question No. 31 Van Grieken; Answer Homans).

In addition to conformity with the Administrative Language Law, the current use of translators and interpreters appears to be in a tense relationship with the non-discrimination and equality principle. These questions differ from the previous analysis of the Belgian language model in light of non-discrimination and equality provisions,[53] as they are in this case rather concerned with the equal use of translation and interpretation services by different groups of non-Dutch speakers. As such, the comparison is concerned with non-Dutch-speaking persons or groups, and not so much with a comparison between Dutch speakers and non-Dutch speakers in Flanders.

Another specific issue is that formal translation and interpreting services are not often used for some languages that are commonly known by at least some civil servants. Formal translation and interpretating in these languages is neither used nor considered necessary in practice in several services, as civil servants or their colleagues use these languages as contact languages. This results in different treatment of persons with knowledge of a common language, as they do not enjoy the benefit of a certified interpreter's assistance. Even the well-intended use of another language by a civil servant, instead of a formal interpreter, might be problematic in light of the general lack of verification of local civil servants' language skills in other languages. Although there might be a reasonable and objective justification for the difference in treatment in these situations, such justifications are currently not entirely evident in local language policies and practices.

4 Conclusion

We have highlighted some of the legal obstacles with regard to local language policies as well as with the organization and use of translators and interpreters. These obstacles are concerned with whether their organization and their use conform, in the first place, with the language-related Articles in the Belgian Constitution and the Administrative Language Law and, second, with the non-discrimination and equality principle.

Consequently, a need for statutory regulations or guidelines on the use of translators and interpreters is apparent (Roels et al. 2015, 163; Meylaerts 2018, 474), especially for certain issues such as the use of child interpreters. Moreover, the diverging use of formal and informal translators and interpreters within one and between several administrations adds to this

---

53 See ECtHR 23 July 1968, nos. 1474/62, 1677/62, 1691/62, 1769/63, 1994/63 and 2126/64; ECommHR 15 July 1965, No. 2333/64.

need for a framework outlining when these services may or must be used. A fundamental question underpinning such a framework, going beyond the topic of translation and interpretation, is how the burden of enabling communication between administrative services and non-Dutch speakers should be distributed. The dominant narrative that Dutch is the common language in Flanders and that newcomers should learn Dutch does not preclude a more structural and consistent approach to translation and interpreting organized by administrations in certain situations.

References

Backhaus, Peter. 2012. "Language Policy at the Municipal Level." In *The Cambridge Handbook of Language Policy*, edited by Bernard Spolsky, 226–242. Cambridge: Cambridge University Press.

Bernaerts, Jonathan. 2019. "Meertaligheid in eentalige administraties." *TBP*, No. 6: 307–328.

Blommaert, Jan. 2011. "The Long Language-Ideological Debate in Belgium." *Journal of Multicultural Discourses* 6 (3): 241–256.

Clement, Jan. 2003. *Taalvrijheid, bestuurstaal en minderheidsrechten: Het Belgisch model: een constitutionele zoektocht naar de oorsprong van het territorialiteitsbeginsel en de minderheidsrechten in de bestuurstaalwetgeving*. Antwerpen: Intersentia.

De Pelsmaeker, Tom, Lennart Deridder, Frank Judo, Johan Proot and Frederik Vandendriessche. 2004. *Taalgebruik in bestuurszaken*, Administratieve rechtsbibliotheek Algemene reeks. Bruges: Die Keure.

Gosselin, Frédéric. 2017. *L'emploi des langues en matière administrative*. Mechelen: Kluwer.

Meylaerts, Reine. 2011. "Translational Justice in a Multilingual World: An Overview of Translational Regimes." *Meta* 56 (4): 743–757.

———. 2018. "Language and Translation Policies in Context of Urban Super-Diversity." In *Language Policy and Linguistic Justice: Economic, Philosophical and Sociolinguistic Approaches*, edited by Michele Gazzola, Torsten Templin and Bengt-Arne Wickström, 455–475. Cham: Springer International Publishing.

———, and Gabriel González Núñez. 2017. "Interdisciplinary Perspectives on Translation Policy." In *Translation and Public Policy: Interdisciplinary Perspectives and Case Studies*, edited by Gabriel González Núñez and Reine Meylaerts, 1–14. New York: Routledge.

Patten, Alan, and Will Kymlicka. 2003. "Introduction Language Rights and Political Theory: Context, Issues, and Approaches." In *Language Rights and Political Theory*, edited by Will Kymlicka and Alan Patten, 1–51. New York: Oxford University Press.

Roels, Britt, Marie Seghers, Bert De Bisschop, Piet van Avermaet, Marie van Herreweghe, and Stef Slembrouck. 2015. "Equal Access to Community Interpreting in Flanders: A Matter of Self-Reflective Decision Making." *The International Journal for Translation & Interpreting Research* 7 (3), 149–156.

Vande Lanotte, Johan, Geert Goedertier, Yves Haeck, Jurgen Goossens, and Tom De Pelsmaeker. 2015. *Handboek Belgisch Publiekrecht: Inleiding Tot Het Belgisch Publiekrecht.* Bruges: Die Keure.

Velaers, Jan. 2001. *Het gebruik van de talen.* Brugge: Die Keure.

———, and Maurice Adams. 1993. "Taalrechten, taalvrijheden en taaldwang in de multiculturele samenleving." In *Recht en verdraagzaamheid in de multiculturele samenleving*, edited by Centrum Grondslagen van het Recht, 169–188. Antwerp: Maklu.

About the editors

Marie Bourguignon holds a master's degree in law and in communication from the UCLouvain. Currently a PhD candidate at the Centre for Public Law (KU Leuven), her research focuses on the translating role of judicial actors, and more specifically notaries, in nineteenth-century Belgium. Marie is also a teaching assistant at the Leuven Institute for Human Rights and UHasselt. She co-edited the book *Can We Still Afford Human Rights?* with Jan Wouters, Koen Lemmens and Thomas Van Poecke.

Bieke Nouws holds a master's degree in history from the University of Antwerp and a PhD in translation studies from KU Leuven. She was earned her doctorate with a dissertation on translation and translators in Belgium's courtrooms and administrations between 1830 and 1914. In other research, she delved into Belgian political history, parliamentary discourse in the Low Countries, the use of humor in parliamentary settings, the history of language politics, translation politics and the challenges and opportunities of combining the disciplines of history and translation studies. She likes to explore digital research methods and has supported the State Archives of Belgium in developing a database of tax jurisdictions in Belgium from the nineteenth century through today, in a project called 'Daphnis'. She currently works as a digital archivist for the same institution.

Heleen van Gerwen holds a master's degree in Western literature and a PhD in translation studies (KU Leuven). Her dissertation focuses on translation and transfer practices in the legal and administrative domains in nineteenth-century Belgium. Her research interests include translation history, intercultural transfer, translator studies and sociocultural roles of translation in multilingual contexts. Her publications include "Translation space in nineteenth-century Belgium: rethinking translation and transfer directions" (co-authored with Lieven D'hulst, published in *Perspectives*) and *Transfer Thinking in Translation Studies. Playing with the Black Box of Cultural Transfer* (co-edited with Maud Gonne, Klaartje Merrigan and Reine Meylaerts, published at Leuven University Press).

About the authors

Jonathan Bernaerts is a postdoctoral researcher at the KU Leuven, Centre for Public Law. He holds bachelor's degrees in Philosophy and Law (University of Antwerp) and obtained master's degrees in international law (University of Antwerp) and comparative international law (University of Toulouse Capitole 1). He was awarded the European MA in Human Rights and Democratisation (European Inter-University Centre, Venice).
Under the supervision of Professor Marie-Claire Foblets and Professor Jan Velaers, Bernaerts obtained in 2020 a Joint PhD from the University of Antwerp and the Martin-Luther-Universität Halle-Wittenberg, in collaboration with the Max Planck Institute for Social Anthropology, Department of Law & Anthropology. His PhD considers the interactions between local authorities and non-majoritarian language speakers from a legal empirical perspective. Bernaerts currently works on a project of the Max Planck Institute for Social Anthropology, Department of Law & Anthropology, regarding cultural and religious diversity in Europe.

Albert Branchadell is a lecturer in the Department of Catalan Studies at the Universitat Autònoma de Barcelona (UAB, Autonomous University of Barcelona) and is currently the dean of the university's Faculty of Translation and Interpreting. He holds a PhD in linguistics from the UAB (1992) and a PhD in political science from the Universitat Pompeu Fabra (Pompeu Fabra University) (2003). The latter of his theses was a comparative study on the legitimacy of the preservationist language policies of Quebec and Catalonia. He has conducted research in theoretical linguistics, Catalan sociolinguistics, translation studies, and political philosophy and, moreover, has recently published on hypothetical language regimes of an independent Catalonia, Alan Patten's 'equal recognition' theory in the face of the Catalan case, translation policy in nineteenth-century Barcelona and the position of 'less-translated languages' in institutional translation (United Nations, European Union, Spain, and Catalonia). He is a member of the Societat Catalana de Sociolingüística (Catalan Society of Sociolinguistics), a branch of the Institut d'Estudis Catalans (the Catalan academy of sciences) and the Spanish representative in the committee of experts monitoring the implementation of the European Charter for Regional or Minority Languages.

Paolo Canavese is a research and teaching assistant at the University of Geneva's Faculty of Translation and Interpreting (FTI), where he is a member of the Italian Translation Unit and the Centre for Legal and Institutional Translation Studies (Transius). He holds a double degree (2014) in applied interlinguistic communication and German-Italian studies from the University of Trieste (Italy) and Regensburg (Germany), as well as an MA (2016) in specialized translation and interpreting from the University of Trieste. He conducts research in the fields of legal and institutional translation and linguistics. He is particularly interested in translation-mediated legal and administrative communication in multilingual institutional settings, with a focus on the Swiss quadrilingual system. More specifically, he specializes in barrier-free state-to-citizen communication, including comprehensibility of legal language and accessibility of institutional texts both in plain and easy language. He regularly attends conferences and publishes papers on these topics. He is currently working on his doctoral dissertation, which consists of a corpus study that, combining a quantitative and a qualitative approach, tries to shed light on the level of clarity of Swiss federal legislation in Italian, both in terms of readability and comprehensibility.

Flavia De Camillis holds a degree in specialized translation and is currently completing her PhD in translation, interpreting and intercultural studies at the University of Bologna. She has been working at the Institute for Applied Linguistics at Eurac Research since 2015, first as a translation trainee, later as a PhD fellow, and currently as a researcher. Her research interests include non-professional translation, institutional translation and machine translation for minority languages.

Chantal Gagnon is an associate professor at Université de Montréal, where she teaches translation in business and economics. As translation scholar and certified translator, she has published articles on the translation of political speeches and journalistic translation in magazines such as *The Translator*, *Perspectives*, *Across* and *Meta*. She is currently leading a research project on the translation of political speeches on the Canadian federal government's budget. Dr. Gagnon is also a member of the Office québécois de la langue française.

Shuang Li holds a PhD in translation studies from KU Leuven. Her research interests include translation policy and complexity theory, on which topics she has published several articles and chapters. Central to her PhD dissertation, entitled "A Complexity Approach to Translation Policy: The Case of

Courtroom Interactions in a Multi-ethnic and Multilingual County in China", are the questions of why translation management, translation practices and translation beliefs are sometimes contradictory, why and how translation policies have become as they are in specific contexts, and how we can cope with the inherent uncertainty of translation policies.

Willem Possemiers is a PhD student and teaching assistant at the Institute for Comparative Law at the KU Leuven Faculty of Law. His main research topics are the Van Dievoet Commission and the development of Dutch legal language in Belgium. Other research topics include the history of the codification of civil law in Belgium and other countries, Belgian constitutional law and Belgian language legislation. He also has a particular interest in the development of private law in the People's Republic of China.

Marketa Štefková (https://orcid.org/0000-0001-8641-2492) is an associate professor at the Chair of German, Dutch and Scandinavian Studies at the Faculty of Arts, Comenius University in Bratislava, Slovakia. Her research initially focused on legal translation in languages with limited diffusion and on the translation of European legal texts. As a practicing sworn translator, she focused on the potential opportunities for the professionalization and lifelong learning of legal translators. Later, she broadened her interest to the definition of public service translation and interpreting in Central Europe, where this concept is insufficiently anchored in theory. She carries out field research aimed at the status and position of sworn translators, their specializations and the quantity and nature of the assignments they conduct for public authorities, natural persons and legal entities. At the same time, she develops didactic material for the training of translators and interpreters for public services.

Helena Tužinská is associate professor at the Department of Ethnology and Museology at the Faculty of Arts, Comenius University in Bratislava, Slovakia. She conducted ethnographic research in refugee camps and the asylum courts in Slovakia which resulted in *Questions of Description and Translation: Use of Data from Anthropology and Ethnology in the Conduct and Interpretation of Interviews with Immigrants* (2011), and *[Between the Lines] The Ethnography of Interpreting in Asylum Court Hearings* (2020, in Slovak). In cooperation with non-governmental organizations, she has facilitated training opportunities in intercultural communication for a range of stakeholders in the migration field. She also co-authored an informal survival kit on Slovakia: *In_different. As Told By Foreigners*. The majority of her texts are available at https://uniba.academia.edu/HelenaTužinská.

Sebastiaan Vandenbogaerde holds master's degrees in history (Ghent University, 2006), law (Ghent University, 2010) and corporate law (KU Leuven, 2021). In 2014, he obtained a PhD in law (Ghent University) on the history of legal periodicals in Belgium, after which he was granted a FWO-postdoctoral scholarship. His research focuses on intellectual legal history and how legal periodicals play a central role in disseminating ideas on law and society. In addition, he works on the impact of both world wars on national and international law. Currently, he is a visiting professor at the universities of Ghent and Antwerp.

Katarzyna Wasilewska graduated from the University of Warsaw (Applied Linguistics) and Warsaw School of Economics (International Economics). She is currently a PhD student at the Faculty of Applied Linguistics at the University of Warsaw, where she is writing a dissertation on administrative reports in both the international European Union and the national Polish contexts. In February 2015, she completed a five-month traineeship at the European Commission, Directorate General for Translation, Polish Unit, after which she participated in the research project The Eurolect: an EU variant of Polish and its impact on administrative Polish (2015–2020).

Index

Administrative Language Law 225, 226, 227, 228, 229, 231, 243, 244
administrative style 69, 82
asylum applicants 157, 158, 160, 166, 170, 176
attractors 50
authentic(ity) 72, 110, 117, 206
Belgium 110, 112, 182, 206, 224
budget speeches 24
Canada 23, 158
Catalan/Catalonia 38, 90, 110
child interpreters 236
China 49, 88, 163
Chinese 52, 164
Civil Code 183, 192, 193, 205
civil servants 17, 30, 89, 148, 185, 224, 227
community interpreting 158, 228, 233, 237, 243
complexity theory 49, 62
consistency 69, 82, 94, 122, 214
constitution(al) 30, 52, 88, 112, 117, 138, 142, 183, 206, 208, 225, 226
constraints 50, 166, 169, 220
context of communication 18, 166
co-official language 91, 113
Council of State 212, 219, 230
court interpreter 52, 163, 167
court interpreting 18, 52
court translator 160, 163
critical discourse analysis 25
cross-cultural communication 177
dialects 88, 89, 169
Directorate-General for Translation 68
discourse internalization 40
drafting 69, 70, 95, 141, 148, 208
Dutch 112, 164, 189, 205, 224
English 25, 77, 125, 144, 162, 169, 238, 243
equality 11, 13, 18, 38, 55, 68, 117, 128, 142, 184, 192, 243
ethics 175
ethnographic 51, 88, 166, 171
EU institutions 68
expert terminology 176
explicitation 36

federal 12, 17, 24, 25, 36, 109, 111, 112, 134, 136
federal Italian 137
Flanders 181, 183, 212, 226
Flemish 182, 207
Flemish Integration Decree 226
flexible language policy 234
formal interpretation 243
formal translation 223
fossilized structures 82
French 25, 90, 112, 114, 136, 169, 182, 205, 224, 238
genre 32, 39, 71, 72, 192
German 90, 110, 136, 161, 162, 213, 221, 224
guidelines 38, 68, 99, 103, 104, 141, 177, 234, 244
habit 51, 82
implicitation 36
in-between policy 234
informal interpretation 241
informal translation 223
inheritance law 214
in-house revision 70
in-house style guide 71
in-house translators 69, 89, 101
institutional discourse 26
integration 74, 157, 159, 225
Italian 89, 118, 134
Italy 88, 110, 141, 143
labor migrants 158
language minorities 90, 158
language policy 92, 114, 122, 160, 229, 234
language rights 91, 115, 159, 160, 183
Law of Equality 182, 189, 208
legal language 16, 182, 187, 210, 211
legal terminology 98, 172, 184, 188, 192, 197
linguistic minorities 49, 88, 115
local language policies 95, 234
manual 33, 69, 71, 72, 74
minority languages 28, 53, 88, 90, 110, 134, 142, 161
multilingualism 8, 11, 54, 88, 110, 134, 135, 137

Napoleonic Code 192
national minorities 90, 157
occasional translator 89
official language 12, 14, 25, 67, 89, 110, 112, 135, 136, 161, 183, 207
Polish 68, 161
power asymmetry 173, 177
problematic expressions 77
professional interpreter 165
public service interpreting 17, 158
quality 10, 16, 61, 68, 73, 100, 104, 139, 148, 149, 150, 158, 159, 172, 173, 176, 184, 198, 205, 212, 217, 238, 242
Quebec 24
refugees 158
regiolects 169
regional language 90, 110, 117
Slovakia 125, 158
sociolects 169
South Tyrol 88, 111
Spain 88, 110
Spanish 110

standardization 14, 17, 83, 104, 158
standards 73, 118, 122, 159, 166, 170, 175, 212
strict Dutch-only policy 234
style guides 68
Swiss Italian 136
Switzerland 31, 110, 134
sworn translator 56, 225
SWOT analysis 147
trajectories 50
translation beliefs 48, 114
translation bureau 30, 95
translation management 9, 48, 114
translation memories 69
translation practices 10, 48, 87, 89, 114, 160
translation process 73, 82, 92, 96, 97, 99, 103
translation services 30, 48, 96, 99, 141, 150, 163, 164, 241
translation shifts 24, 26, 31
translator training 13, 97, 141, 167
trial 49
Van Dievoet commission 209

Titles previously published in the series Translation, Interpreting and Transfer

1. Kayo Matsushita, *When News Travels East. Translation Practices by Japanese Newspapers* (2019)
2. Jan Van Coillie and Jack McMartin (eds), *Children's Literature in Translation. Texts and Contexts* (2020)
3. Olha Lehka-Paul, *Personality Matters. The Translator's Personality in the Process of Self-Revision* (2020)
4. Maud Gonne, Klaartje Merrigan, Reine Meylaerts and Heleen van Gerwen (eds), *Transfer Thinking in Translation Studies. Playing with the Black Box of Cultural Transfer* (2020)
5. Raquel Pacheco Aguilar and Marie-France Guénette (eds), *Situatedness and Performativity. Translation and Interpreting Practice Revisited* (2021)

More info at
https://lup.be/collections/series-translation-interpreting-and-transfer

www.ingramcontent.com/pod-product-compliance
Ingram Content Group UK Ltd.
Pitfield, Milton Keynes, MK11 3LW, UK
UKHW021848140426
5217IPUK00022B/1651